# Mainstreaming Gender, Democratizing the State

**Institutional Mechanisms for the Advancement of Women**

Edited by **Shirin M. Rai**

**Transaction Publishers**
New Brunswick (U.S.A.) and London (U.K.)

First paperback printing 2007
© 2003 United Nations.

This book is printed on acid-free paper that meets the American National Standard for Permanence of Paper for Printed Library Materials.

Library of Congress Catalog Number: 2005054873
ISBN: 1-4128-0570-8 (pbk. : alk. paper)
Printed in the United States of America

Library of Congress Cataloging-in-Publication Data

Mainstreaming gender, democratizing the state : institutional mechanisms
    for the advancement of women / Shirin M. Rai, editor.
        p. cm.—(Perspectives on democratization)
    ISBN 1-4128-0570-8 (pbk. : alk. paper)
    1. Women—Government policy.  2. Women in politics.  3. Women—
    Social conditions.  4. Democratization.  5. Equality.  I. Rai, Shirin.
    II. Series

HQ1236.M3425  2006
320.082—dc22                                                          2005054873

# Contents

# Figures and tables

## Figures

## Tables

# List of contributors

**Selma Acuner** got her PhD at the Public Administration and Political Sciences Faculty of Ankara University, Turkey. She is a part-time lecturer at the Women's Studies Center of the same University and an adviser on gender issues at the Prime Ministry. Her area of studies includes equality policies, the European Union and equal opportunities, and the institutionalization of gender equality at all levels.

**Brigitta Åseskog** is a deputy Director at the Division for gender equality in the Ministry of Industry, Employment and Communications in Sweden. During 1998–99 she was the manager of a gender mainstreaming project launched by the Nordic Council of Ministers. Since 2001 (and during a leave of absence from the Ministry) she has been employed by the European Commission as a senior official.

**Anne Marie Goetz** is a Fellow of the Institute of Development Studies at the University of Sussex, UK. She is a political scientist who studies the politics of promoting and implementing gender and development policies. She has conducted research on this subject in Bangladesh, and has studied women in politics in Uganda and South Africa. She is currently working on the challenge of improving state responsiveness to poor and marginalized citizens. This has involved research into the anti-corruption struggles of the poor in India. She is the editor of *Getting Institutions Right for Women in Development* and is co-author of *Contesting Global Governance: Multilateral Economic Institutions and Global Social Movements*.

**Jurgette Honculada** is the Women's Secretary of the National Federation of Labor and Vice-Chair of both PILIPINA and the Women's Action Network for Development in the Philippines. She is a commissioner of the National Commission on the Role of Filipino Women.

**Zuzana Jezerska** is Executive Producer of the independent film and video company EMERGE Productions, Slovakia. She has been involved in women's issues since 1992. She is currently collaborating as expert and project manager of the Slovakia-based Gondwana Foundation in the human rights division and is preparing a regional project on gender sensitization of the media in Central and Eastern Europe and the Commonwealth of Independent States. Her professional interests include, in addition to creative writing and directing, media and communication theory related to gender.

**Nüket Kardam** is Associate Professor of Political Science at the Monterey Institute of International Studies, California, USA. She is author of *Bringing Women In: Women's Issues in International Development Programs*. She has written a number of articles and book chapters on gender-related policy change in international development organizations and governments, on the establishment of global gender equality norms and their implementation, as well as on the politics of gender in Turkey. In her research and consultancy work she focuses on Turkey and the former Soviet Union countries. Most recently, she has completed an evaluation of an innovative women's human rights education programme in Turkey.

**Joy C. Kwesiga** is Dean of the Faculty of Social Sciences, Makerere University, Uganda. She is former Head of the Women and Gender Studies Department. She has been actively involved in the Uganda women's movement, particularly in the founding of an influential national association, Action for Development (ACFODE), of which she was Chair during the period 1993–97.

She was also involved in reactivating the Uganda Association of University Women in the early 1980s. She participated actively in the Fourth World Conference on Women in Beijing (1995) and was involved in many preparatory meetings within and outside Africa.

Dr Kwesiga's research interests cover women's education, the women's movement, analysis of women's non-governmental organizations and the wider civil society, women and politics, gender and management, gender training and gender issues in higher education. She has published articles in these areas. She has also conducted training programmes and carried out evaluation of developmental projects within the East African region. Her book, *Access of African Women to Higher Education*, is due for publication by Fountain Publishers in Uganda.

**Rosalinda Pineda Ofreneo**, PhD, is a Professor at the Department of Women and Development Studies, College of Social Work and Community Development, University of the Philippines, Diliman, Quezon City. She has been active in various women's organizations for the last thirty years, and has worked with the National Commission on the Role of Filipino Women on various projects.

**Shirin M. Rai** is Reader in the Department of Politics and International Studies, University of Warwick, UK. She has written extensively on issues of gender, governance and democratization. She is the author of *Gender and the Political Economy of Development* (Polity Press, 2002). She has edited *International Perspectives on Gender and Democratisation*, (Macmillan, 2000) and has co-edited *Women in the Face of Change: Soviet Union, Eastern Europe and China* (Routledge, 1992); *Women and the State: International Perspectives* (Taylor and Francis, 1996); *Global Social Movements* (Athlone Press, 2000) and *Rethinking Empowerment* (with J. Parpart and K. Staudt) (Routledge, 2002). She is Series Editor (with Wyn Grant) for *Perspectives on Democratization*, Manchester University Press.

**Marian Sawer** is Head of the Political Science Program, Research School of Social Sciences, Australian National University, Canberra. Her books include *Sisters in Suits: Women and Public Policy in Australia* (Allen & Unwin, 1990); *Working from Inside: Twenty Years of the Office of the Status of Women* (with Abigail Groves, Australian Government Publishing Service, 1994); and *Speaking for the People: Representation in Australian Politics* (edited with Gianni Zappalà, Melbourne University Press, 2001). She has worked as a policy practitioner inside and outside government.

**Kathleen Staudt**, who received her PhD in Political Science from the University of Wisconsin in 1976, is Professor of Political Science at the University of Texas at El Paso. Among her latest books are those that focus on international borders: *Free Trade? Informal Economies at the US–Mexico Border* (Temple University Press, 1998), and *The US–Mexico Border: Transcending Divisions, Contesting Identities* (with D. Spener) (Lynne Rienner Publishers, 1998) and *Rethinking Empowerment* (with J. Parpart and S. Rai) (Routledge, 2002). Kathy has consulted with the United Nations Development Programme, the UN Division for the Advancement of Women and the UN Research Institute for Social Development.

**Wendy Stokes** is Lecturer in politics and sociology at Richmond, the American International University in London, where she is developing courses on gender and environmentalism. She is at present working on a book, *Women and Politics*.

**Silvia Ugalde** is an activist and leader of the Ecuadorian Women's Political Coordinating Organization.

# Acknowledgements

This book is a result of an expert group meeting on 'National Machineries for Gender Equality' organized by the United Nations Division for the Advancement of Women in collaboration with the Economic Commission for Latin America and the Caribbean (Santiago, Chile, 31 August–4 September 1998). In an effort to provide a wide picture of national machineries in different countries, the book draws from the background papers prepared by the participants who attended the meeting, as well as from other experts working on national machineries.

The book was prepared by the Division for the Advancement of Women under the direction of Dorota Gierycz, Chief of the Gender Analysis Section. It has benefited greatly from the work of the consultant Shirin M. Rai who, in addition to contributing two chapters and the conclusion, also undertook the initial editing of the book. On the part of the Division, it is the result of a team effort, involving a number of staff of the Gender Analysis Section, particularly Emanuela Calabrini, Elizabeth Leitman, Santiago Martinez-Orense and Sharon Taylor. The book draws on inputs by Yakin Ertürk, the then Director of the Division for the Advancement of Women, who provided insightful comments on the framework as well as on each chapter of this volume.

The Division for the Advancement of Women would like to express its appreciation to the authors and to the team at Manchester University Press — Nicola Viinikka, Philippa Kenyon and Tony Mason — who provided precious assistance in editorial and publishing matters.

The authors are responsible for the choice and presentation of the facts contained in this book and for the opinions expressed therein, which do not necessarily reflect the views of the United Nations Division for the Advancement of Women.

# Foreword

The publication *Mainstreaming gender, democratizing the state?* is reflective of the commitment of the United Nations, and in particular of the Division for the Advancement of Women (DAW), to the promotion of mechanisms that aim to be instrumental in the achievement of equality between women and men. National machineries for the advancement of women are such mechanisms.

The idea of national machineries was conceived in a recommendation of the World Conference on the International Women's Year held in Mexico City in 1975. Since then, the subject of national machineries has been taken up systematically by the subsequent world conferences on women in 1980 (Copenhagen), 1985 (Nairobi) and 1995 (Beijing), as well as the various sessions of the Commission on the Status of Women. The Beijing Platform for Action identified institutional mechanisms for the advancement of women, including national machineries, as one of the twelve critical areas of concern. However, national machineries are not only perceived in the Platform as one of these areas of concern but also as the primary institutional mechanism entrusted with the implementation of the strategic objectives contained throughout the Platform at the national level. The outcome document adopted at the 23rd special session of the General Assembly on Beijing +5 has reiterated the significant role that national machineries play in promoting equality between women and men, gender mainstreaming and monitoring of the implementation of the Platform for Action as well as the Convention on the Elimination of All Forms of Discrimination Against Women.

In the course of time, the mandate of these national institutions has evolved from promoting women-specific projects to ensuring that equality concerns are integrated into all government legislation, policy, programmes and budgetary processes. The ability of member states to subscribe to the global agenda for equality between women and men has been significantly enhanced by the creation of these national-level institutions. Yet the review and appraisal of the implementation of the Beijing Platform for Action conducted by DAW (E/CN.6/2000/PC/2) revealed that national machineries face serious constraints in fulfilling their mandate, including inadequate financial and human resources; relatively powerless locations within government structures; and insufficient linkage with civil societies. They are also affected by a general lack of understanding of, and commitment to, gender issues by concerned actors in governments and societies at large. The Committee on the Elimination of Discrimination Against Women has repeatedly expressed similar concerns in the consideration of state parties' reports.

Since the Mexico City Conference, these issues have been a topic of debate and research, resulting in a rich array of publications. However, a volume bringing together discussions on theory and practice, as well as comparative analysis and in-depth case studies of national machineries, has been a long-standing need. This book responds to this need.

On behalf of the Division for the Advancement of Women, I am pleased to present this publication to the international community. We hope that this endeavour will contribute to furthering the understanding of the role and functioning of national machineries for the advancement of women and inspire further innovative work in this area.

Yakin Ertürk
Director
Division for the Advancement of Women
August 2001

# List of abbreviations

| | |
|---|---|
| APEC | Asia-Pacific Economic Cooperation |
| BJP | Bhartiya Janata Party (India) |
| BNP | Bangladesh National Party |
| CAWP | Civic Assembly of Women in the Philippines |
| CBO | Community-based organization |
| CEDAW | Convention on the Elimination of All Forms of Discrimination against Women (the term also refers to the Committee on the Elimination of Discrimination against Women) |
| CEE | Countries of Central and Eastern Europe |
| CHR | Commission on Human Rights |
| CIDA | Canadian International Development Agency |
| CNMD | National Coalition of Women for Democracy (Chile) |
| CONAMU | National Women's Council (Ecuador) |
| CPME | Ecuadorian Women's Political Coordinating Organization |
| CSW | Commission on the Status of Women |
| CSWI | Committee on the Status of Women in India |
| CTB | Bipartite Technical commission (Ecuador) |
| CWDS | Centre for Women's Development Studies (India) |
| DAC | Development Assistance Committee (of the OECD) |
| DAW | Division for the Advancement of Women |
| DAWN | Development Alternatives with Women for a New Era |
| DINAMU | National Office for Women (Ecuador) |
| DWA | Department of Women's Affairs |
| DWCD | Department of Women and Child Development |
| ECA | Economic Commission for Africa |

| ECE | Economic Commission for Europe |
|---|---|
| ECOSOC | Economic and Social Council |
| EDSA | Epifanio de los Santos Avenue |
| EOC | Equal Opportunities Commissions (UK) |
| EU | European Union |
| FPOs | Focal Point Officers |
| GABRIELA | General Assembly Binding women for Reform, Integrity, Equality, Leadership and Action |
| GAD | Gender and Development |
| GDI | Gender Disaggregated Index |
| GEM | Gender Empowerment Measure |
| GO | Governmental organization |
| *HDR* | *Human Development Report* |
| INSTRAW | United Nations International Research and Training Institute for the Advancement of Women |
| JÄMKOM | Gender Equality in the Municipalities (Sweden) |
| MGCD | Ministry of Gender and Community Development (Uganda) |
| MGCSD | Ministry of Gender, Culture and Social Development (Uganda) |
| MGLSD | Ministry of Gender, Labour and Social Development (Uganda) |
| MGSD | Ministry of Gender and Social Development (Uganda) |
| MIS | Management Information System |
| MP | Member of Parliament |
| NAWOU | National Association of Women's Organizations in Uganda |
| NCRFW | National Commission on the Role of Filipino Women |
| NCW | National Council for Women (Uganda) |
| NDPB | Non-Departmental Public Body |
| NGO | Non-governmental organization |
| NRM | National Resistance Movement (Uganda) |
| NWM | National women's machinery |
| OECD | Organization for Economic Cooperation and Development |
| OSW | Office of the Status of Women (Australia) |
| PAM | Political Coalition of Andean Women (PEM) |
| PfA | Platform for Action |
| SALA | Swedish Association of Local Authorities |

| | |
|---|---|
| SERNAM | National Service for Women (Chile) |
| SRA | Social Reform Agenda (Philippines) |
| UKP | Alliance of Women in Politics (Philippines) |
| UN | United Nations |
| UNDP | United Nations Development Programme |
| UNESCO | United Nations Educational, Scientific and Cultural Organization |
| UNGASS | United Nations General Assembly Special Session |
| UNICEF | United Nations Children's Fund |
| UNIFEM | United Nations Development Fund for Women |
| UNRISD | United Nations Research Institute for Social Development |
| VWU | Vietnamese Women's Union |
| WAD | Women and Development |
| WBG | Women's Budget Group (UK) |
| WEL | Women's Electoral Lobby (Australia) |
| WHO | World Health Organization |
| WID | Women in Development |
| WNC | Women's National Commission |
| WTO | World Trade Organization |
| WU | Women's Unit (UK) |

# Introduction

SHIRIN M. RAI

The role of national machineries, as a way to promote the status of women, acquired international relevance during the World Conference on the International Women's Year, held in Mexico City, Mexico, in 1975, which called for their establishment. The World Decade for Women (1976–85), during which two other World Conferences on Women were held (in Copenhagen,[1] 1980 and Nairobi,[2] 1985), gave further impetus to the setting up of institutional mechanisms at the national level, to promote the status of women. By the end of the decade, 127 member states of the United Nations (UN) had established some form of national machinery.[3]

Since then, the international community has given increased attention to the role and structure of national machineries. The Commission on the Status of Women (CSW) was at the forefront of the discussion of this issue, which was considered as a priority theme at the CSW thirty-second and thirty-fifth sessions held, respectively in 1988 and 1991. At the time, the discussion centred on the role of national machineries in promoting women-specific issues. The report provided to the thirty-second session of the Commission defined the national machinery as being a body 'recognized by the Government as the institution dealing with the promotion of the status of women'.[4] Its functions were described as being, *inter alia*: supporting the effective participation of women in development; promoting the situation of women in education, political decision making and the economy; ensuring the highest level of government support for this policy; combating negative cultural attitudes and stereotyping of women in the media; facilitating research on the status of women; and collecting sex-disaggregated data.

The report to the Commission in 1991[5] focused on information systems and identified the acquisition, analysis and dissemination of information on the advancement of women as essential factors for the success of national machineries. It suggested that location, staff improvement, access to modern communication technologies and networking, especially with non-governmental organizations (NGOs) and with the UN system, were crucial indicators for success.

During the thirty-fifth session of the Commission, many representatives of member states drew the attention of the Commission to the efforts undertaken in various countries to restructure the national machineries, which resulted in an improvement in their status and increased development of their technical potential. Others instead highlighted the obstacles to the success of their national machineries, including lack of human and financial resources and the persistence of certain cultural phenomena, such as patriarchy.[6]

By the time of the Fourth World Conference on Women held in Beijing, China, in 1995, the discussion on the role of national machineries had shifted from a focus on women-centred issues to gender equality. The main task of the national machinery, as defined in the Platform for Action adopted at the Conference, was 'to support government-wide mainstreaming of a gender-equality perspective in all policy areas'.[7] The Platform proposed strategic objectives with concrete actions to address mechanisms to promote the advancement of women at all levels and in all areas to make them more effective and relevant. The issue of 'institutional mechanisms for the advancement of women' was chosen as one of the twelve critical areas of concern of the Platform for Action. Among the actions to be taken by governments proposed in the Platform were to 'encourage and promote the active involvement of the broad and diverse range of institutional actors in the public, private and voluntary sectors to work for equality between women and men'[8] and the need to 'report, on a regular basis, to legislative bodies on the progress of efforts, as appropriate, to mainstream gender concerns'.[9]

After the Fourth World Conference on Women, the UN addressed the issue of national machineries on two other occasions. In 1996, the Division for the Advancement of Women (DAW), jointly with the United Nations Development Programme and the Economic Commission for Europe, organized a subregional conference on the implementation of the Beijing Platform for Action in Central and Eastern Europe.[10] This conference, *inter alia*, elaborated recommendations on how to strengthen national machineries in the region, including through governmental action to 'address the need for consultative mechanisms aimed at fostering cooperation with parliamentarians', 'establish coordination mechanisms among NGOs at the national level' and 'support the dialogue and bilateral and multilateral cooperation with all social partners'.[11] In the same year, the United Nations Economic and Social Commission for Asia and the Pacific held a Regional Meeting on Strengthening National Machineries for the Advancement of Women which drafted recommendations for Asia and the Pacific. Besides having co-organized these meetings, the United Nations Regional Commissions have played, and continue to play, an important role in facilitating linkages, interaction and the exchange of experiences among national machineries at the regional level.

In July 1997, the Economic and Social Council (ECOSOC) adopted agreed conclusions (1997/2),[12] which provided a definition, a set of principles and practical recommendations for action on gender mainstreaming in the UN system, including the need to enhance interaction among UN entities and national machineries for the advancement of women. Following the adoption of the agreed conclusions by ECOSOC, DAW organized a Workshop on Gender Mainstreaming, held in Geneva, Switzerland, from 15 to 17 September 1997. Its purpose was to share experiences and lessons learned between and among bilateral and multilateral organizations about mainstreaming for gender equality as a crucial element in the transformation of the development agenda. At the national level, institutions set up for the advancement of women would be the main mechanisms through which mainstreaming would be pursued.

In 1998, DAW, in collaboration with the Economic Commission for Latin America and the Caribbean, organized an expert group meeting on 'National Machineries for Gender Equality'[13] in Santiago, Chile. The expert group meeting aimed, *inter alia*, to create a better understanding of the institutional and other factors related to national machineries which would stimulate actions, policies and the allocation of resources to strengthen their role, efficiency and effectiveness in implementing the Beijing Platform for Action. One of the recommendations of the expert group meeting was the compilation of a UN publication on good practices in order to facilitate exchange of information among people working for the strengthening of national machineries in different countries. The present book, *Mainstreaming Gender, Democratizing the State? Institutional Mechanisms for the Advancement of Women*, is a response to that recommendation.

Furthermore, the results of the expert group meeting were fed into the agreed conclusions adopted by the Commission on the Status of Women in 1999 (1999/2) on the institutional mechanisms for the advancement of women containing recommendations for further implementation of this critical area of concern of the Beijing Platform for Action. The CSW stressed that 'the effectiveness and sustainability of national machineries [were] highly dependent on their embeddedness in the national context, the political and socio-economic system and the needs of and accountability to women'.[14] The Commission also recommended that national machineries be placed at the highest possible level of government and be invested with the authority and resources needed to fulfil their mandates.

In June 2000, a special session of the United Nations General Assembly (UNGASS) on 'Women 2000: Gender Equality, Development and Peace for the Twenty-first Century' was held in New York, in order to review the progress made, and obstacles remaining, to the implementation of the Beijing Platform for Action. In preparation for the special session, a thorough review and appraisal of the implementation of the Platform was made, with a detailed analysis of its twelve critical areas of concern, including the area of institutional mechanisms for the advancement of women.[15] UNGASS adopted an outcome document which showed that, in many countries, 'national machineries [have] been instituted or strengthened and recognized as the institutional base acting as "catalysts" for promoting gender equality, gender mainstreaming and monitoring of the implementation of the Platform for Action'.[16] 'Progress [has] been achieved in terms of the visibility, status, outreach and coordination of activities of these machineries.'[17] However, the outcome document also revealed the existence of factors which still hindered the activities of the national machineries in many countries, including 'inadequate financial and human resources, lack of political will and commitment (at the highest level), insufficient understanding of gender equality and mainstreaming among government structures, unclear mandates, and structural and communication problems within and among government agencies'.[18]

The issue of national machineries has been central to the work of DAW. In addition to the organization of the expert group meeting in Chile and the various events held in relation to the implementation of the Beijing Platform for Action, in 1996, DAW conducted a survey of national machineries among member states in order to study the situation of national machineries in terms of their location, authority to review legislation, activities, and access to the internet and other resources. The Division also issues, twice a year, a global directory of national machineries for the advancement of women, and undertakes technical cooperation activities to support efforts by member states aimed at strengthening national machineries, particularly in developing countries.

One of the current technical cooperation activities undertaken by DAW is a project on 'Capacity Building of National Machineries for Gender Equality' in the African region. The project aims to strengthen existing national machineries and support the establishment of machineries where they do not exist as well as to strengthen capacities of women in decision making in the public sector; in particular, by increasing women's ability to participate in, and have influence on, the policy-making process.[19]

This book, which reflects DAW's long-standing interest in the area of national machineries, brings together the experiences, research and insights of experts. The chapters are reflective of diversities in types of national machineries, political systems and socio-economic contexts, as well as geographic regions, and therefore allow the reader to reach important comparative insights.

This volume contributes towards a critical assessment of the experience of national machineries in three ways. First, it attempts to deliver a critique of existing practices; second, an analysis of 'good practice'; and third, forward-looking strategies for national machineries. The book is divided into three Parts — 'Conceptual frameworks', 'Comparative Analyses' and 'Case Studies' — and ends with a concluding chapter.

Part I sets out the major issues facing national machineries at the conceptual level. In chapter 1, Shirin M. Rai examines the major issues that need to be considered in the evaluation of national machineries. Rai argues that national machineries are part of the process of democratizing the state and hence of good governance. She reflects upon five aspects of democratization that are critical for national machineries: devolution or decentralization; the role of political parties; monitoring and auditing systems of the national machineries themselves, making for more accountable bodies with stronger links to civil society associations; leadership commitment to gender equality agendas; and the importance of increasing the presence of women within broader political institutions of the state and government.

In chapter 2, Kathleen Staudt reflects upon the ways in which the move from focusing on women to gender has, among other things, opened up the issue of gender analysis for policy making, which is a core concern of national machineries. The focus of this chapter is on exploring the historical and contemporary debates on gender mainstreaming. Staudt is clear that the framework of gender mainstreaming must begin with 'institutional *outcomes* rather than inputs and promises'. She argues that 'the language of gender provides analysts with the most socially significant categories of people, next to nationality, about whom policy actions are significant: women and men' (p. 58). Such an outcome-driven process would result in a 'policy dialogue' that would influence the appropriate training of state personnel at all levels, as well as sex-disaggregated budgeting. Thus Staudt asserts that the 'gender mainstreaming framework is ultimately a framework about good governance' (p. 61).

Part II is a comparative analysis and sets out the major issues facing national machineries at the political level. In chapter 3, Anne Marie Goetz, provides a comparative analysis of five national machineries. She suggests that a national machinery will be successful in promoting gender equality if it is able to 'mobilize resources and public concern to support its demands', if the 'nature of the political system and the organization of political competition' are supportive of their agendas, and if 'the state and its bureaucracies . . . [have the will] and capacity to enforce change in the culture and practices of [their] bureaucracies' (pp. 91–2). A combination of factors, including civil society, state bodies and political actors, need to come together for national machineries to function effectively in the interest of gender equality.

In chapter 4, Nuket Kardam and Selma Acuner focus on 'lessons learned' by national machineries in mainstreaming gender. Linking this assessment to the debates on 'good governance', they argue that national machineries are limited as well as enabled by a clear understanding of 'the constraints posed by conceptual, political and organizational factors' (p. 98) in particular national contexts. Kardam and Acuner argue that national machineries should have an achievable agenda, an important part of which must be 'a re-definition of gender issues in alliance with international donors, women's NGOs and their own governments, that is appropriate to their own contexts' (p. 112).

The third Part contains case studies that build upon the specific experiences of national machineries in different countries. In chapter 5, Silvia Vega Ugalde argues for the importance of the 'political' in the agenda setting for gender equality. This implies reflecting on the importance of the political affiliation of the party in office, making links with the middle-level state personnel who are critical to the process of implementation of policies, and the strengthening of the role of women's groups and organizations in 'proposing, pressuring, negotiating, overseeing, criticizing, demanding explanations' (p. 125).

In chapter 6, the theme of the importance of the political role of women's movements is further developed by Jurgette Honculada and Rosalinda Pineda Ofreneo within the context of the national machinery of the Philippines. Honculada and Ofreneo argue that 'a vibrant women's movement plays a critical role vis-à-vis a national women's machinery —

lobbying for its creation, providing leadership and direction, pioneering new initiatives such as gender training . . . , and serving as gadfly when the government fails to deliver' (p. 131).

In chapter 7, Birgitta Åseskog examines the successful experience of Nordic countries in gender mainstreaming. Åseskog links the attainment of gender equality with the 'Nordic welfare state model'. She argues that in the Nordic countries, the 'political view prevails that society can progress in a more democratic direction only when the competence, knowledge, experience and values of both women and men are acknowledged and allowed to influence and enrich developments in all spheres of society' (p. 148). The argument here is also that a consensus about the equality of men and women within a political and social system 'imposes demands on the fundamental structure of society and its various functions' (p. 148). The participation of women in the economy, in political movements, political parties and welfare state ideology all combine to bring about such a consensus, which is crucial to the effective functioning of national machineries for the further advancement of women.

Also taking a regional perspective, Zuzana Jezerska in chapter 8 focuses on the nature and mandate of national machineries in the countries of Central and Eastern Europe. In Central and Eastern Europe the status of a national machinery can 'vary from NGO status to very strong mandate within the government' (p. 167). She argues that, given the relatively recent concern with issues of gender mainstreaming in Central and Eastern Europe, 'we not only need gender awareness but also awareness of the role and importance of national machineries for the advancement of women *per se*' (p. 168). Like all the other chapters in this section, Jezerska also emphasizes that while international organizations such as the UN have been important in putting gender mainstreaming as an important item on the international agenda, women's groups in individual countries have been influential in the establishment of national machineries at the national level.

In chapter 9, Wendy Stokes reflects upon the experience of the United Kingdom and argues that while 'the legitimacy of the [Women's National Commission; WNC] derives from the broad range of its Partners, the question arises as to what extent there can be a shared point of view amongst such divergent groups' (p. 198). She concludes that 'At present the informal factors appear to be working for the WNC, but it is not hard to imagine that a change of government or even personnel could disrupt this. For this reason, if no other, stronger institutional support for gender equality is required' (p. 201).

Joy C. Kwesiga examines the experience of the Ugandan national machinery in chapter 10, and establishes that the lack of political will and, as a consequence, the under-resourcing of the machinery are the two main obstacles to the efficient functioning of the Ugandan Machinery for Gender Equality. Political and economic instabilities in Uganda also adversely affect the machinery, as do the lack of a clear mandate and trained personnel. Despite these obstacles, the machinery has been able to formulate 'a National Gender Policy aimed at providing policy makers, and other key actors ... with guidelines for identifying and addressing gender concerns' (p. 214).

In chapter 11, Shirin M. Rai argues that 'the work of the National Commission for Women provides a useful focal point not only to address specific policy issues but it also allows us to raise the broader issues of differences among women' (p. 241). However, she suggests that while the National Commission for Women in India is potentially an important means for mainstreaming gender within the state policy-making structures, its weakening links with the women's movement are a cause for worry as they are eroding its legitimacy in the very constituency from which it needs support. Together with the lack of political will of most political parties to mainstream gender in policy making, this constitutes an important obstacle for the Indian National Commission for Women.

The thrust of Marian Sawer's argument in chapter 12 is that even successful and self-confident national machineries need to be aware of the changing political and economic climate in order to guard against the erosion of their work. Examining the Australian national machinery, she argues that the 'structures for gender accountability within government, which Australia helped pioneer, have been threatened by discursive shifts within government' in the context of shifts in economic policy towards market liberalization and

and the consequent attack upon the role of the state in addressing broad social issues (pp. 260–1). She calls for resisting further erosion of the work done by the women's national machinery in Australia, which could build upon the still present 'institutionalized acknowledgement that all government policy needs to be analysed for gender effects and that no policy can be assumed to be gender neutral' (p. 262).

Finally, in the Conclusions, Shirin M. Rai examines the lessons learned from the experiences of different national machineries examined in this volume, and reflects upon some of the ways forward. She suggests that as national machineries expand in their numbers and roles, they need to develop more transparency in agenda setting and resource management, and develop strong links with civil society organizations which will allow them to strengthen their position *vis-à-vis* state bodies.

## Notes

1 World Conference of the United Nations Decade for Women: Equality, Development and Peace, 1980, Copenhagen, Denmark, 14–30 July.

2 World Conference to Review and Appraise the Achievements of the United Nations Decade for Women: Equality, Development and Peace, 1985, Nairobi, Kenya, 15–26 July.

3 As listed in the Directory of National Focal Points for the Advancement of Women, quoted in *Women 2000*, No. 3. 1987:7, New York: United Nations.

4 E/CN.6/1988/3, para. 21. The definition is based on the outcome of the seminar on 'National Machinery for Monitoring and Improving the Status of Women', 1987, Vienna, Austria, 28 September–2 October. *National machinery for monitoring and improving the status of women, Report of the Secretary-General to the thirty-second session of the Commission on the Status of Women*, doc. E/CN.6/1988/3, para. 21, United Nations.

5 Report of the Secretary-General on *Development: National, Regional and International Machinery for the Effective Integration of Women in the Development Process, including Non-governmental Organizations* (E/CN.6/1991/3), New York: United Nations.

6 Official Records of the Economic and Social Council, 1991. *Report on the Thirty-fifth Session of the Commission on the Status of Women* (E/CN.6/1991/14): New York: United Nations 58.

7 United Nations, *Fourth World Conference on Women, Platform for Action and Beijing Declaration*, 1996, Department of Public Information, United Nations, New York.

8 Ibid.:117, para. 203 (f).

9 Ibid., para. 203 (e).

10 Subregional Conference of Senior Governmental Experts on the 'Implementation of the Platform for Action adopted by the 1995 Fourth World Conference on Women in Beijing, Central and Eastern Europe', organized by the United Nations Division for the Advancement of Women, the United Nations Development Programme and the Economic Commission for Europe, 1996, Bucharest, Romania, 12–14 September.

11 Report of the Subregional Conference of Senior Governmental Experts on the 'Implementation of the Platform for Action adopted by the 1995 Fourth World Conference on Women in Beijing, Central and Eastern Europe', organized by the United Nations Division for the Advancement of Women, the United Nations Development Programme and the Economic Commission for Europe, 1996, Bucharest, Romania, 12–14 September, 1996:11.

12 Agreed Conclusions of the Economic and Social Council 1997/2, doc. A/57/3/Rev.1, Chapt.IV.A, Report of the Economic and Social Council for the year 1997. New York: United Nations.

13 Report on the Expert Group Meeting on 'National Machineries for Gender Equality', organized by the United Nations Division for the Advancement of Women and the Economic Commission for Latin America and the Caribbean, 1998, Santiago, Chile, 31 August–4 September (EGM/NM/1998/Rep.1), New York: United Nations.

14 Official Records of the Economic and Social Council, 1999. *Report on the forty-third session of the Commission on the Status of Women*, 1999, doc. E/1999/27, Chapt.I.B.IV.II, para. 2, New York: United Nations.

15 Report of the Secretary-General on the *Review and Appraisal of the Implementation of the Beijing Platform for Action* (E/CN.6/2000/PC/2), New York: United Nations.

16 Official Records of the General Assembly. *Report on the Ad Hoc Committee of the Whole of the Twenty-third Special Session of the General Assembly* (A/S-23/10/Rev.1), New York: United Nations.

17 Ibid.:15.

18 Ibid.:15–16.

19 Further information on the project can be found on the web site of the Division for the Advancement of Women at www.un.org/womenwatch/daw.

# Part I

# Conceptual frameworks

# 1

# Institutional mechanisms for the advancement of women: mainstreaming gender, democratizing the state?

SHIRIN M. RAI

Institutionalizing women's interests in all areas and sectors of policy at all levels has been a concern of women's movements worldwide, as well as of international institutions such as the United Nations (UN). Gender mainstreaming has emerged as a strategy for addressing this issue, relevant to all states and public institutions. National machineries for the advancement of women are regarded as appropriate institutional mechanisms for ensuring that gender mainstreaming agendas are implemented and issues of gender equality remain in focus in public policy. Gender mainstreaming and national machineries have found added salience in international public policy through UN-led and national governments' endorsed agreements on these issues, such as the Beijing Platform for Action (1995) and Economic and Social Council (ECOSOC) Agreed Conclusions[1] (see also Staudt, chapter 2, this volume).

Certain themes emerge in the analysis that follows. First, are national machineries as state institutions the most appropriate instruments for furthering women's interests? Two sets of debates inform this issue — the viability of women's engagements with the state and the nature of women's interests. The second theme is about the viability of national machineries as bodies promoting women's interests — do these institutions command the necessary resources to be able to promote women's interests? In this context I address issues of resources — economic and political, the setting of goals and targets for national machineries, as well as the political environments in which these machineries are embedded. Here, the stability of governance institutions, for example civil society and the relative strength of women's movements, and issues of accountability of the machineries are also important. The third theme focuses on the processes of democratization which a state needs to undergo to mainstream gender effectively — the hierarchical nature of state bureaucracies and political parties, the presence or lack of auditing mechanisms within state machineries, leadership commitment to gender mainstreaming and, of course, increasing the presence of women within state bodies at all levels.

## Defining issues

What is gender mainstreaming? It can be defined as 'the process of assessing the implications for women and men of any planned action, including legislation, policies or programmes, in all areas and at all levels. It is a strategy of making women's as well as men's concerns and experiences an integral dimension of the design, implementation, monitoring and evaluation of policies and programmes in all political, economic and societal spheres so that women and men benefit equally and inequality is not perpetuated. The ultimate goal is to achieve gender equality' with the aim of transforming structures of inequality (UN, DAW, 1998:4). In this book the term is used largely to address issues of gender mainstreaming in public policy institutions although the impact of such policy shifts is expected to create a political context in which the process of gender mainstreaming in private institutions also proceeds.

There has been a debate among those concerned with issues of gender justice about whether to use the language of equality or of equity. The position of those concerned to emphasize issues of difference between men and women is that the equality discourse tends to erase the differences between women and men, that sameness becomes the focus rather than an acknowledgement of the different needs and interests of women and men. The argument is also made that the language of equality is a language of universalism, and that universal norms are really the norms of Western hegemonic societies which are inappropriate, or even counter-productive, in different cultural contexts (Ali,

2002). International bodies such as the UN and some other feminist scholars, however, have asserted the need for universal rights to be made the centrepiece of gender justice strategies. So, for example, it is argued that

> the term 'equity' ... is conditioned by subjective criteria, [and therefore] cannot become a substitute for the fundamental legal principle of equality ... [Further] that reference to [the] 'dignity of women' does not encompass and cannot be substituted for the principle of the 'dignity and worth of [the] human person and the equal rights of men and women' enshrined in the Preamble of the Universal Declaration of Human Rights. (UN, 2000:5)

The argument is that any dilution of equal treatment of women and men on grounds of culture undermines the very basis of gender justice. It also allows women of some countries, and some religious and ethnic groups, to be left out of the discussions about refining and contextualizing the rights of women and men. Hegemonic cultural discourses often reinforce traditional gender roles and the focus shifts away from the needs of women outside the boundaries that define these roles. Codification of women's social role within these cultural boundaries then comes in the way of processes of democratization of the state and within civil society. In this volume, we have used the term 'equality' rather than 'equity'.

What are national machineries? Despite attempts at a common definitional understanding of these institutions, differences remain in the ways they are conceptualized which depend on the political contexts obtaining in individual states. National machineries emerged as instruments of advancing women's interests after the World Conference of the International Women's Year in Mexico City (1975), but were particularly strengthened in the Platform for Action adopted at the Fourth World Conference on Women in Beijing (1995). They can be defined as 'the central policy coordinating unit inside the government. [Their] main task is to support government-wide mainstreaming of a gender equality perspective in all policy areas' (Platform for Action, para. 201). National machineries are thus 'catalysts' for promoting gender equality and justice. However, as Kathy Staudt points out in this volume, 'we find vastly different institutional cultures, leaders and leadership styles, degrees of coordination, birthing periods, disciplinary specializations, missions and staff demographics, gender and otherwise — all protecting their autonomy to likewise different degrees' (p. 46; see also Goetz, chapter 3, this volume). The nation-state thus continues to be the focus of women's movements that remain embedded in particular cultural, historical and political contexts. In order to embed gendered perspectives into policy, the spotlight most often turns to how national states are performing on this score, though global institutions themselves are also increasingly under scrutiny in this regard.

### Can state institutions promote women's interests?

I would suggest that one of the most important questions for analysing national machineries is whether state-based or promoted institutions such as national machineries can be effective in advancing the interests of women given the embedded nature of these machineries in structures of inequality.

I have argued elsewhere that the question of engagement with the state and state institutions cannot be seen in terms of binary opposites. Indeed, we need a position which allows for a mobilization of women's interests and their articulation within the space of civil society which would challenge the gender status quo. In parallel, it would allow for an engagement with the policy-making machinery of the state in order to institutionalize the gains made through discursive and political shifts brought about through these mobilizations. I have termed such a dialectical position 'in and against' the state (Rai, 1996). In terms of the national machineries for women, I would argue that an 'in and against' the state position allows us to consider mainstreaming gender through and within the state seriously and critically. Thus, on the one hand, as the different case studies in this volume show, women's movements, non-governmental organizations (NGOs) and international institutions such as the UN have striven for state institutions in the form of national machineries committed to the gender equality agenda to be recognized, and given political space and resources. This strategy has been seen as addressing the continued marginalization of women in the public sphere and to continued gender inequality more generally. However, on the other hand, there has also been a concern that national machineries might well be used, especially where a strong women's movement does not exist, to co-opt the gender agenda within state policy, thus divesting it of its radical edge. Holding these two positions together, at times in tension with each other, does not take away from the importance of the state as an arena for furthering gender justice. It also suggests that the state is a fractured and ambiguous terrain for women, needing complex negotiation and bargaining by those working within its boundaries as well as those on the outside. So the answer to the question of whether national machineries can be effective in advancing women's interests must be yes, but under certain conditions which include issues of location and resources as well as of strong democratic movements holding these bodies accountable. This position has not always been acceptable within women's movements or among feminist scholars, as will be evident below. However, if we examine the position of women in politics today, we can see that the scale of women's exclusion from political bodies needs to be addressed urgently if the nature of these bodies is to be changed.

## Women in political institutions

A head count of the officers of the state in all sectors — legislature, executive and the judiciary — in most countries of the world reveals a massive male bias despite many mobilizations furthering women's presence at both national and global levels. An Inter-parliamentary Union study found that the number of sovereign states with a Parliament increased sevenfold between 1945 and 1995, while the percentage of women Members of Parliament (MPs) worldwide increased fourfold (Pintat quoted in Karam, 1998:163). The UN *Atlas of Women in Politics* (1999a) shows that women form 13.4 per cent of MPs as a whole. The Nordic states lead, with women constituting 38.8 per cent of members of both Houses of Parliament, while the Arab states have only 3.5 per cent (UN, 1999). Furthermore, data show that there is no easy positive co-relation between economic indicators and the presence of women in public bodies. While in Europe (without the Nordic countries) women comprised 13.4 per cent of the total number of MPs, the figure in Sub-Saharan Africa was 11.7 per cent, in Asia 14.3 per cent and in the Americas 15.3 per cent. In recognition of the slow improvement in women's representation in national Parliaments, enhancing women's presence within state bodies is now being pursued by both women's movements and international institutions. This suggests that an engagement with state structures is now considered an appropriate means of bringing about shifts in public policy.

I now sketch out the major positions that have been articulated in feminist state debates, and the shifts that have occurred within them. A familiarity with these debates sheds light on the difficulties that women's groups have had in engaging with national machineries and, therefore, on the process of mainstreaming gender through institutional strategies.

**Feminist state debates**

There have been two separate shifts in feminist debates on strategy and theory. First, within the women's movements there was a significant shift in the 1980s towards engaging positively with state feminism as a strategy that could be effective in furthering the cause(s) of women. Women recognized that interests need to be articulated through participation and then representation in the arena of politics. The argument about presence, as Anna Jonasdottir (1988) pointed out, concerns both the *form* of politics and its *content*. The question of form includes the demand to be among the decision makers, the demand for participation and a share in control over public affairs. In terms of content, it includes being able to articulate the needs, wishes and demands of various groups of women. The interest in citizenship was also prompted by the shift in women's movements, in the 1980s, from the earlier insistence upon direct participation to a recognition of the importance of representative politics and the consequences of women's exclusion from it (Lovenduski and Norris, 1993; McBride Stetson and Mazur, 1995; Rai, 2000). It is here that politics — public and private, practical and strategic — begins to formalize within the contours of the state.

Second, in the 1970s, feminists began to engage with theories of the state, as opposed to theorizing politics. There were several reasons for this shift, many of them mirroring the shift in the study of citizenship. Traditional political theory has defined the state as a 'set of political institutions whose specific concern is with the organization of domination, in the name of the common interest, within a delimited territory' (Rai, 2000:1569). Weber, in his work *Politics as a Vocation*, gave a modern definition of the state as an organization with a territory, with a monopoly of violence and legitimacy to be able to use that violence (Weber, 1972). Together with Marxists and socialists, feminists have sought to move beyond this description of an organizing agency, which was seemingly not embedded in the structural power relations of the economy and patriarchy. Some have questioned the liberal presumptions of the state as a means of overcoming the state of nature and the establishment of the patriarchal state. Others have attempted to use class analysis to understand how women's position within the family and wage labour regimes is regulated by the capitalist state, and still others have analysed the state in parallel with their analysis of the law which systematizes male power (MacKinnon, 1987; Pateman, 1985).

Political responses to the theorizing of the state have also been varied. While some, like Judith Allen, posed the challenging question: 'Does Feminism Need a Theory of "the State"?' (1990; Pringle and Watson, 1992), others have seen the state as a potentially legitimate agency of the politics of change (Eisenstein, 1978). Similarly, while some have queried whether state organizations such as national machineries for women 'transform gender equality activists into technocrats/bureaucrats first and foremost, or is it that they have tended to attract technocratic feminists?' (Tsikata, 1999:17), in other contexts, such as Australia and Canada, feminists insisted that they needed to engage with the state bureaucracy to influence policy making within state bodies in the interests of women outside. As Marian Sawer explains in chapter 12 of this volume, an 'important aspect of the Australian model of women's policy machinery was that it was originally developed by the women's movement rather than invented by government' (p. 244). In many Southern states too women have chosen to engage with the state after a period of maintaining a sceptical distance. In some countries this shift has come about in tandem with the process of democratization, such as in South Africa. In other states, such as India, this has been due to a realization of the need to shake up consolidated privilege within state structures in order to make them sensitive to growing gender demands. Women have also analysed state power in the context of communist states to show how class-based understanding of gender relations need not translate into policies that speak to the strategic interests of women (Einhorn, 2000).

**The state response**

Most states have also undergone a shift in their policies towards accepting gender mainstreaming as a valid political agenda. This has been primarily due to pressure from global institutions such as the UN (see Kardam and Acuner, chapter 4, this volume). States' acceptance of the outcome of the World Conferences on Women, particularly the Beijing Platform for Action and the outcome document of the twenty-third special session of the General Assembly on Gender Equality, Development and Peace for the Twenty-first Century, has resulted in a commitment to some form of institutional change. The political and discursive shifts within women's movements discussed above have added to this pressure on the state to engage with gender equality agendas. Support of global institutions through training sessions and particular projects, as well as political pressure from international NGOs and women's movements, have also been helpful in moving forward states' agendas on the issue of mainstreaming. Finally, practical issues such as filing state reports on the status of women under the Convention on the Elimination of All Forms of Discrimination against Women (CEDAW) has shown the need for a body to oversee the process (see Ali, 2001).[2]

So, for a multiplicity of factors, national machineries for the advancement of women are now in existence in many states. However, if these bodies raise issues about the nature of the state and women's engagement with it, they also raise questions about what and whose interests are they going to promote, mainstream and embed in political institutions. Identifying, aggregating and representing interests is thus a core element of the work of national machineries. National machineries have been envisaged as nodes for acknowledging, listening to, recognizing and articulating the interests of different groups of women within the national political community. Representing women's interests to governance circuits at different levels is one of the important tasks of national machineries. Thus they are also seen as conduits between civil society and the state. What have been the debates on women's interests that were needed to inform this mandated function of the national machineries?

### Representing women's interests

What are interests? Interests can be defined as shared understandings and articulations of concern to an individual or group. The term includes both the objectives of the individual or group and the power of the individual or group to attract attention to those objectives. While traditional liberal theory has largely focused on individual interests, collective action and social conflict frameworks of analysis have shifted this focus to groups (Young, 1995; Kymlicka, 1995). These frameworks also allow us to reflect upon strategies for the pursuit of interests — demonstrating, lobbying, going on strike or other such forms of collective action.

There is a comprehensive literature about theorizing women's interests. The concept has been examined in two different ways. The first is to challenge the view that equates women's interests with identity politics and particularistic demands. As Jonasdottir (1988) has emphasized, interests are formulated within particular contexts which frame the processes of making choices. She has also argued that women are not just another 'interest group' because they exist in a historically determined conflictual and subordinate relationship to men. There is of course the issue of difference among women that has challenged both feminist scholars and women activists. While women exist in a historically conflictual relationship with men, they also do so with women of a different class, ethnicity, sexuality, dis/ability, and so on. So, for example, economic interests divide women, just as their subordinate position *vis-à-vis* men places them on the same side. Economic interests, especially in the context of global restructuring, have become important markers of difference among women, even as globalization is bringing women closer together across national boundaries through technological and global governance networks (Hoskyns and Rai, 1998; Parpart, Rai and Staudt, 2002). Whose interests, in this context, is not always an easy question to answer. There has also been some debate among feminist scholars on women's interests and gender interests. The latter are interests addressing the structure of relations between women and men, the former those concentrating on women's lives.

Maxine Molyneux has made an analytical distinction between women's 'practical' and 'strategic' needs. Practical interests reflect women's immediate and contained demands — for better conditions of work, equal opportunities, child care, housing, water, and so on. These interests do not challenge the wider framework of patriarchal structures of power. Strategic interests reflect the need to shift the paradigms of power. In the words of Molyneux, 'In the formulation of practical interests there is the assumption that there is compliance with the existing gender order, while in the case of strategic interests there is an explicit questioning of that order and of the compliance of some women with it' (1998:235).

From a different standpoint, Chantal Mouffe (1992) and Mary Dietz (1992) have made the point that framing women's interests — both practical and strategic — in terms of the general interests of a just society can be an effective way of giving them greater salience in wider political debates and policies. This would be an effective way of mainstreaming — as opposed to adding gendered analysis on to existing paradigms of power. The current climate of global restructuring could be a good starting point of such reformulations. This might include suggesting, and insisting upon, new policies addressing women's interests and, participating in making discursive shifts — the language of politics, agenda setting for the next phase of gender politics, challenging the reversal of already fought for and won freedoms and benefits.

Some have claimed that Molyneux has made too rigid a distinction between the two sets of interests. However, Molyneux argues that the 'pursuit of particularistic interests . . . is of course not necessarily at variance with strategies that pursue broader goals and interests and may be framed in terms of general principles' (1998:239). The distinction also allows political strategizing to take place. As Molyneux points out, 'The political *links* between practical and strategic interests are ones which can only emerge through dialogue, praxis and discussion' (1998:236). National machineries need to be able to participate not only in making these distinctions clear, but to be able to strategize according to the specific contexts within which they function. If this is to happen, national machineries need clarity of mandate, sufficient resources and a stability within governance networks.

In the following section I examine the second theme of the book — the mandate and resources of the national machineries for the advancement of women.

## National machineries for women

The mandate of national machineries places a great deal of stress on their agenda-setting role, while their legitimacy derives from the close contact they are able to maintain with women's groups. Finally, they represent national states at international bodies. The following is a survey of different issues that arise for national machineries in performing their roles.

### A variety of national machineries

National machineries vary considerably from country to country. In most countries the national machinery is part of the government structure. The particular issues here relate to the status of the governmental body, its closeness to the highest offices within the government, the resources — both economic and political — available to it, and the access or otherwise it has to other sectors and bodies of government. In some countries, national machineries remain outside government, though the government recognizes their role as an important forum at both the national and international levels. Here the resource issue is critical at both the economic and political levels, as are issues of flexibility, voice and consensus building across political boundaries. These bodies might be considered more autonomous, or less influential, depending on how they are able to negotiate political boundaries, to become effective in improving the status of women.

All national machineries are embedded in specific socio-economic and political contexts. Comparisons between them are therefore not always useful. However, we can identify five elements that are critical for all:

1 Location [at a high level] within the decision-making hierarchy [and authority] to influence government policy.
2 Clarity of mandate and functional responsibility.
3 Links with civil society groups supportive of the advancement of women's rights and enhancement of women's status.
4 Human and financial resources' (United Nations, 1999b).
5 Accountability of the national machinery itself.

I discuss the first four points in turn in the following sections. I will return to the question of accountability in the Conclusion to the book.

Location

In a survey conducted by the Division for the Advancement of Women in 1996 it was noted that two-thirds of all national machineries are located in government, and one-third are either non-governmental or have a mixed structure. Of those within the government, more than half of the national machineries are part of a ministry, one-third are located in the office of the head of state and the rest are free-standing ministries. Of those within ministries, half are situated in Ministries of Social Affairs and one-third in that of Labour (ECOSOC, March 1999; see also Jezerska and Kwesiga, chapters 8 and 10 in this volume). Why is there a preponderance of national machineries in Ministries of Social Affairs and Labour? What does it say about the assumptions regarding 'women's needs/concerns'? Does this indicate a 'low status' within the governmental structure itself — the high-status ministries being either the 'earning' ministries such as the Treasury or Industry, or regulating ministries such as Home and Foreign Affairs, while Social Affairs is a high-spending area? (see NGO Coordinating Committee for Beijing +5, 2000:73) What does this mean for opening up or 'democratizing' the state through the presence and activities of the national machineries? As the Ugandan case (see Kwesiga, chapter 10 in this volume) suggests, the comparatively low status of the Social Work Ministry has meant that restructuring of the state machinery under the structural adjustment policies has led to frequent downsizing and relocation of the national machinery for women. However, government portfolios which were traditionally considered 'soft' — Welfare, Health and Education — are also, under regimes of economic restructuring, where fundamental arguments about resource allocation are taking place. It is at this time that national machineries can be most effective in insisting upon a 'reassessment both of priorities of states and of the normative social order' (Molyneux, 1998:242).

Free-standing machineries too have strengths and weaknesses. One danger of an autonomous entity is the lack of political clout and therefore of political and economic resources. No ministry or politician need feel responsible for this body, and its achievements bring no benefit to ministers who might then develop a stake in the functioning of the machinery. As Marian Sawer comments in chapter 12 of this volume, 'Australian feminists decided against a self-standing bureau or ministry on the grounds that it might simply become a "waste-paper basket for women's problems" and an alibi for gender-blind policy in the rest of government [and] would lack policy clout' (p. 245). Second, the resourcing of such a body would pose considerable problems. While project-based grants could provide it with some resources, this would not provide the stability of organization needed to develop medium- and long-term strategies. If the machinery was funded by international agencies, the political consequences of this resource might be unacceptably high in some political contexts where the political system might label the machinery as a 'tool of Western agencies'. Such a loss of legitimacy would make the work of the machinery extremely difficult indeed.

Location at the highest level raises the profile of the machinery, and arguably enhances its economic and political resources. In some countries the success of the national machinery derives from its cross-ministerial location (see Åseskog, chapter 7 in this volume). This is possible only when the head of government takes responsibility for opening up the governmental structure in this lateral way. However, to be effective at the highest possible level, several factors have to be considered, together with the location and the commitment of the head of government. The position of the head of government within the political system is crucial — the weaker this position, for example, as part of an unstable coalition, the less likely is the national machinery able to be to use this political resource (see Rai, chapter 11 of this volume). A more general political instability, military coups for example, can also threaten the work of machineries at the highest level. As Honculada and Ofreneo point out in chapter 6 of this volume, 'In the great divide between those for and against martial law [in the Philippines] the [National Commission on the Role of Filipino Women] was perceived by second-wave feminists to be an ally of government' (p. 133). However, in other countries, such as Turkey, the number of women in the government has increased since the military intervention. Times of transition can also be moments of opportunity for the national machineries to strengthen their position (see Zulu, 2000; Jezerska chapter 8 of this volume). The Algerian case also suggests that the political context in individual countries is of primary importance in any analysis of gender mainstreaming through institutional mechanisms (Mehdid, 1996). While visibility provides resources it can also be a burden. A head of state might adopt populist agendas that are not in the interests of women for immediate political gain. As Ugalde urges in chapter 5, 'It is thus effective to create "alliances" with mid-level state personnel who are, in general, more open and more stable than appointed and/or elected officials at the top of the political machinery'

(p. 125). In some contexts, location at the highest level within the governmental structure that is not accountable to the citizenry can lead to the alienation of the national machinery from civil society groups. 'In Chile, Kardam and Acuner point out that some civil society organizations saw the [National Women's Machineries] as an arm of a state which does not represent their interests' (p. 103). An eight-country study by the UN in Africa also reveals that 'being located in the highest level of government does not guarantee national machinery influence and effectiveness . . . An often ignored issue in the location debate is whether the location which is viewed as advantageous, because of its proximity to the powers that be, is also the best location when the mandate and functions of the national machinery are taken into account' (African Agenda, 1999:13 and 15). Autonomy for the work of the machinery can be low at the highest levels of government. Co-optation thus remains a crucial issue for national machineries.

Location is also important for the role that national machineries might play at the regional and global levels. Here the national machineries function to participate in international forums, represent the governmental and non-governmental debates on gender equality, and collect and disseminate information, ideas and good practice from the global to the national level. Location at the top levels of government would provide the machineries with increased credibility at these forums, as well as the negotiating power to make contacts, strategic cross-border contacts and projects. This has happened successfully in South America (see Vega Ugalde, chapter 5 in this volume). However, the South Asian experience has not been so rewarding regarding cross-border contacts between state-based national machineries. The tense political situation between India and Pakistan dominates, and the contact between women remains productive only at the NGO level. National machineries are thus embedded not only in historical and cultural contexts, but also in more immediate intra- and interstate politics.

Clear mandates and functions

Clarity serves a political purpose — it does not allow national machineries to be held responsible for areas that are beyond their remit. It also allows an assessment of why certain areas are outside the remit of the women's national machinery. Such an assessment can prompt questions about the openness of state structures to the agendas of gender equality. A review of the mandates and functions of various machineries illustrates this.

Some national machineries exclusively focus on their role as policy advisers and catalysts for gender mainstreaming, leaving the actual implementation of policies, programmes and projects to other bodies. Other women's machineries not only devise programmes but also monitor their implementation. An implementational role for the national machineries also has its merits. First, a successful project implementation raises the profile of the machinery involved and provides credibility. The 3R project, carried out with the support of state funding and of the Equality Affairs Division by the Swedish Association of Local Authorities, which analysed the effectiveness of gender mainstreaming in local committees and boards, would be one such example (Åseskog, chapter 7 of this volume). Second, involvement in implementational processes could lead to cross-sector liaising that could spread the influence of the national machineries and open new areas for mainstreaming. Finally, taking responsibility for implementing policies could increase both political and economic resources as the process of implementation gathers pace. However, there are also disadvantages of being involved in the implementation of policies. Under federal and/or multiparty political systems, for example, an implementational role can lead to confrontation and divisiveness within the civil society groups and the national machinery where these groups are affiliated with political parties not represented at the central level of government (see Rai, 1997). Most studies in this volume show that national machineries for women do not take on (and neither are they expected to) the role of implementing policies. It was for these reasons that the UN Expert Group Meeting on National Machineries in 1998 specifically recommended that national machineries 'at the governmental level [are] a catalyst for gender mainstreaming, not [agencies] for policy implementation. [They] may, however, choose to be involved in particular projects' (UN, DAW, 1998:10).

A catalytic role of national machineries can be useful for strengthening their profile within the state and in civil society in the following ways. First, mainstreaming works through its 'ownership' by cross-ministerial structures of government. The responsibility of developing policy initiatives can involve the machineries in negotiations with other ministries that can expand the network of bodies involved in the process of mainstreaming gender equality agendas. Second, raising the profile of gender equality agendas is a more effective use of political and economic resources than trying to use scarce resources to implement policies which might best be done by individual ministries. Third, the role of national machineries as a catalyst within government allows these bodies to develop and conduct research on the policies being implemented and feed these through into policy forums, and to develop methodologies and 'the political ability to anticipate and judge key opportunities and possibilities for effective political impact' (Vega Ugalde, p. 124). This would make machineries proactive rather than reactive to state initiatives.

While approaches to the functioning of the national machineries vary, there are major functions that all these bodies need to carry out, though with varying degrees of effectiveness. These are, in terms of their relations with civil society, making gender visible through media campaigns or other means; developing links with civil society groups that support gender equality in order to strengthen the lobbying process; and to channel resources to community organizations, enabling them to participate in the processes of mainstreaming gender. While research and feeding through the results of research into both civil society and policy-making bodies overlap, other state-oriented functions include the following: ensuring gender training for governmental officers; developing new initiatives and methodologies to ensure gender equality in government policy-making processes; reviewing proposed legislation in all appropriate areas; monitoring government policy through insisting on gender-disaggregated budgets, for example; and disseminating good practice. At the global level, the national machineries function to participate in international forums, represent the governmental and non-governmental debates on gender equality, and collect and disseminate information, ideas and good practice from the global to the national level.

## Links with civil society

The relationship between national machineries and civil society is mutually reinforcing.

> Civil society groups have often played a crucial role in establishing national machineries. Support from civil society also strengthens the position of national machinery vis-à-vis other parts of government . . . National machineries need strong links with non-governmental organizations . . . Whenever possible, they should institutionalize their relationship with these organizations. (United Nations, 1999b:18).

While civil society is a crucial factor in the functioning of the national machineries, it is often not theorized enough to distinguish how it might support or in fact be a hindrance to the work of national machineries. Some clarificatory analysis is thus important in this context. First, 'it is necessary to hold together the constituent elements of civil society — including the system of needs (the market), the system of rights (the law) and non-state associations — rather than highlight one of these aspects of civil society at the expense of the other' (Fine and Rai, 1997:2). This is important especially in the context of the growing need to assess how the globalizing markets on the one hand, and legal initiatives of international institutions on the other, are affecting women. Such an analysis would be important for national machineries in order to advise, strategize and make alliances with different groups within civil society. Without an understanding of how markets are gendered and how this affects their functioning, for example, changing labour markets and the shifting position of women and men within them would be difficult to map out (Evans, 1993). Similarly, an assessment of how CEDAW might be used by national machineries to push the state to enact laws that are in the spirit of the aims of CEDAW, while at the same time embedded in local political culture, is needed. NGOs would be useful participants in any strategizing by national machineries. However, an analysis of the variety of NGOs that are supportive of women's rights would reflect both the political concerns of national machineries and the political positions of NGOs. As Stokes points out in chapter 9 of this volume, 'the question arises as to what extent there can be a shared point of view amongst such divergent groups. Are the Union of Catholic Mothers, Stonewall (a gay rights group) and the Women's Engineering Society ever likely to share an opinion?' (pp. 198–9). Strategizing to build on groups that are sympathetic and oppose those which are not requires a complex analysis that goes beyond categorizing all civil society groups as beneficial to the work of national machineries.

Second, and equally important, 'we need to highlight the exclusionary aspects of civil society in relation to those who find no place in its system of needs or in its associational life, and therefore to question the description of civil society as a sphere of "uncoerced action" for all' (Fine and Rai, 1997:2). As the Pakistan's NGO Review of the Platform for Action states, 'increasing violence in society and violent conflict that has accompanied the rise of militant sectarian and conservative politico-religious and ethnic groups not averse to using violent armed tactics . . . to silence . . . those with different or opposing views have militated against women's groups espousing the cause of enhancing women's rights (NGO Coordinating Committee, 2000:47).

Third, 'in terms of the civil society–state relation, we should emphasize the importance of the state beyond simply maintaining (or not maintaining) the parameters of civil society itself, and of politics in mediating between the particular interests of civil society and the universalist claims of the state' (Fine and Rai, 1997:2). As the 'Recommendations of the Expert Group Meeting on National Machineries . . .' suggest, governments are critical to the effective implementation of the Platform for Action by encouraging NGO participation on policy agencies, in setting up accountability mechanisms, and indeed, '[w]henever possible, Governments should utilize NGO volunteer capacities' (UN, 1998:12). However, the restrictive power of the state is also evident in the many studies in this volume (see chapters 6, 8 and 10). Taking the above into account it is, however, important to note that women's groups that have organized outside state boundaries are critical to the continued strength and accountability of national machineries.

Resources

One could argue that the question of resources is fundamentally about politics. It is the political will of national
leaderships that determines the resourcing of bodies such
as national machineries. Without a commitment of the
leadership to gender equality, and to the mechanisms
important for monitoring its pursuit, resourcing of these
institutions is bound to be poor. An additional pressure is
the economic restructuring of the state itself. The pressures of liberalization and the consequent shrinking of state
budgets are resulting in cut-backs to the budgets of bodies
such as the national machineries. This phenomenon is not
only confined to countries in the global South such as
Uganda but is also prevalent in countries that are more
economically secure such as Australia (Kwesiga and Sawer,
chapters 10 and 12 of this volume). While resources can
and need to be enhanced through project funding from
multilateral bodies, the political costs of such support can
also be significant. One way of enhancing political resources
is to link up with civil society groups that have an important voice in the political system. While this strategy is not
always feasible, it is important that we consider it seriously. Given that resources are political, the state elite's
political will (or lack of it) can determine the extent to
which national machineries are considered important political actors and given access to the policy making and
implementational infrastructure of the state. The strength
of the women's movement and the corporatist nature of
the state can be important factors here, as is clear in the
study of Nordic states (Åseskog, chapter 7 of this volume).

## National machineries and democratization

Democratization as a concept and process is informing the
governance agendas of both international organizations and
development agencies. Loans are often tied to democratization of state institutions and bureaucracies, and political
pressure is applied to ensure compliance in this regard.
However, it is not always the case that ensuring gender

equality is built into the definition of such 'democratization'. Considerations of cultural specificity often dilute the message of women's equal rights. As Anne Marie Goetz points out in chapter 3 of this volume, 'the hierarchical and undemocratic nature of bureaucracies, and their hostility to agendas which challenge accustomed organizational patterns . . . is compounded by the high boundaries erected between different sectoral Ministries and by the patronage politics preserved by Ministerial boundaries' (p. 89). In this context, national machineries need to be part of the process of democratization of the state from the outset if gender equality is to be made integral to it. If, as the Platform for Action and subsequent recommendations on the issue suggest, there is a need for greater consultation between NGOs and national machineries and the state bodies involved in policy making, then the question of access to government becomes critical. There are five areas where a democratization of the state/government is required in this context. First, there is the issue of devolution or decentralization. This might be considered at the two different levels of political devolution and of privatization.

While many states are considering devolved government under pressure from ethnic or regional movements and economic possibilities within their polities, we need to consider the gender-specific implications of decentralization and whether such decentralization is beneficial to the work of national machineries. The particularity of political systems would have to be considered here. If decentralization takes place with a strong central bias then the national machineries for women at the devolved levels would have to consider their relationship with the central national machinery. Here, the relationship between civil society organizations and the national machinery would take on another layer of complexity. Given the paucity of resources available to national machineries in most countries, another layer of organization might not be the most efficient way of maximizing budget support and garnering influence for addressing gender equality agendas. On the other hand, decentralization in large, multi-ethnic and multi-religious states could benefit gender mainstreaming as it would be more clearly 'owned' not only by governmental elites at the centre but also by local governmental and state elites.

Decentralization under globalization is also occurring as privatization of welfare regimes. For example, as the state retreats from its role in the provision of health services in order to stabilize the economy under conditions of structural adjustment, two issues might arise for national machineries. First, how to campaign for ending discrimination within the private sphere in terms of women's access to privatized health provision. Second, how to influence the health machinery in terms of recruitment policies, as well as gender-sensitive provision of health facilities.

Second, the role of political parties is also an important issue for the democratizing of the state. As several chapters in this volume suggest, the place and ideology of political parties within the state system can either promote or hinder gender mainstreaming. A monopoly of state power poses difficult questions for gender equality. On the one hand, as Jezerska points out in chapter 8, 'In a political sense, the women were officially equal with men under the communist system. For example, "the greatest number of women in the unicameral parliament [in Poland] under the communist regime was 23 per cent in 1980–1985, far higher than in many Western democracies" ' (p. 171). However, the lack of political space for women to organize meant that this formal equality was not translated into gender equality agendas, and women who did attempt to push the boundaries of state policy faced threats of political persecution. In consolidated democracies such as India political parties pose different sorts of question. The selection process of candidates for election has routinely favoured men even when the gap between men and women in terms of their electoral participation has never been very wide (Rai, chapter 11 of this volume). In South Africa, this issue has been dealt with by encouraging political parties to introduce quotas for women on their party list, with varying degree of success (Zulu, 2000). As many countries experience the 'third wave' of democratization and transitions from single-party to multi-party governance take place, the role of political parties in gender mainstreaming remains critical, and should be the focus of attention of both national machineries and NGOs.

Third, democratization of the state is also needed in the area of monitoring and auditing mechanisms. These mechanisms have to be seen at different levels. First, in terms of democratic elections of the government, which would include a democratic audit of political parties and the functioning of state institutions. Second, intra-state accounting and monitoring mechanisms. This involves the national machineries holding other areas of government accountable in terms of gender mainstreaming. As the Australian and Canadian examples show, 'gender budgets', also adopted by South Africa and the Philippines, require all government departments and agencies to prepare a budget document which disaggregates outlays in terms of their gendered impact (Sawer, chapter 12 of this volume; UN, 1998). Finally, the openness of the state to civil society scrutiny is required if gender agendas are to be monitored, implemented and audited. Strengthening the mechanisms of consultations with civil society groups, including the establishment of formal channels for such consultation, where possible ensuring that the mass media carry the message of gender equality or at least do not carry materials inimical to it, and including women's NGOs in international conferences would be some of the ways in which this scrutiny could be carried out. The openness of the state to such auditing will be premised upon the openness of the political system in general, and critically upon the leadership of political parties and governments. The question of the political will of the leadership remains extremely important, but also unpredictable in any equation regarding gender mainstreaming. Auditing and monitoring require training. This training must involve existing personnel and new recruits and officers of the state at all levels. The training can be provided through national machineries — in which case the machineries need to develop in-house technical capacity — or through civil society consultants at both national/local and international levels. The role of multilateral organizations such as the UN becomes critical in this context.

Fourth, leadership commitment to gender mainstreaming can be affected by different elements within the political system, as well as the personal commitment (or the lack of it) that leaders bring with them. Populist politics can work both ways — leaders can take advantage of a general civil society mobilization by women to push for gender equality. This has been the case in many countries covered in this volume, such as Uganda (see Kwesiga, chapter 10). The reverse can also be the case, whereby civil society mobilizations in the name of 'culture' or religion can undermine the leadership's commitment to gender equality (Karam, 1998). Individual leaders' perceptions of themselves can also have an impact upon whether or not they take up gender matters. In India and the United Kingdom strong female leaders — Mrs Indira Gandhi and Mrs Margaret Thatcher — did not choose to pursue gender agendas. Their understanding of their own meritocratic entry into public life did not allow them to see the social exclusion of women as a political problem (Rai, 1997). Leadership commitment can also be affected by political instability. As Kardam and Acuner point out in chapter 4 of this volume, 'Instability leads to job insecurity, . . . lack of motivation and ineffective performance' (p. 102).

Fifth, democratizing the state also needs to address the issue of the presence of women within political institutions. Different states have addressed this in a variety of ways, or not at all. Quotas for women in political institutions — in local and national representative bodies, political parties' lists and administrative recruitment — has been one strategy, and is increasingly being demanded by women's groups. It has been adopted in some states (see Åseskog Rai, chapters 7 and 11 in this volume). The argument here is well rehearsed — the presence of women in state institutions allows women's interests to be considered at the time of political debates, policy making and implementation. This presence needs to be at a 'threshold' level for women in state institutions to feel confident enough to take up issues across party and sectoral lines. While the evidence of the impact of a quota-based strategy is mixed (see Rai, 2000), national machineries can benefit from these in two ways. First, they could lobby women more directly on women's rights and, second, they could use the expertise and access to state bodies of women parliamentarians or bureaucrats.

Democratization processes are therefore crucial for embedding national machineries in the architecture of governance. These processes include democratization of state and political systems, as well as gender mainstreaming within state and policy structures. As national machineries for the advancement of women become an established part of the political landscape of countries, their success will depend upon the way they are able to address issues of governance and democratization both within the state and in their relationship with civil society associations at both the national and global levels.

## Notes

1 Agreed Conclusions of the Economic and Social Council 1997/2, New York: United Nations doc. A/57/3/Rev.1, Chapt.IV.A, Report of the Economic and Social Council for the year 1997.

2 The implications of CEDAW for states party to it are potentially far reaching indeed. Not only must they abolish all existing legislation and practices that are discriminatory, they are also under a positive obligation to eliminate stereotyped concepts of male and female roles in society. 'Traditional customs and practices' as an argument is not considered valid.

# 2

# Gender mainstreaming: conceptual links to institutional machineries

KATHLEEN STAUDT

We enter the new millennium with a quarter-century of experience in reflection and practice about women and sub-sequently gender in development. This experience builds on the voices of many diverse people who share stakes in and support a broad definition of development, used here to mean the enhancement of human capacity in a world that sustains, rather than undermines, its natural resources.[1] Such enhancement can hardly occur in a world lacking good governance, a world with more than a billion people living in desperate poverty, or a world with so much violence and personal insecurity that it disrupts the everyday lives of innocent bystanders, many of whom are children.[2]

This chapter reviews and acknowledges the emergence, development and increasing sophistication of that body of knowledge and action associated with integrating women and then consolidating the attention to gender in institutional core missions and strategies. These strategies are pursued in the complex political and bureaucratic policy-making contexts, wherein decisions are made every day that embrace and ensnare men and women alike, but that *always* affect them differently given historical and persistent gender inequality. The multiple contexts and institutions by definition defy uniform recipes about internal institutional *processes*.

Process and results are quite different. Although no one best strategy exists to consolidate gender-fair results in the mainstream, world conferences and global mandates clearly focus on gender equality outcomes. As far back as 1970, advocates initially called for women to be integrated into select policies. After a considerable transition in thinking and action, advocates now call for gender to be embedded in *all* policies. Gender equality outcomes cannot occur in sideline, peripheral units — the usual predicament of women's bureaus and ministries, often called 'machineries'. Gender equality must be addressed in the budget and institutional core of mainstream policies and agencies. Gender analysis should be as central to mainstream policies in employment, enterprise, agriculture, criminal/civil justice and education as mainstream attention should be to once sidelined 'women's' issues such as domestic violence and reproductive health (see Staudt, 1998). Yet advocates must start somewhere, and that somewhere often begins in national machineries.

However, to celebrate multiple strategies is not to praise our still-lacking means of measuring the *policy outcomes* in meaningful ways at the global, national and local levels — means that respect the rich and diverse historical and multi-cultural realities of those grandiose to minuscule spaces. While we enjoy the complex and profound thinking of those who measure human development, from sex disaggregation to empowerment (the GDI and GEM[3]), these quantitative scores still leave us with gaps in understanding gender inequality in ways that are difficult to reduce to numbers. Moreover, empowerment measures should be linked to poverty reduction, given women's over-representation below poverty lines. To count some women in economic and political decision-making positions does not necessarily connect to power relations that relegate many desperately poor women to lives stripped of entitlement and endowment.[4]

## Preliminary global perspectives, grounded in governance institutions

Socially constructed categories perpetuate inequalities. The most persistent of these categories that perpetuate inequality include nationality, gender and class. According to the annual UNDP *Human Development Reports* (*HDRs*) of the 1990s, global disparities in wealth are not only marked, but worsening, with income ratios between the top and bottom fifths of the world population rising from 30:1 in 1960 to 78:1 in 1994 (*HDR*, 1997:9). To be born in Swaziland versus Switzerland makes for profound differences in life opportunities and circumstances. *HDRs* methodically count, measure and compare national differences. But gender threads itself through unequal national relations in ways that are hardly visible to those who count and measure. A United Nations (UN) report circulated for the 1985 United Nations World Conference to Review and Appraise the Achievements of the United Nations Decade for Women: Equality, Development and Peace, held in Nairobi, focuses on the structure of opportunities and endowments: to paraphrase, women provide the majority of labour, are formally counted as less than a third of employees, earn a tenth of income and own 1 per cent of the land (see Baden and Goetz, 1997). We need to make unequal gender lines as prominent in analysis as national lines to poverty reduction outcomes.

Although global perspectives provide a framework for understanding the full dimensions of inequalities, global citizens have limited political spaces in which to share voices about regional and international trade agreements, capital flows and computerized trading. Instead, decisions are made at the commanding heights, behind the closed doors of corporate and selective government and international bureaucracies. What we *do* have are those nearly two hundred nation-states, non-governmental organizations (NGOs), and bilateral and multilateral technical assistance organizations that range in their degrees of openness and responsiveness. These institutions operate in more or less accountable ways. For these reasons, *good governance* — whatever the institution — is a necessary condition from which to act on gender equality.

Good governance matters a great deal. Much ink has been spilled over what that means, ranging from the narrower international banking approach ('honest governance that facilitates market transactions') to broader approaches that emphasize increasingly democratic spaces in which people exercise voice and power to hold officials accountable for their decisions. A majority of countries claim to be democratic, but thus far democratic accountability has rarely operated with vigour for most women, the working class and/or the unemployed. Contemporary thinking on democracy and good governance is virtually silent on gender. Men's near monopoly of political decision making has been so long taken for granted that women's absence goes on hardly noticed.[5] Gender must be embedded in the ways we conceptualize, define and measure good governance, for representation, responsiveness and accountability to its stakeholders, a balance of women and men alike.

In the sections below, I address the historical development of women and gender in integrating and mainstreaming terms. I ground these ideas in the knowledge accumulated thus far about institutional practices and movements towards mainstreaming. Considerable accomplishments have occurred in expanding public policy agendas and establishing connections to mainstream policy. Although the bodies of knowledge about women and gender have grown and become differentiated, there is a remarkable convergence of thought that builds an action momentum. Yet neither gender strategies nor visions have *transformed* institutional missions. Ultimately, institutional missions must change, for those missions set the stage for the institutional incentives and penalties that structure the opportunities, attitudes and behaviours of decision makers and staff, ranging from their chief executives through mid-level to street-level bureaucrats.[6]

### An expanding policy agenda

In the 1970s, when research and action first began on women and development, public policies, UN meetings and textbook treatment on development were oblivious to women in production, reproduction and community. Since the International Year of Women (1975), the World Decade for Women (1976–85) and subsequent women's World Conferences, the range of public policies with gender stakes has expanded to include virtually all areas of society and economy, largely due to grassroots actions around the world. The line once drawn between the public and the sacred terrain of everyday private life has been crossed, thereby embracing the former 'non-decisions', in the mobilization of bias that perpetuated hierarchical power relations, sub-ordinating women (see Staudt, 1985).

The scope of issues now on the agenda is breathtaking. Consider the broad range of issues (i.e. the critical areas of concern) about which a coherent and consensus Platform for Action emerged at the Fourth World Conference on Women in Beijing. These critical areas of concern, found in the left-hand column of table 1, are central to the missions of key international and national institutions, listed in the right-hand column, with which civil organizational stake-holders interact.

This comprehensive list grapples with the *whole* mandate of governments and international organizations, though many issues cut across agency and ministerial lines. To respond to the mandate is to enhance good governance at international and national levels. Yet how many of the

**Table 1** Issues and institutional responsibilities

| Critical area of concern | Responsible institutions |
| --- | --- |
| Poverty reduction | Banks at all levels<br>Economic and planning ministries<br>World Trade Organization (WTO)<br>United Nations Development Programme (UNDP), Commission on Human Rights (CHR), Bretton Woods institutions |
| Education and training | Banks at all levels<br>Education, youth, employment ministries<br>Teacher-training institutions<br>United Nations Educational, Scientific and Cultural Organization (UNESCO) |
| Health | Banks at all levels<br>Health ministries and sector institutions<br>World Health Organization (WHO), United Nations Fund for Population Activities (UNFPA), United Nations Children's Fund (UNICEF) |

**Table 1** (*continued*)

| Critical area of concern | Responsible institutions |
|---|---|
| Anti-violence against women | Justice and law ministries<br>CHR, United Nations Development Fund for Women (UNIFEM) |
| Armed conflict; rape as war crime | Defence, foreign affairs ministries<br>CHR |
| Economic growth/ opportunity, anti-occupational segregation and work–family harmonization | Employment, justice, cultural ministries<br>Banks at all levels<br>UNDP, WTO, Food and Agriculture Organization, International Fund for Agricultural Development, International Labour Organization United Nations Industrial Development Organization |
| Women's equal participation in transparent and accountable government | Interior, justice ministries<br>UNDP, CHR<br>Public administration/personnel training |
| ⚹ Institutional capability to integrate gender perspectives and data in policies, programmes and laws | Planning, education, and justice ministries<br>UNDP<br>Public administration/personnel training |
| Promotion and protection of women's human rights | Justice and law ministries<br>CHR, UNIFEM |
| Balanced, not degraded images of women in the media | Cultural, communication ministries<br>UNESCO |
| Environmental sustainability | Banks at all levels<br>Environment, planning ministries<br>United Nations Environment Programme, WHO, UNICEF |
| Enhancing the potential of girls | Education, health, justice ministries<br>UNICEF, WHO<br>Banks at all levels |

standard operating procedures in these institutions are designed to draw on knowledge about people — women and men — in ways that respond to their needs and interests in ways that can be documented and accounted for? Are gender-aware dialogues in place in transparent budgetary decisions? In the drive towards people-centred development, these institutions must clarify how and what they actually do, spend and connect with the everyday lives of women and men. The Platform, however, is not fully known, used or linked to institutional missions.

If institutions are to act on the Platform, they must understand how people and institutions are *gendered*; that is, they must address, compare and assess their missions and programmes for burdens and benefits on women and men in the given asset and opportunity structures of unequal power relations. Such a task is easier said than done, for institutions and their missions share little in common save what sociologist Max Weber once referred to as the 'Iron Cage of Bureaucracy'. In that cage, we find vastly different institutional cultures, leaders and leadership styles, degrees of coordination, birthing periods, disciplinary specialization, missions, and staff demographics (gender and otherwise) — all protecting their autonomy to different degrees.

The Beijing Platform for Action is remarkable for the strength of the language and the ways it builds common ground among diverse groups of women and men, committed to gender equality. It has continued its long-standing emphasis on work and health, so important for the efficiency and instrumental rationales to which most institutions listened and responded, however meagrely. As an example, support for micro-enterprise programmes — *and* for the policy and legal changes that would make them effective to entrepreneurs whatever their gender — have taken hold in our state-downsized, market-oriented global context. NGOs such as the Grameen Bank have been celebrated, analysed and cloned in many parts of the world. At the 1997 Micro-enterprise Summit in Washington, DC, which many heads of state and NGOs attended, one might have got the impression that micro-enterprise has become a code word for women or gender-equality efforts. Yet fully transparent documentation of the key questions — who gets what, with what consequences (the outcomes) — shows the overwhelming statistics: over nine out of ten investments are not only in men, but also in public rather than NGO conduits.[7] The Beijing Platform for Action put political representation and institutional accountability on the agenda, the full piece of the picture in understanding the great lengths to which we must go in realizing gender equality on seemingly compatible programmes such as these.

The Platform also gave priority to issues once muted for their seemingly radical threat — such as human rights, violence and rape — to which institutions have begun to respond. As an example, women's rights *are* human rights and official 'war crimes' now include rape (Gallagher, 1997; Staudt, 1998). Even among the early Women in Development (WID) advocates, these priorities were once isolated among activists who viewed the state as suspect or of so-called 'rights-oriented liberals' who sought to strengthen rules of law that would take crimes against women seriously. Now these disparate groups not only come together on common ground, but also elevate their concern to the policy mainstream. It is important to take this strong consensus into the mainstream of institutions and governance. What analytical language best enables this transformation towards people-centred development: women or gender?

## From women to gender (or both?)

In the 1970s, the term 'gender' was submerged in obscure and academic texts, relegated mainly to sociology and linguistics. But now it seems to be the term of preference, at least in the English-speaking world, for the term does not translate consistently well into other languages (Jahan, 1995). Why the transition? The shift had as much to do with the broader embrace of language as with the ambitions to move from the margins to the centre of institutional policies.

Conceptually, gender language has some advantages over the language of women, woman or female (and certainly sex, still given to chuckles, multiple meanings and the like). Gender emphasizes the *social construction* of people's identities, giving contextual and historical meaning to the biological (and therefore seemingly immutable) referents of male and female, women and men, or sex. Public policies are about reconstructing society and economy, and are thereby linked to constructivist thinking. Gender is also more inclusive and relational, addressing women *and* men, along with the relations between them. It responds to that quip that early women advocates often heard: Why not men in development? (Those who made such quips rarely comprehended the depths to which men's interests had been institutionalized in policy practice.) Gender also had the advantage of defining problems and analysing alternative solutions in more far-reaching ways. The nineteenth-century 'woman problem' could in the late twentieth century be a 'man problem' as well, whether dealing with sexism, reproduction or the perpetrators rather than the victims of sexual violence (see Zalewski and Parpart, 1998). As examples, family planning and sexuality education aims to reach boys and men as the partners in reproduction and the potential perpetrators of attitudes which reduce women to one-dimensional sexual/reproductive beings. Programmes work with young men to reduce the aggression, superiority complexes and hostility that lead to battery and rape (see Staudt, 1998; www.unfpa.org).

Strategically, the term 'gender' also had advantages for turning what was disparaged as a political issue into a technical term with hoped-for due respect among the professionals and scientists who inhabit institutional life. Politically, WID advocates operated outside the institutions. They sought entrée but got stuck at the margins, housed in a women's office, at a women's desk and with pocket change in terms of overall budgets. The occupation of such limited space left gendered power structures intact, the holders of that power perhaps hoping to pacify the critics with a few resources. The outsider advocates, now on the inside, helped massage the policy rhetoric of their institutions, developing procedures of intent and effort, of which they compared and measured the progress. Some early work treated this as 'institutionalization', the language of public administration that transitions the innovative to the routine. Policy rhetoric and procedures of good intent (summarized as 'inputs') however, can never substitute for implementation, action, results and outcomes. The analyses of 'women's machinery', now part of virtually all national governments, offer parallel conclusions (see Staudt, 1985; Kardam, 1990; Moser, 1993; Goetz, 1995; Jahan, 1995; UN, 1995; Razavi and Miller, 1995a).

One of the first conceptual distinctions among WID, Women and Development, and Gender and Development (GAD) emerged from Canada. As an example, the Canadian International Development Agency (CIDA), with support from its technical and research counterpart arm, was among the first bilateral agencies to develop what it called a 'corporate' strategy to gender and development. This strategy shifted responsibility from a single advocacy office to broad accountability, relying on staff training and personnel and evaluation. In its admirably thorough evaluation notes of the early 1990s, however, CIDA still lacked a thorough embedding of gender analysis throughout its corporate structure. So-called 'mandatory' gender training fell short of those implied universal goals; numerous contractors were never reached (a perennial problem with UN agencies as well). Besides, short-term training for a day or two can hardly undo or unlearn a lifetime of gender obliviousness. Yet other opportunities emerged to foster dialogue about and establish gender monitoring (and potential outcome) indicators through the reorganization of CIDA's Management Information System (MIS). With the crisis created by the year 2000, the MIS required re-engineering and thus the opportunity to incorporate gender in the results-oriented approach (Rathgeber, 1990; Razavi and Miller, 1995b; Rivington, 1997; Staudt, 1998).

Although many institutions have renamed projects by changing the word 'women' to 'gender', their actions do not uniformly demonstrate a corresponding shift in behaviour or gender equality outcomes. In fact, some confusion seems to prevail on the different meanings of the terms. Part of the confusion involves polarized interpretations among some who view the word 'gender' as an attempt to politicize, while others regard it as an attempt to depoliticize. Of course, any shifts in public spending and priorities ultimately involve politics and power, no matter what economists or sector specialists want to believe about this or their own work, including work that dismisses women or gender. Others see gender being used to divert attention to a new high-priority 'men at risk', as exemplified in Jamaica's

GAD-oriented Women's Affairs Bureau (see Goetz, 1995; Baden and Goetz, 1997). The translation of 'gender' in multiple languages is an issue mentioned earlier. Consequently, stakeholders on women and gender will likely see, read and experience the use of both terms for many years to come, including at world conferences and in future Platforms for Action.

### From sideline to mainstream

At least a decade of separate WID offices produced noteworthy projects and principled thinking about rationales linked to integration. Like the 'masters' houses' in which women's offices operated, development was compartmentalized and fragmented into discrete, timetabled projects (see Staudt, 1998). But a larger shift was taking place from project approaches to programmes and grand policy approaches in the context of government downsizing and structural adjustment. So also did the locus of decision making shift within and between institutions.

The project approach rarely added up to anything approaching equality or any of the many ways those noble principles can be conceptualized and measured. Measured by numbers of projects or by funding allocated (for those rare institutions prepared or willing to make such accounts public), the efforts to include women resulted in paltry outcomes, usually single-digit proportions of institutional effort. Among the rare institutions to document double-digit efforts, or up to 20 per cent of funding to women, we find organizations with missions that departed from the orthodox mainstream (such as Scandinavian bilateral technical assistance agencies) and CIDA, already mentioned above for its institution-wide efforts (Jahan, 1995).

Overall missions and budgetary priorities *do* make a difference. The UNDP *HDR* consistently advocates '20–20' proposals, calling for international and national good governance commitments to 20 per cent human development funding (primary education, health and family planning care, and mass-supply water and sanitation). The range is from 10 per cent in the World Bank to 78 per cent in UNICEF, and significantly below 20 per cent in many national governments (*HDR*, 1994). Good intentions or paper commitments are not enough. Some institutions made the clever but ultimately deceptive claim that the mention of women in design documents (an intent? rhetorical device?) was tantamount to integration. All too often, this sort of 'paper compliance' was what characterized WID at the sidelines.

By the 1985 Women's Conference in Nairobi, activists hungered for a strategy to spread and diffuse responsibility across institutional mandates down to the very core of institutional missions. Mainstreaming was born as a strategy, before accumulated experience on what did and did not work in mainstreaming could be analysed. From all historical and research accounts, gender lines permeate everyday life; public policies and programmes often perpetuate those lines or have disparate impacts on women and men because of the structure of social inequality. And women and men participate differently in what some forward-looking economists call the 'care economy': domestic or reproductive work and voluntary community work, 'vital in developing and maintaining the health and skills of the labour force; and in developing and maintaining the social framework' (Elson, 1996a: 8–9; see also Moser, 1996). Policies, then, have gendered effects, even if those who make and implement policy are blind to that way of understanding and measuring analysis. The shift to mainstreaming paralleled the shift from women to gender. But a decade of attempted mainstreaming prompted some to worry about the disappearance of gender in subsequent decades. In actuality, gender mainstreaming has hardly begun.

Thus began the era of gender training, defined as 'a way of looking at the world, a lens that brings into focus the roles, resources, and responsibilities of women and men within the system under analysis' (Rao, Stuart and Kelleher, 1991:7). Through gender training, it was hoped, staff would understand and link knowledge about gender to sound technical development practices. Such hopes do not materialize unless staff are grounded in a structure of expectations, recognition and rewards for a new kind of job performance. Institutions had not yet established serious evaluation systems that took gender perspectives into account for either their programmes or their personnel. Training was not coupled with recruitment and replacement strategies in which selection criteria and job definitions included gender expertise and experience.

Several types of gender training approaches emerged (Kabeer, 1994; Razavi and Miller, 1995b). In the first, the Gender Roles Framework, trainees learned the division of labour, assets and returns for effective projects. In the second, the Triple Roles Framework, also associated with the Gender Planning approach, trainees learned about the productive, reproductive and community demands on women's time and labour burdens.[8] In the Social Relations Framework, trainees learned the power relations between men and women in the context of other inequalities such as class and race. In moving from roles to planning and to relations, we also move the level of analysis from local project fields to the institutional level, whether national or international. This is obviously a move from the relatively simple to the complex. Gender relations analysis is especially complex because it insists on understanding diversity among women and men (see Mohanty, Russo and Torres, 1991). It attends to gender inequality as well as attending to income inequality or poverty and does not assume all women are alike.

These three approaches give more or less attention to the power relations of institutions and the contexts in which they operate (table 2). Gender Roles approaches have no institutional agenda, outside of more enlightened staff. Gender Planning seeks to infuse institutional operations and procedures with gender perspectives. Social Relations attends to diagnosing institutions in all their comparative complexity. Such diagnoses are far more complex than the earliest WID strategies which prescribed common ingredients, most of them in the area of procedural intent,

**Table 2** Approaches to gender training

| Approach | Level of action | Effect on governance |
|----------|-----------------|----------------------|
| Gender Roles | Local project field | None intended |
| Triple Roles | Programme, policy, budget | Institutional |
| Social Relations | All | Institutions in society |

about the existence of policy, checklists, guidelines, sex-disaggregated data bases, and so on.

The Organization for Economic Cooperation and Development's (OECD's) Development Assistance Committee's (DAC's) WID Committee developed increasingly complex reporting tools about its bilateral institutional membership's commitment to integration. The very existence of what came to be thirty-nine practices in four categories gave institutions not only legitimized ideas but the leverage that visible reports can provide to stimulate change (OECD, 1992).

The OECD/DAC/WID's position as a clearinghouse provides a loosely centralized network. But, by institutional definition, it has stopped short of establishing rules and outcomes for its sovereign member states. While UN family institutions are not in comparable circumstances, some of those institutions have the explicit mission to respond to sovereign state agendas, such as the UNDP. While many states are on official record for ratification of the Convention on the Elimination of All Forms of Discrimination against Women, or in support of various outcomes of women's conferences, their governance relations vary markedly, from those wherein men monopolize political power with a narrow policy agenda to those making a transition towards gender-balanced democracies with women-friendly policy agendas.


## Mainstreaming: transforming institutional missions?

Both official organizations and NGOs took up the banner for mainstreaming. One of the first comprehensive analyses to reform mainstream development visions came from the Southern-based DAWN, the Development Alternatives with Women for a New Era. The vision is ambitiously breathtaking, but one to which few institutions subscribed, both then and now. Consider DAWN's summary:

> We want a world where inequality based on class, gender, and race is absent from every country, and from the relationships among countries . . . where basic needs become basic rights and where poverty and all forms of violence are eliminated . . . where massive resources now used in the production of the means of destruction will be diverted to areas where they will help to

relieve oppression both inside and outside the home . . . where all institutions are open to participatory democratic processes, where women share in determining priorities and making decisions. (Quoted in Sen and Grown, 1987:80-1)

The first institution to put thought into mainstreaming was UNIFEM. While it worked with women and gender units on their expertise, it sought to strengthen those units with funding leverage to spread commitment and responsibility to the other parts of government (Anderson, 1993).

During the 1980s, several analyses emerged which categorized the rationales and principles on which women and gender action were based: welfare, efficiency or effectiveness, poverty reduction, equality and justice, and empowerment. They were, and are, used, misused and criticized in confused ways. Gender mainstreaming will not produce consensus on one rationale. Bankers and economists, engrained in a market model, are not likely to respond to terms such as 'empowerment'. However, conceptual spaces in their model open to 'human capital investments' in education and health (Bangura, 1997:21).

The mid 1990s saw several pathbreaking analyses of institutional mainstreaming. One, deriving from a slogan to get prices right, focuses on 'getting institutions right', whether governmental or non-governmental. The mainstreaming, or 'gender-sensitive institutional change', effort is 'to routinize gender-equitable forms of social interaction and to challenge the legitimacy of forms of social organization which discriminate against women' (Goetz, 1997:5-6). Another compares two multilateral and two bilateral institutions, with practices traced to outcomes in two nation-state settings. The work is set within a framework of two kinds of mainstreaming, one that *integrates* existing institutional missions and the other, agenda-setting type, that *transforms* institutional missions (Jahan, 1995). Such analysis allows us to make a bridge to institutional mission and alternative development models. In the 'triumph of capitalism', or the late 1980s transition to market economies, one leading economist warns of the flaws and distortions that easily emerge in such triumph: the collusion of economic and political elites and growing inequalities (Heilbroner, 1989). Without saying as much, these warnings are calls for good governance: to open public space and spread voice beyond elites; to construct people-friendly policies that distribute assets, incomes and opportunities among people in more equitable ways.

Elsewhere, the attention is paid to alternative models and decision-making processes 'on the allocation of values that is likely to result in new policies or modification of existing ones', called 'policy dialogues' (Bangura, 1997:8–17). Three are relevant, listed from the most to least hegemonic:

- *Technocracy, especially the neo-liberal economic model,* which vests authority in government technocrats and international finance experts who reduce deficits and inflation, open markets, and promote competition and efficiency.
- *Corporatism,* the 'historic class compromise' which manages national conflict through bringing organized interests into policy making.
- *Global sustainable pluralism,* inspired by UNDP *HDR* thinking about development as equitable, gender balanced, participatory, sustainable and respectful of diversity.

Women fare least well in the simplistically elegant model of neo-liberal economics; better under corporatism (particularly in Europe, in contrast to Latin America); and between the two in the open and eclectic global sustainable model. Corporatism thus far has been viewed with national boundaries, rather than at global levels, except for some rare exceptions such as the International Labour Organization with its tripartite stakeholders, none of which prioritize gender. With a solid analytical base along with the strong language of the Beijing Women's Conference, the UN family has formulated a clear foundation for gender mainstreaming. Note the frequent use of the word *all* in this language, as well as the shift to 'policies'. The clear message herein is that institutions should no longer relegate gender equality strategies to the isolated margins of separate projects, disconnected from the institutional mandates and all the bureaucratic divisions:

> We hereby adopt and commit ourselves as Governments to implement the following Platform for Action, ensuring that a gender perspective is reflected in all our policies and programmes. (*Beijing Declaration, para.* 38)

> [We call upon] States, the United Nations system and all other actors to implement the Platform for Action, in particular by

promoting an active and visible policy of mainstreaming a gender perspective at all levels, including the design, monitoring and evaluation of all policies, as appropriate, in order to ensure effective implementation of the Platform (*General Assembly, on follow-up to the Fourth World Conference on Women, Res. 50/203*)

[We define mainstreaming a gender perspective] as the process of assessing the implications for women and men of any planned action including legislation, policies, and programmes, in any area and at all levels. It is a strategy for making women's as well as men's concerns and experiences an integral dimension in the design, implementation, monitoring and evaluation of policies and programmes in all political, economic and societal spheres so that women and men benefit equally and inequality is not perpetuated. (*ECOSOC Agreed Conclusions 1997/2*)

Moreover, the UN now has multiple strategically placed people and committee stakeholders in place for coordination and oversight, among them the Division for the Advancement of Women, an Assistant Secretary-General for Gender Issues and the Advancement of Women, an Inter-Agency Committee on Women and Gender Equality, the International Research and Training Institute for the Advancement of Women, and the United Nations Development Fund for Women. Human Rights oversight embraces theoretical mandates that are broader than single-sector institutions or multiple-sector technical assistance agencies such as the UNDP. Still necessary, however, are basic tools for use in evaluating outcomes and deconstructing budgetary cores of institutions with good governance, including gender-balanced governance. One by one, institutions are in transition towards mainstreaming.

A gender mainstreaming policy requires that various staff — from top to bottom and in all divisions — be aware of and/or trained in awareness of how each policy and operational decision will benefit and burden different groups of women and men. No action is free of gender implications, for in all societies the structure of gender relations creates different opportunities, experience and benefits.

Gender mainstreaming begins a process of understanding the baseline of institutional capabilities, measurements and actions with respect to consequences of inequality in different degrees. The track record will initially appear faulty, but it will be a tribute to those well-governed institutions to be open, transparent and honest about documented performance. The highlights which follow illustrate how top-level administrative commitment, backed up with resources and measurable goals, can alter the incentives that support gender equality within large institutions, even those that are decentralized in complicated ways. For example, a 1996 memorandum from the UNDP Administrator reports that 6.7 per cent of resource allocations in 1994/5 were in the category of advancement of women, compared with 20 per cent each in the categories of poverty, the environment and governance. An internal report of 417 projects, cited in this memorandum, observes that 'gender was superficially added to the project background to pass the screening process, but rarely integrated into the operating assumptions of the development sectors'.

From this analysis, the UNDP Administrator took steps to enforce commitment, steps with numerical funding objectives and reporting requirements, all of which necessitate ongoing monitoring. For example, a 10 per cent commitment from global programme resources was allocated to gender mainstreaming, to which allocations from other thematic areas (especially poverty) would be added, totalling 20 per cent. In that global programme, resources support gender mainstreaming tools and models as well as partnerships that include women in decision making. Additionally, 20 per cent of regional programme and 20 per cent of country allocations are designated for 'the advancement of women'. This comes from that same 1996 memorandum from the UNDP Administrator.


**Gender mainstreaming framework**

After imbibing the historical and contemporary considerations above, we are now in a position to establish a basic framework for gender mainstreaming. The task is a daunting one, given the need to respect the integrity, complexity and diverse missions of institutions at global, country and within-country levels. But it is a task long overdue, for the Beijing Platform for Action speaks loudly, clearly and in consensus about the goal of gender equality.

*women + difference change*

*outcome*

The framework would begin with institutional *outcomes* rather than inputs and promises. These outcomes must be people oriented, surely a common ground that even the most orthodox of economists would acknowledge. When the promotional literature of the largest international bank says it 'makes a difference in people's lives', the outcomes oriented among us would hope that the difference is positive, that it reduces gender and income inequalities, and that it can be documented. The language of gender provides analysts with the most socially significant categories of people, next to nationality, about whom policy actions are significant: women and men.

*Discursive*

The framework would operate at the macro level of *policy dialogue*. As such, the framework recognizes the competing dialogues that operate in global and national society and occasionally within institutions themselves. Policy dialogue can be as grandiose as a hegemonic orthodox economic model (wherein counter-hegemonic forces frequently operate), to institutional mission, to sector objectives. Within the context of this policy dialogue, the framework asks the Chief Executive Officer and major stakeholders to establish answers to two basic questions:

- What, in documentable people outcomes, does it mean for our institution to pursue its work?
- What, in documentable people outcomes, does it mean for our institution to pursue that work in gender-sensitive ways?

To answer the second question, those involved in the dialogue must also ask about policies and programmes:

*gender analysis*

- What policies and practices institutionalize preference to men?
- What policies and practices would de-institutionalize such preferences?
- What new policies or compensatory practices would equalize future policies?
- What assumptions are made about the (aforementioned) 'care economy', and how do those assumptions distort traditional ways to measure efficiency and cost–benefit calculations?

Once outcomes are established, the central operating mission unit wherein planning and budgetary approval are housed should establish funds along with data, monitoring

*Process*

*Inputs*

and operating procedures to move towards those outcomes. Those significant commitments now become the 'inputs' rather than promises to put the word 'women' in design documents, checklists or the women-impact statements of years past. Of course, those minimalist, but bureaucratically cumbersome, techniques could reorient staff. At the *Actors* bottom line, though, staff selection, orientation and training programmes, followed up with personnel evaluation and rewards, would recognize gender-sensitive work as central to institutional missions. Each significant division, *Institution* bureau and department should have a critical mass of focal points with gender expertise and experience to make gender-sensitive outcomes happen. Critical mass is taken here to mean more than one or two and, within larger units, at least 20 per cent representation of women.

In most institutions, the dialogue, as well as the institutional machinery to operationalize people- and gender-sensitive outcomes, will require *new* staff with gender expertise and experience to replace those who leave under attrition and retirement. Selection criteria for new staff should contain gender expertise and experience along with the other factors. Such criteria will shift some of the mainstreaming burden to educational institutions, public administration institutes and the schools that educate faculty and teachers for all levels of schooling. Gender analysis should occupy as critical a place in curricula as other forms of social analysis.

Gender expertise is linked to technical capabilities, political and diplomatic skills, and sector-specific expertise. *Tasks* In the words of those who analyse women's policy machinery in Australia, Canada and New Zealand, 'bilingualism' is required in both the dominant and gender discourses, coupled with connections to outside constituencies, which themselves understand the institutional structures, pressure points in budget cycles and procedural issues (Sawer, 1996:23). Typically, small groups of officials deal with budget *range of* policy. Those in dialogue need to be a broader group than the few who generally meet 'behind closed doors'. This *Actors* group would include spending ministries, women's and other groups in the general public, and researchers and policy (including gender) analysts, who will increase the *demand* for integrating gender into budget policy — a sure counter

*Budgets*

to the small *supply* in that policy. 'Budget hearings' with women parliamentarians and NGOs are another means (Elson, 1996b:16).

Precedents have been set for viewing the budget as a mechanism to facilitate outcomes. Among these examples we would identify South Africa, Australia and Canada. The framework for Australia is quite complete, as a pictorial outline illustrates (Elson, 1996b:10; Figure 1).

Commonwealth ministers responsible for women's affairs heard and discussed these approaches in the context of moving from 'gender blind' (also known as 'gender neutral') to 'gender-sensitive budgets'. Of particular interest is the effort of budget analysts to understand the 'care economy', guided by neither commercial nor altruistic principles. In this economy, wherein women especially pursue socially valuable tasks, what might appear to be cost-saving measures in downsizing the state may have significant burdens on women, who assume responsibility for some of those tasks. At some point, even women cannot bear extra burdens and the tasks go undone, at a major cost then to the whole society. Downsizers cannot assume that women's time and labour are 'available in unlimited quantities ... perfectly elastic' (Elson, 1996a:10). The calculation of costs and benefits in the care economy is part of the toolkit of gender-aware outcome and budget analysis.

With disparate national and international institutions developing institution-specific outcomes and budgets, we

**Figure 1** Australian women's budget: outline

Total budget equals:

By department:
Specific gender-based expenditures, i.e. in employment and health

+

Equal employment opportunity expenditures on employees

=

Budget, minus above two expenditure types, for gender impact:
Who uses?
Who receives?

still need global summary outcomes reported with honesty, integrity and technical competence. For its track record of attention to people-centred outcomes, as well as its gender-sensitive staff, the UNDP *HDR* office seems a logical choice. However, *HDR* should pursue data and outcome measures that go beyond the current indexes (GDI and GEM). Gendered decision making counts are in part outcome but in part assumptions about the means (inputs) towards equit-able outcomes. Global citizens need *gendered* summary outcomes about poverty reduction, assets and incomes, and good governance.

This gender mainstreaming framework is ultimately a framework about good governance. Those who conceptu-alize and support good governance need also to go to their central drawing boards to consider outcome, meaning and strategy in gender-equal terms. Outside the rhetorical and pronoun approach (women and men, he and she), governance documents do little to clarify what the de-monopolization of male politics will mean for governance outcomes and procedures.[9]

## Obstacles to gender mainstreaming

The obstacles to an ambitious gender mainstreaming strat-egy are both contextual and conceptual. In part, these are obstacles associated with transforming institutional mis-sions and policy dialogues with gender tools that attend to the very heart of development as capacitating human beings: budgets and evaluation outcomes.

Gender analysts confront the first huge challenge of move-ment towards 'good governance'. Good governance is about many things, ranging from opening democratic spaces to performing governance tasks well, justly and equitably. Thus budget and evaluation matters are at the heart of these concerns. Heretofore, budgetary processes have been less transparent than they would have been had notions of good governance been a standard. Evaluation offices have been rendered impotent in institutions that relish the opportun-ity to promote the 'good news' about their work but avoid accountability for the 'bad news'. Even evaluation units have avoided conceptualizing their work in ways that document outcomes for people, meaning both women and men. Instead, evaluators have attended to the concerns of funders rather than determining how effectively that money is spent in improving human capabilities. Fortunately for gender analysts, good governance has begun to preoccupy many within both national and international institutions. Once those associated with good governance comprehend the centrality of gender equality to the tasks at hand, their stakes in this work will deepen.

A second obstacle to gender mainstreaming results from a context of limited resources and of downsized institutions (see Kwesiga, chapter 10 in this volume). Whatever the gender unit and wherever it is located, analysts and focal points could use what in public administration literature was once termed 'slack resources', or flexible monies to leverage change. Moreover, it takes resources to recruit new staff and to reorient existing staff towards gender-aware analysis in outcome and budgetary tasks. As the analysis of 'femocrats' (versus 'ecorats', or economic rationalists) in Australia, Canada and New Zealand warns about operating within downsized government, actions are sometimes limited to preventing further damage to women (Sawer, chapter 12 of this volume and 1996).

Yet if institutions are to take their gender mainstreaming seriously, other institutional resources will be freed up for equality outcomes. Such funding 'liberation', however, always involves struggle for those who lose, or who perceive loss. And the loss may be more than budgetary privilege and preferential spending to men. The movement towards gender equality is a movement away from arbitrary male control and authority. Yet will downsizing and economic downturn, affecting men and women alike, lead resentful men to resist equality and their loss of control rather than resist political-economic decisions that burden people? Under such circumstances, good governance needs to ensure safety against domestic violence, rape and other backlash hate crimes.

A third obstacle to gender mainstreaming is found within the hegemonic neo-liberal, orthodox economic model — one that pays no heed to the care economy. Yet as outlined earlier in this paper, multiple models exist along with space therein for gender analysis. As institutions and people move and shift to new models, however long that process, analysts should be eclectic and open to opportunities to stretch and/or critique existing models within spaces that exist for policy dialogue. Even the orthodox, or the ecorats, understand the importance of what they term 'human capital investments'. The challenge here is to ensure that investments are adequate, approaching or exceeding the 20–20 human development funding goals that were cited earlier.

Besides the larger, contextual obstacles outlined above, gender mainstreaming also confronts several conceptual challenges. One involves the way we conceive of households and the winners and losers therein. At one time, simplistic analyses assumed that householders shared income and benefits. Economic rationalists continue to use such simplified assumptions for elegant model making and computation. WID analysts brought the 'female-headed household' on to the analytical platter, as well as household diversity on the degrees to which incomes are separate or shared. Households are complex units which, according to one conception, are places of 'cooperative conflict' (Sen, 1990).[10] This sort of complexity is a large obstacle to interpreting gender-aware budgets. The second conceptual obstacle is associated with assessing gender equality outcomes in global, quantitative, qualitative and contextual ways. Numbers, and our obsessions with them, are tools to begin gender-aware dialogue, rather than to close those matters.

Fundamentally, gender mainstreaming is at the very core of public and democratic efforts in development. For this reason, it seems fitting to close with the troubling, yet eloquent words of the UNDP *HDR* in its call for gender-sensitive conceptions and outcomes: 'Human development, if not engendered, is endangered' (1995:1). Such a grave threat cannot be addressed with a single 'machine' within a nation or institution. Gender mainstreaming must permeate governance rather than rely on a piece of machinery.

## Notes

1 This definition draws on the work of the UNDP's *Human Development Report*, issued annually and published by Oxford University Press

in New York, hereinafter referred to as *HDR*, with the appropriate year.

2 *HDR 1997* was focused on poverty. The billion-person figure is based on both income and human development criteria.

3 The Gender Disaggregated Index (GDI) and Gender Empowerment Measure (GEM), pioneered in the 1995+ *HDRs*, are composite scores. As *HDRs* routinely say, 'no society treats its women as well as its men'. The word 'equality' (the same share for everybody), which seems fixed, absolute and simple in its implications, as Deborah Stone (1997, chapter 2) discusses, is complex in the polis: same shares among those with interest or need, or all? Same share based on the value of the good? Same share based on equal competition, or compensation for past burdens? Same statistical chance in share allocation? Same share based on opportunity to participate politically? And on and on . . .

4 Entitlement and endowment come from Amartya Sen's work on poverty (see, for example, Sen, 1990), which in turn feeds into *HDR* thinking. Yet Sen's focus on assets such as land do not show up in *HDR* methodologies. *HDR*'s Capability Poverty, or more recently (1997) Human Poverty Index, composites could use gender disaggregation.

5 The rich and elaborate UNDP website for Good Governance contains little conceptualization which embeds gender (www.undp.org). The World Bank's concern with governance is largely related to stable, legal contractual systems for market exchange. The Freedom House, which produces an annual Map of Freedom showing the global shift to majority free and partially free countries (www.freedomhouse.org), is gender neutral, or to use Diane Elson's term for the budget, 'gender-blind' (see, for example, Elson, 1996a, b). Its eight-item political rights checklist asks whether 'cultural, ethnic, religious and other minority groups' have participation, but says nothing about gender. It asks about freedom from 'economic oligarchy' but seems oblivious to male oligarchy. But see *HDR 1995*, focusing on gender and highlighting 'men's monopolization' of politics.

6 Much institutional analysis, whether gendered or not, focuses on inducements or structures of rewards and penalties that affect staff from top to bottom. Street-level refers to those front-line staff who interact with the public.

7 The Summit is analysed in Staudt, 1998, chapter 5, with a table from the conference directory showing the overwhelming responses from NGOs that serve majority women. Yet literature from South Asia, also reviewed therein, shows 'pipelining' loans through women to their husbands (which surely expands stakeholders and supporters, but confuses the understanding of evaluation outcomes). In Bangladesh, the renowned Grameen Bank issues a minuscule proportion of credit in the country context, even though its participants now number two million. *HDR(s)* have reported that micro-enterprise credit still goes to a 95 per cent male majority; the 1997 *HDR* says that less than 1 per cent of credit reaches the poorest billion (*HDR*, 1997:109). The 1993 *HDR* says that the Grameen Bank accounts for 0.1 per cent of national credit in Bangladesh (*HDR*, 1993:6–7).

8 Gender Roles has also been associated with the 'Harvard' model, while Kabeer is wedded to Gender Relations. Moser's foundational work is Triple Roles, and these ideas have given birth to the care economy considerations in Elson's conceptualization of gendered budgets.

9 The UNDP web site is beautifully complete, save conceptualizations and references on gender. Yet the definition of good governance is potentially inclusive: participatory, transparent and accountable . . . effective and equitable . . . rule of law . . . wherein the 'voices of the poorest and the most vulnerable are heard in decision-making over the allocation of development resources'.

10 Razavi and Miller (drawing on Buvinic) point out (1995a) that an emphasis on female heads is 'less threatening to male bureaucrats' and that it 'does not raise intra-household redistributive questions' Razavi and Miller:7. See also Baden and Goetz (1997) on credible sources.

# Part II
# Comparative analyses

# 3

# National women's machinery: state-based institutions to advocate for gender equality[1]

ANNE MARIE GOETZ

## Introduction

This chapter considers the effectiveness of National women's machineries (NWMs), examining their record of promoting women's interests in five countries: Bangladesh, Chile, Jamaica, Morocco and Vietnam.[2] These countries are each at different stages of integrating gender into development processes. They also differ in their degree of economic development, their political histories and the nature of their main economic constraints. What they have in common is a reasonable degree of political stability since 1990, though the specific characteristics of civil society and governance in each country differ. The singling out of these countries is not intended to give the impression that they are either particularly remiss or progressive in their approach to institutionalizing women's interests in development — when it comes to institutionalizing women's interests in policy processes, no country in the world can be considered 'developed'.

NWMs are created on the premise that the state must take a lead in promoting gender equality. They are a form of institutionalized or bureaucratic representation of women. The reason the state has been such an important focus of feminist efforts to redress gender injustices is because the state is assumed (or hoped) to have a degree of autonomy from patriarchy and hence, to the degree that the state assumes responsibility for women's interests, it can provide a resort of appeal against the power of men in more intimate institutions such as the family.

But few states have distinguished themselves in championing women's rights. Indeed, the injustices worked in women's lives by the power asymmetries attached to gender differences across most social institutions have historically commanded a very weak response from public authority all over the world. In the Platform for Action from the 1995 UN Fourth World Conference on Women in Beijing it was asserted that a lack of political will was the reason for the slow implementation of gender equality policy measures in many countries. This 'lack of political will' explanation is too vague to be of much use; it does not direct attention to the real problems of generating political support for socially unpopular policies and, in any case, it underestimates the rather high degree of political will which does exist among many national leaders, but which cannot be translated into results because of insufficient backing from political parties or civil society, or insufficient power over the permanent government: the civil service. In addition, the 'lack of political will' explanation for policy failure ignores the problem of the deep institutionalization of gender differences and male privilege in the public sphere. This is the prime concern of this chapter, which concentrates on efforts to integrate women's interests into state institutions.

## Institutionalizing WID/GAD

In most of the cases in this study, measures to institutionalize the Women in Development (WID)/Gender and Development (GAD) machinery in the state bureaucracy have been in response to pressures exerted either by foreign donors or the international feminist movement through the United Nations (UN) system. This is not to suggest that women's organizations had not been actively pushing for the state to take responsibility for gender equality. However, in some of the cases (Bangladesh and Vietnam), the energy of the women's movement in the 1960s and 1970s was co-opted by political parties in an effort to harness additional political support from the country's female constituency. In other cases such as Morocco, the efforts of women's organizations were oriented towards more conventional women's welfare projects. In only two of the case countries — Chile and to a lesser extent, Jamaica — did a national concern with WID/GAD and the establishment of government machinery emerge in direct response to pressure from the women's movement.

## Structural and sectoral location

Two responses to the question of finding an institutional location for the WID/GAD agenda have been common. One is to set up an advocacy unit at a central level with a mandate to influence planning processes across all development sectors. Staudt's detailed analysis of this kind of response in the United States Agency for International Development shows how this can be a method for placating troublesome constituencies while at the same time ensuring that the issue is contained because of the inherent difficulties of pursuing cross-sectoral change, especially where the advocacy unit is desperately under-resourced, as tends to be the case (Staudt, 1990). The other response is to set up a WID/GAD desk in a sector which is seen as most closely identified with the issue, or indeed to create a new WID/GAD sector. Typically this enclaves the WID/GAD issue in a social welfare sector, where it may share in a general derogation of social welfare issues as being marginal to main development concerns such as growth. Alternatively it may be lumped in as a new quasi-sector with a range of residual and marginalized concerns — such as culture, youth and sports. The institutional location of WID/GAD bureaucracies can thus be discussed in terms of their proximity to power in the central state directorate (vertical location) and their thematic or sectoral location (horizontal location).

The different formal roles that WID/GAD units have been assigned fall into the following typology:

- *'Advocacy' or 'advisory' units,* located either in a central political unit, such as the office of the Prime Minister or President, or in a central economic planning unit, such as the Ministry of Planning. This WID/GAD unit is responsible for promoting attention to gender issues and giving advice to various government units. Very often, however, it is under-equipped in terms of staff numbers and technical skills, and becomes the representative of a 'special issue' in an often resented or easily dismissed policy-pleading role.

- *Policy 'oversight' or 'monitoring' units*, which may have rather more robust powers to the degree that they may be granted automatic rights to review projects before approval by central economic planning units, or to review submissions for Cabinet decisions.

- *Units with implementation responsibilities*. These WID/GAD units create programmes which are designed to have a demonstration effect, inspiring replication in other areas of government activity. They also respond to policy needs not well catered for elsewhere, for example by setting up shelters for victims of domestic violence. But the typically low level of resources for policy implementation means that these efforts are isolated and cannot produce broad-based policy changes across the public administration.

Central advocacy or 'oversight' WID/GAD bureaux within the central state directorate have been set up in Chile and Vietnam. Chile's National Service for Women (SERNAM), set up in the early 1990s, has a curious statutory basis: it is a unit within the Ministry of Planning yet it is headed by a state minister. Neither a full Ministry with an input to Cabinet decisions, nor an established boundary-bridging body, it straddles two administrative identities in a way which diminishes its potential impact. In principle its institutional location provides it with access to the 'technical core' of policy making, and indeed rhetoric about gender equality now figures in the Ministry of Planning's work. However, it lacks clear mechanisms for ensuring changes in government decisions, such as automatic review of all new investment decisions, or clear means of ensuring cross-ministerial compliance with the WID/GAD policy mandate. Women's desks and gender-sensitive programmes do exist in some other ministries, and SERNAM supports these. Its formal mandate explicitly excludes project implementation functions, except for demonstration and experimentation purposes. However, its limited impact on cross-ministerial decision making has made it focus instead on public awareness building and on implementing pilot projects which are donor funded and often executed by non-governmental organizations (NGOs), prompting the observation that SERNAM behaves more like an NGO than a part of the public administration (Pollack, 1994a:20). In its operational work it focuses, importantly, on activities which are neglected in other areas of government, such as sexual violence, adolescent pregnancy and female-headed households.

In Vietnam, the Vietnamese Women's Union (VWU) is the *de facto* national women's bureaucracy. It is one of several important mass organizations which make up the 'Fatherland Front of Vietnam' — or the ruling Communist Party. Although by official statute it is an NGO, it has strong links to government and has been influential since the 1950s in promoting progressive legislation for women, in particular labour legislation protecting women's conditions of employment and rights to maternity leave. During the war years, however, its main function was the mobilization of women as combatants, suppliers and supporters of the war effort, and as a result its main skills are in 'agit prop' (Tran Thi, 1994:29) rather than in structured policy advocacy. One feature of its wartime organization was the development of an extensive grassroots network in villages, as well as representation in trade unions, giving it a valuable structure for coordinating gender and development efforts nationally. However, with just 150 staff members, the VWU is grossly under-resourced, and its level of influence in villages and trade unions is highly uneven (Olin, 1988:16).

Although the VWU gained the formal right, in a 1988 decision by the Vietnamese Council of Ministers, to be consulted and involved in any decision regarding women in the country, its lack of resources, and lack of veto power over unsatisfactory government policy, mean that it has to rely primarily upon the uncertain mechanism of the good-will of government members to include it in decision making. It is in any case curious for an 'NGO' to be recognized to have privileged access to state decision making, and this may have been more of a rhetorical gesture than an effort to institutionalize the VWU's influence on policy making.

While its formal mandate as an arm of the Party is to focus on issues of national concern to women, since 1990 it has increasingly turned to the implementation of gender and development projects (such as income generation) in response to the new availability of funds from international donors.

In Bangladesh the WID/GAD agenda has been institutionalized in a distinct Ministry, but it shares space with marginalized public concerns such as children. The Ministry suffers from under-resourcing, significant power distance from the central state directorate, association with residual welfare or community issues, and overlapping roles with ruling party-linked women's units. This central WID/GAD unit has had a long but very administratively discontinuous history. It has been hostage to shifting political currents, having been promoted to ministerial status under the Bangladesh National Party (BNP) regime of President Zia ul-Rahman in the 1970s, demoted to a Department of the Social Affairs Ministry under President Ershad in the 1980s, and reinstated as a Ministry under the BNP regime of Zia's widow, Begum Khaleda Zia in the mid 1990s. These changes owe less to any significant variation in the official commitment to the WID/GAD agenda than to its utility at various times in generating international political capital in demonstrating a progressive national position. The credibility of these positions has been highly compromised by simultaneous concessions — which have increased in significance over time — to Islamic interests. What has remained a constant in this opportunistic administrative tergiverzation has been an unclear mandate and deficiencies in staff, financial resources and administrative privileges.

The Ministry's formal mandate combines an advocacy role with a programme implementation role. However, it is under-equipped to carry out either role. Its one direct link to national economic planning processes is through the Women's Desk in the Planning Commission, where a sole officer is also responsible for sports, culture, youth, social welfare and media, a cluster of responsibilities which signals women's place among a residuum of planning concerns. It has begun to experiment with WID focal points across sectoral ministries, which will be discussed in the next section. Since 1990 it has been granted right of oversight and appraisal over projects of other ministries and agencies, where it is given ten days to review new projects before they are forwarded to the Planning Commission. However, just two staff members are available for this and they are constrained by the tight time limit and by a lack of gender analysis skills. On the operational side, its tiny budget for implementing programmes (just 0.22 per cent of the national development budget) restricts it to small projects which are largely urban centred, although it uses these to promote issues neglected by other ministries, such as working women's need for hostels and child care, shelters for survivors of domestic violence, legal education and legal aid, and vocational training. Many of its top-level posts are vacant, and have been for years, and it is quite unable to fulfil its functions as a line Ministry, with staff in less than a quarter of sub-districts.

In Jamaica the Bureau of Women's Affairs has had an uneasy history on the administrative peripheries of the state, shunted back and forth between the Ministry of Youth and Community Development, and the Ministry of Social Affairs. Only once, in response to heightened awareness of the issue provoked by the 1975 UN World Conference of the International Women's Year in Mexico City, was it located in the Office of the Prime Minister, from 1975 to 1978. After 1989, however, it was located in the Ministry of Labour, Welfare and Sport. This is significant and appropriate, given women's very high participation in the country's formal labour force. However, this latest institutional placement may have owed less to women's strong labour force attachment than to the fact that at the time that Ministry was headed by the only female Cabinet minister, who was assumed, because of her gender, to be likely to provide the right home for the Women's Bureau.

The Bureau has had a combined mandate of advocacy and project implementation, and has been highly dependent on outside funds to carry out these functions. In the late 1980s these funds were withdrawn in reaction to the government's persistent failure to provide counterpart funding, forcing the Bureau to withdraw from project activities, most of which had an income-generating focus, and to focus on efforts to influence the national planning process. Though this shift in focus is regretted by Bureau members

(Mariott, 1994), it is a mixed blessing, as the Bureau was never properly equipped to implement projects. Also, curiously, the majority of these projects were conventional small-scale and informal-sector income-generating ventures. In a country which has one of the highest rates of female participation in formal employment in the world, this conventional WID focus seems unjustifiable. It perhaps best reflects the Bureau's intellectual and financial dependence on outside donors and their externally-derived WID perspectives.

Of all the case countries, Morocco has invested the least in setting up a coherent WID/GAD administrative entity. Instead, women's desks have been set up in an *ad hoc* manner across a range of Ministries, in response to new funding opportunities available through the international community. The Women's Desk in the Ministry of Employment and Social Affairs has had nominal responsibility for responding to international pressures for WID policy statements, but has no policy oversight role, no advocacy role and no policy coordination role. Otherwise, there are women's units in the Ministries of Youth and Sports, Public Health, Agriculture, Planning and Foreign Affairs, and in the National Agricultural Credit Service. It is impossible to speak of a coherent WID strategy emerging from any of these units. Each responds to Ministerial priorities, and usually each is focused around women-specific and foreign-funded project activities which make few encroachments on broader Ministerial activities.

Overall, then, in none of the case study countries except Vietnam has the WID/GAD concern found a secure and sustainable institutional expression. When located in advocacy units close to central state decision-making units, they tend to be inadequately resourced to fulfil their functions. When set up as separate Ministries they can become isolated as a peripheral enclave and associated with marginal concerns. There are cases where the WID/GAD issue has been seen by the dominant political party as a useful political resource, as a means of demonstrating national progressive attitudes to the international community, as in Bangladesh. In these cases the WID/GAD issue risks appropriation by, and hence association with, the ruling political party, which compromises its future in the administrative structure. This kind of politicization of the WID/GAD agenda also undercuts its legitimacy and may cut it off from its natural constituency, where autonomous women's groups may shun association with party-linked WID units. The overwhelming degree to which WID/GAD advocacy and project activities in every one of these case countries depends on outside funding underlines the shallowness of national commitment to the issue and fundamentally undermines the sustainability of efforts to institutionalize the gender equality mandate.

## Mechanisms for influencing other ministries: 'mainstreaming'

Most of the WID/GAD units in question here have a mandate to pursue their agenda across other government departments — a project sometimes called 'mainstreaming'. For this they have devised a range of policy instruments, such as gender-monitoring checklists, guidelines, inter-ministerial committees, gender awareness training and WID Focal Points. Gender-specific national policy statements or plans have also been formulated; these will be reviewed in the next section. Mainstreaming measures are intended to provoke gender-sensitive institutional, policy and operational changes across the public sector in order to make responsiveness to women's interests a routine part of each sector's activities. At the very least, they are also hoped to tap the technical and administrative resources of other departments to make up for resource deficiencies in the WID/GAD sector in research, advocacy and implementation. Vietnam and Morocco will not be discussed in this section as the state units charged with gender equality in both countries do not appear to be equipped with mainstreaming mechanisms. In Morocco, the gender units of various ministries appear not to benefit from central coordination. And while the VWU has extensive links downwards to villages and horizontally to trade unions, it lacks mechanisms for coordinating policy with government units.

Jamaica is the only case country to have elaborated detailed gendered project guidelines and checklists. Jamaica's

Project Profile format for all new projects incorporates a procedural step for assessing potential gender-differential impact issues. Linked to this, methods for assessing gender-differential impact have been incorporated into the training for civil servants at the Administrative Staff College. To ensure adherence to this measure, the Bureau of Women's Affairs has a seat on the project Pre-selection Committee of the Planning Institute. For projects in process, a Gender Monitoring Checklist specifies five benchmarks against which development actions are assessed: whether sex-disaggregated data are used or collected; whether the project adheres to national policy commitments; whether mechanisms exist to consult with women and men on gender issues; whether the project takes action on equality issues; and whether the context for the project is gender sensitive, in the sense of incorporating women's specific needs.

Chile and Bangladesh have experimented with designating WID Focal Point officers in other ministries. In Chile, this has been an informal process. SERNAM lacks institutional measures for communication and coordination with other Ministries, and hence requested that each Ministry designate a contact person with whom SERNAM can communicate. There are no institutional rewards associated with the Focal Point position and, unsurprisingly, the position has often been occupied by individuals uninterested in the issue and hence unwilling to commit time to it. The Ministries of Labour and Education are notable in that there has been committed top-level support for the gender issue from male ministers. This is not enough, however, as the strongest resistance comes from mid-level male staff. Training is only a partial solution, as it reaches only a few individuals, and often, as in the case of the highly resistant Ministry of Agriculture, the majority of staff reject training opportunities by failing to attend seminars on gender awareness (Pollack, 1994a:17).

In Bangladesh, a formal Focal Point system was introduced in the early 1990s, where designated contact individuals in twenty-seven ministries constitute an inter-ministerial coordination committee intended to meet every three months. Again, these positions have often been given to lower-ranking individuals who lack commitment to the gender issue. WID planning cells in ministries are under-staffed and lack technical skills, and hence are unable to arm their Focal Points with relevant information or policy analyses. Ideally, the Bangladesh Department of WID would provide this technical support, but it is equally under-resourced in this area.

By and large in the cases under review, 'mainstreaming' has been interpreted as a project of simply gaining access to other ministries; as a means of inserting staff charged with the WID mandate into the administrative structure and inserting women as a target or client group in every devel-opment sector. The difficulties of achieving this alone have postponed a more transformative project of challenging the basic operating assumptions of each sector and their under-lying disciplinary biases. The sorts of gendered project guide-lines and monitoring checklists developed in Jamaica do indicate means of pursuing this more transformative project. However, tools of that sort can too easily be dismissed if their use is not policed or supported by effective sanctions on non-compliance, such as vetoes on gender-insensitive pro-ject proposals. The experiments with Focal Point officers show, disappointingly but predictably, that success relies on committed individuals in that position and that com-mitment cannot be engineered by training alone.

There is a more general problem inherent in projects of seeking cross-ministerial compliance to a new policy man-date. This has to do with the embeddedness of bureaucratic interests and their defence within bureaucratic boundaries. Most public administrations feature a strong propensity to protect ministerial territory and to resist cross-cutting in-terests. Especially in contexts of resource scarcity, adminis-trative units tend to guard their own territory because development resources attached to programmes and projects offer opportunities for patronage. This imposes competi-tion between ministries, which defend privileged access to resources by evolving distinctive mandates and operational processes tied to disciplinary and sectoral concerns. These same kinds of incentive operate in national WID units as well, producing a strong incentive to concentrate on women-specific projects which provide a visible justification for their continued existence.

### Promoting national ownership of the WID/GAD agenda: integrating gender to national planning processes

National development plans and budgets are important public statements expressing politically chosen priorities for change and progress, and are based on a macroeconomic framework designed to create the conditions under which this national vision can be realized. Integrating gender into this process requires both political and economic groundwork by WID/GAD policy advocates. This involves securing top-level commitment to WID/GAD priorities, agreeing action programmes and earmarked funds for every planning sector, generating sex-disaggregated data, and designing gender-specific achievement targets and progress indicators at the macro and sectoral levels.

In Chile SERNAM has formulated a national Equal Opportunity Plan. This is designed to 'promote an equal distribution of resources and social tasks, of civil rights, and participation, and access to power between men and women, and to value women's contribution to economic development' (Pollack, 1994a:3). SERNAM has been successful in providing a new impetus for collecting sex-disaggregated data, both within the Ministry of Planning, where it is located, and in other governmental departments. Within the Ministry of Planning, the annual socio-economic population survey is disaggregated by sex, and all new analytical work related to poverty and labour market issues makes an effort to address gender issues. As of 1995 households have been disaggregated by sex of headship in living standards studies. Across other government departments, the National Statistical Institute of the Ministry of Economics has introduced measures to sex disaggregate new data related to economic and employment variables, and has created a sex-disaggregated index of wages and salaries which illuminates problems of discrimination against women in the labour market.

In Bangladesh issues related to women have been raised in each successive five-year development plan from the first (1973–78) to the current plan. All of these plans have put primary emphasis on enhancing the quality of women's domestic role, through, initially, handicraft training and family planning, and later through improved provision of rural credit and better access to education. The second plan (1980–85) was the first to propose a multi-sectoral approach to women's development. But in this and subsequent plans, only the social sectors show significant expenditure allocations for women. The third and fourth five-year plans raised employment issues for women, but these were almost entirely oriented to informal micro-enterprise opportunities which enable women to raise the productivity of their home-based work. No measures were detailed to increase the number of women participating in the formal labour force, save for a 15 per cent quota for women in public sector employment. Rarely are resources or institutional mechanisms specified in these plans to enable the Women's Ministry to discharge its coordinating, information generation and policy design functions.

An alternative approach to the promotion of women's interests in national planning documents has been the formulation of separate gender-focused national perspective plans by WID/GAD units. In Jamaica a *National Policy Statement on Women* was produced by the Bureau of Women's Affairs and adopted by the Cabinet in 1987, and a five-year *National Development Plan on Women* was produced by the Bureau and the Planning Institute in 1990. The 1990 Plan details actions to be taken in each major development sector and identifies main agencies responsible for implementation. But its implementation remains the sole responsibility of the Bureau of Women's Affairs. It has neither a budget nor details of budgetary implications for other government departments, and it has not been internalized by other departments because it was elaborated without any participation from them. Further, since it was elaborated separately from the Jamaican Five-Year Development Plan to 1995, it remains essentially external to the main planning framework.

In Morocco there is no WID presence in the Ministry of Planning or other central government departments, which means that there has been no clear point from which gender-sensitive planning guidance could emerge. The Centre of Demographic Studies in the Department of Statistics in the Ministry of Planning does, however, produce valuable sex-disaggregated data, particularly in relation to the formal workforce. But no women or gender-trained researchers are part of this team, nor is it animated by any concern to illuminate significant information on gender for planners. This restricts the potential impact of sex-disaggregated data on the policy-making process, and it has also meant that a range of important gender issues are not included in national surveys — for example, the legal and political aspects of women's lives (Barkallil, 1994:17).

Vietnam, like Morocco, has no system for mainstreaming gender equality concerns in national planning. No systematic attention to gender equality is paid in the State Commission on Development Planning or in technical or line ministries. A national employment generation programme launched in 1992 did not include a component for women until the VWU put pressure on the government to allocate some of the funding to a credit programme for women (in the end, just 1.8 per cent of the funding from the national programme was allocated to women) (Van Anh, 1988:26). Observers feel that gender equality concerns have tended to be addressed in national planning only when problems caused by gender relations impede national production goals (Olin, 1988:16). For example, the concern to free women's labour for employment in public sector services and industries during the war turned attention to the need to replace women's domestic labour through the provision of child care.

But in spite of this lack of clear mainstreaming mechanisms, the VWU has played an important role in promoting women's rights. It was involved, for example, in fiercely lobbying the government to retain the provision for six months' maternity leave in the new Labour Code adopted in 1994. In this, it actually clashed with another women's department, the Board for Women's Affairs in the Confederation of Labour, which was promoting a reduction of maternity leave to four months, lowering the costs of maternity benefits as an incentive to newly privatized businesses to hire women. Another motive behind this was popular resentment at women's capacity to moonlight in a second job during paid maternity leave. The Labour Code eventually adopted ambiguous wording guaranteeing six months' maternity leave to state workers and four months for women employees in private business.

A problem with this process is that neither the sectoral gender policy statements nor the draft national policy statement detailed budget implications of any of the proposed policies. As with national planning experiences in Morocco, Jamaica and Bangladesh, this failure to follow through recommendations with clear calculations of public expenditure implications is an important reason why WID/GAD policy commitments tend to stay trapped on paper.

In sum, WID/GAD institutions in many of the case studies have developed a capacity for strategic planning, but what they still lack is a capacity to ensure that national policy commitments to the integration of gender in development are clearly tied to budget allocations. Here, skills are needed in budget analysis, and in the identification of important policy documents — such as public expenditure reviews or published national budget statements — for analysis and exposure. In some other countries, notably South Africa, Australia, Canada, some Caribbean countries and, lately, Uganda and Tanzania, techniques in gender-sensitive budget analysis have been developed which are now being used in planning and budget analysis in some of the countries under study here (Hurt and Budlender, 1998). For this to be effective, however, more sex-disaggregated data are needed about the extent to which government spending actually reaches women and, more generally, about women's income, consumption and contribution to production. There have been some examples of noteworthy successes in challenging definitional biases in some data bases used for planning purposes — most particularly, in labour force statistics. Less success has been achieved with data on expenditure and consumption, such as Living Standards Measurement Surveys, or Integrated Household Surveys which continue to regard the household as the main unit of analysis. It has also proven difficult to introduce indicators relating to gendered asymmetries of power — such as participation in local and national politics, sexual violence and juridical rights — to official data used in planning. With regard to the latter, the strategy of WID/GAD units has been to focus on raising public awareness of these issues, as a preliminary step in legitimizing them as matters for policy and planning. These efforts, many of which involve liaising with constituencies and amplifying women's 'voice' within the administration, are the focus of the next section.


## Developing WID/GAD constituencies in and outside the state

*Making space for women in the state*

A theme which emerges powerfully from the review of the experiences of NWMs is the chronic short-staffing of these units; the general paucity of women in the higher levels of the civil service and in government; the lack of awareness of, and commitment to, gender issues generally among state personnel; and the critical importance of allies in government and in the administration. Some WID/GAD units have been staffed and headed by men who are not necessarily gender sensitive. As career civil servants, they consider placement in a marginal administrative unit to be a demotion (which indeed it may often be). Women civil servants in the same positions may share these characteristics and attitudes. As a range of studies of women bureaucrats in other contexts show, women bureaucrats and politicians cannot by any means be assumed automatically to be predisposed to work in women's interests (Dahlerup, 1988; Hale and Kelly, 1989; Hirschman, 1991). Their class status distances them from the concerns of poorer women. More importantly, the few women who do gain access to administrative or political positions tend to be isolated from other women and are under powerful pressures to conform to the dominant orientations of their institutions and the work patterns and concerns of their male colleagues. These pressures limit possibilities for developing sensitivity to, and acting in, women's interests (see Rai, 1997, and the Conclusion to this volume).

Association with an under-prioritized agenda such as WID/GAD can exacerbate problems of individual marginalization and, ironically, problems of personal disaffection with the issue. High-flying careers in the civil service are not often made on its 'softest' peripheries and certainly not in stigmatized 'women's' sectors. Many WID/GAD bureaucrats feel great frustration at their lack of resources and limited impact, their uncertain mandate and, worst of all, at the lack of legitimacy the issue appears to have. It is worth quoting Barkallil on the perspectives of Moroccan civil servants in WID units:

> They [WID bureaucrats] find themselves engaged on an issue for which they often do not feel prepared, all the more so because their mission is in no way defined by written directives coming from higher levels of the administration like the Ministries concerned or the Prime Minister. One has the impression that they are assigned to a delicate question which they have been left to manage as best they can, not with a view to satisfying objectives of effectiveness but in a manner such as to appear to be doing something, from the perspective of national and international opinion, but above all, from the perspective of foreign donors. (1994:22)

Where there has been a positive reception for WID/GAD policy goals in line ministries, this almost invariably relies upon the support of a gender-sensitive civil servant — often, but not always, a woman. This speaks not just to the importance of gender training for state agents, but to the importance of building up what Dahlerup terms a 'critical mass' of women in public administration (Dahlerup, 1988).

Obstacles to the increased representation of women at senior levels in the bureaucracy are considerable the world over. Quite aside from structural problems stemming from sex typing of women in the education system and labour markets, and from the competing demands of women's private lives, women who do gain access to the bureaucracy eventually bump into glass ceilings maintained by the bureaucratic fraternity. In Morocco, this process is personally managed by the representative of traditional patriarchy — the King — who makes all appointments to high administrative office, and has not once conceded this honour to women civil servants.

In Bangladesh, there is a recruitment quota system in the civil service. Since 1972, 10 per cent of gazetted and 15 per cent of non-gazetted posts have been reserved for women. No special training is provided to enhance their performance in the civil service, let alone their gender sensitivity. The system has evolved into a maximum ceiling for women recruits, rather than a minimum threshold. Quotas have had the effect of stigmatizing women's presence in the civil service, where they are regarded as having gained access by virtue of their sex, rather than through merit. On the other hand, they have without question allowed for a greater presence of women in public service than would have occurred without special measures.

In Vietnam, quotas for women's employment in the public administration do not appear to have generated the same problems as in Bangladesh. To begin with, quotas were much less a reluctant and tokenistic gesture towards gender equality than a campaign to ensure adequate staffing levels in the civil service given men's absence on the war front. In 1967 the then Prime Minister suggested an increase in the quota of women civil servants in education and public health offices, as well as trading and light industry establishments, from 50 per cent to 70 per cent (Tran Thi, 1994:9). Though the proportion of women in public administration has not appeared to exceed the high point of 48 per cent in the 1980s, this nevertheless suggests an extremely gender-balanced bureaucracy. The picture is rather different when scrutinized by status levels: women have never held more than 5 per cent of directorships in state-run firms. Nevertheless, the high numbers of women in the rank and file of the public administration may account for the consistency with which gender-sensitive legislation on issues such as labour and property rights has been promoted and implemented, unlike other contexts in which top-level policies for gender equality encounter bureaucratic resistance at the implementation levels.

Several general observations can be made about efforts to gain allies and to increase women's representation in politics and the administration in the case countries. First, most often women who are already in the administration, even if gender sensitive, are too isolated to risk association with the GAD issue. However, efforts to network among them, as is happening in Chile, sometimes through the Focal Points mechanism, can strengthen their resolve and effectiveness. Second, quota systems for increasing women's representation in the administration are not necessarily effective in building up an internal GAD constituency. This should not, however, be taken as an argument against minimum quotas for women, as the possibility remains that they may eventually constitute a 'critical mass' with enough mutual support to venture allegiance to the GAD agenda, as may be the case in Vietnam.

*Cultivating a constituency: mechanisms for public advocacy, coordination with NGOs and linkages to women's organizations*

NWMs and domestic women's movements are, in an important sense, mutually constituting. Often it is the women's movement's pressure on the state which leads to the creation of an NWM. Once in place, the femocrats within the NWM benefit from an active constituency of women's groups in civil society to help demonstrate the legitimacy and urgency of the policy reforms they are promoting. But this relationship can be compromised where domestic women's movements are not strong enough to provide legitimacy to the NWM, particularly where NWMs have been set up in response to donor pressure. In these contexts, official WID/GAD units often find themselves trying to build up a domestic constituency that includes but goes beyond women's groups, through raising public awareness of gender issues, promoting the development of women's organizations and establishing links with sympathetic NGOs.

In Bangladesh, which has a strong women's movement, the Department of Women's Affairs maintains an impressive register of women-friendly NGOs. But women's organizations prefer to maintain distance from the Department, because, at least in the past, it was staffed by members of the Bangladesh Jatiyo Mahila Sangstha (National Women's Association), linked to the right-wing BNP, in and out of power since democratization in 1990. Also, the Department of Women's Affairs is an unappealing partner for the women's movement because of its limited institutional capacity to influence development processes, particularly in rural areas. It has offices in just 22 of the 64 districts and has staff in just 100 of the 460 sub-districts.

In Jamaica, processes of constituency outreach on the part of the Bureau of Women's Affairs are well institutionalized, but its relationships with NGOs and women's organizations have been uneven and very much dependent on the economic situation — both of the Bureau itself and the country. Over the years, the Bureau has come to work more closely with NGOs as its own capacity to initiate research and implement projects withered with the withdrawal of donor funds consequent on the government's failure to provide counterpart funding (Mariott, 1994:5). Disappointingly, however, its relationship with women's organizations was not strong over the 1980s and 1990s. Observers suggest that the women's movement has been decimated by the economic hardships brought by austerity measures in the 1980s, diverting efforts from advocacy to economic survival (Mariott, 1994:6).

In Morocco, reflecting the uneven institutionalization of WID units across the administration, there is a notable absence of a point of communication or coordination between the government and women's groups or NGOs. Some degree of consultation with women's organizations has occurred in women's units in certain Ministries and government units (particularly the Ministry of Youth and Sport, the Ministry of Agriculture and the National Agricultural Credit Service), but these are isolated instances such as seminars which tend to be sponsored by external donors and focused on particular projects.

With regard to cross-sectoral issues of critical relevance to matters of equality and redistribution, consultation with women's organizations has been almost insultingly cursory, showing an astonishing degree of condescension and disregard for women's perspectives on public policy. For example, in the recent process of reforming the country's Islamic family law code, the *Moudouana*, managed by the King, women's organizations were only peripherally consulted. They were contacted in writing; public debate and the risk of conflict were avoided. Not a single woman from the women's movement sat on the commission charged with revising this critical piece of legislation. The resulting legislation reproduced a patriarchal family model, ignoring changes in women's social and economic roles in Morocco.

Chile differs from the above cases in that SERNAM has had no formal mandate to work with women's organizations or NGOs. This may to some degree reflect a desire on the part of the main coalition of feminist organizations (the National Coalition of Women for Democracy; CNMD) to preserve its autonomy and to pursue a more radical agenda outside government. SERNAM has pursued a project of putting gender issues on the public agenda primarily through the creation of Centres of Information on Women's Rights, concentrating on democracy, poverty and human rights. It has collaborated with NGOs for the purpose of research into employment and domestic violence issues, and only when funded by international agencies. According to some observers, this relative detachment may be due to a reluctance to become embroiled in political differences within the NGO and women's communities (Pollack, 1994b:4). In a context of highly politicized forms of associational life in civil society this reticence is perfectly understandable and probably healthy. In any case, the dynamism of CNMD and its autonomy from the administration are probably the best guarantors of the continued development of a feminist constituency in the country.

Finally, Vietnam differs radically from the other cases in that women's activism in civil society, independent of the Indochinese Communist Party, was one of the political freedoms denied in socialist Vietnam. In the current environment of liberalization, controls on civil society are being relaxed and formal Party units such as the VWU are becoming more autonomous. In the meantime, the VWU's contact with its constituency has been strong, made possible through its extensive grassroots network.

One serious obstacle to effective collaboration between NWMs and the women's movement in all the case countries stems from bureaucratic norms. Too much interaction with outside constituencies can be seen as a violation of professionalism to the extent that it is regarded as politicizing the administration and eroding its integrity. For example, in a relatively open and transparent administration, a WID/GAD unit might rightly illuminate deficiencies in the government's accountability to women, thereby providing outside constituencies with 'ammunition' with which to lobby for change. This means divided loyalties for many WID/GAD bureaucrats, which can undermine their credibility in the bureaucracy. A similar set of constraints operates in the opposite direction. Women's organizations in particular may resist association with an administration linked to a government which is not seen as responsive to their concerns. This appears to be the case in Bangladesh. The transformative potential inherent in an iterative relationship between an active women's constituency and WID/GAD agents in the administration is perhaps best exploited where both retain a degree of autonomy, yet attempt to ensure that their activities on either side of the state/civil society divide are mutually supportive. This appears to be the pattern in Chile.

## Conclusions: towards accountability for gender equality

Efforts to integrate gender in development through NWMs have produced many strategic gains. Above all, they have legitimized a place for gender issues in development. Government units dedicated to promoting gender equality in development have innovated policy analysis and monitoring tools such as gender checklists and guidelines for cross-government use. Other new instruments for coordinating gender-sensitive planning across the government have been WID/GAD Focal Points in line ministries and synoptic gender-sensitive national development plans. NWMs have had pockets of success in gaining allies and have made critically important gains in revising data bases used for development planning to include aspects of women's lives.

At the same time, NWMs have encountered constraints which include marginalization through under-resourcing in staff, skills and funding, and through patterns of institutional location and role assignment which stigmatize and condemn in advance their ambitions for gender-transformative policy change. Beyond the problem of bureaucratic resistance, there seem to be two main constraints on the effectiveness of NWMs' policy efforts. One is that gender-sensitive policy proposals tend rarely to be traced through to actual budgetary implications, and fail to make a direct impact on the main instrument for national development planning and indeed for accountability systems: the public expenditure planning process. The second serious shortcoming regards the nature of connections between NWMs and the women's constituency in civil society. Ideally a strong constituency base among women's organizations and gender-sensitive NGOs would strengthen the position of the WID/GAD agenda in government, while at the same time sensitizing it to the needs of the national female citizenship. But it has proven difficult to build up or to exploit this iterative relationship.

It is worth asking why so many governments the world over have appeared willing to make commitments to women's rights and to gender equality in the development process and to set up institutions to promote this. Similar support is rarely given to other issues — such as class inequality — which also represent deep social cleavages and which envisage profound structural change. The reason has to do with politics. No government or bureaucracy feels it has anything to fear from women. In civil society they rarely represent a highly mobilized constituency, at the domestic level their interests are often closely bound in with those of men in the family, and in politics and public administration they are under-represented and have rarely acted to entrench a new feminist corporatism. As such, the chance of fundamental changes towards gender equality actually being realized is negligible, given the relative absence of forceful and demanding constituencies within and outside of the state. As a result, far from having anything to fear from women, many governments can make important political gains at the international and domestic levels by espousing gender equality, without serious risk of being held accountable and having to operationalize the promises made in top-level rhetoric.

The experience of NWMs obliges us to develop a more sophisticated understanding of the opportunities for promoting gender equality through the public sector. This chapter concludes with a sketch of a framework for studying this. The extent to which pro-gender equality groups within civil society and the state will succeed in promoting women's interests in public policy, and the extent to which states will respond, will depend upon the interaction of three major factors:

- *The social, cultural and economic power of the gender equality lobby in civil society* — its power to mobilize resources and public concern to support its demands.
- *The nature of the political system* — the depth of procedural and substantive democracy, the different levels of government at which women can express their concerns — and *the organization of political competition* (the

number and types of parties, their ideologies and memberships, the relative importance of high finance or crime in political contests).

- *The nature and power of the state* and its bureaucracies — whether it is a developmental state, whether it has the will and capacity to enforce change in the culture and practices of its bureaucracies, whether the public service has internalized a commitment to social equity, poverty reduction, and so on.

The prospects of women influencing policy will be further shaped by the institutions which organize opportunities for consultation and dialogue with officials, for formal representation in public decision-making forums and, finally, for accountability to citizens. These distinctions between participation, representation and influence emphasize that the creation of opportunities for consultation do not lead, on their own, to policy influence. Nor do opportunities for women to be represented in political forums or in the administration (through quotas for local government councillors or through NWMs) mean actual influence and power (see table 3).

Beginning with the women's movement, this framework allows consideration of accountability issues within women's civil society organizations. Thus, for instance, in

**Table 3** Aspects of the relationship between advocacy and influence

|  | Participation/ consultation | Representation/ presence | Accountability/ influence |
|---|---|---|---|
| The power of the women's movement in civil society |  |  |  |
| The nature of the political regime and of political competition |  |  |  |
| The nature of the state and its bureaucracies |  |  |  |

an organization claiming to represent poor women, the top row of the table could be filled in to make note of the arrangements for the participation of poor women in the organization's activities, the extent to which they are represented in leadership structures, and the mechanisms through which poor women can demand accountability from the organization.

Politics is the intervening variable determining the effectiveness of women's 'voice' in civil society and public sector response. The women's movement may be equipped with all it needs to press demands on the state — a united and well-organized membership, allies in the right places, generalized social support and even a crisis event to concentrate public concern on the group's needs — but the political environment may undercut its impact if the gender equality constituency is not seen as relevant to prevailing political agendas or patronage systems.

Political systems have a critical impact on the calculations that women's groups make about the value of engaging with the state. Formal democracy and the existence of basic civil and political rights are crucial preconditions for virtually any kind of civil society activism which engages critically with the state. Beyond this, the relative strength of oppositional political energies in society, and the ways in which they are represented politically, will shape women's civil society strategies, as will the relationship between the legislature, the executive and the judiciary. For instance, where there is robust multi-party competition, as in Chile, women's groups may pursue confrontational, high-visibility strategies in the hope of interesting opposition parties in taking up their concerns in the legislature.

The nature of the state is of great significance to the effectiveness of women's 'voice' in civil society. The nature of access opportunities to policy-making arenas, and redress mechanisms when policies go wrong, will empower some citizens over others. The coherence, probity and managerial capabilities of the administration will dictate the value of attempting to engage the public sector in partnerships for more responsive administration. The civil service culture will determine the degree of professional defensiveness and resistance with which bureaucrats will respond to initiatives to improve their receptivity to women's needs.

The impact of women's efforts to encourage the public sector to respond to their needs and interests will, most importantly, be shaped by accountability systems in the public administration, which differ according to the model of political-administrative control in the particular country. As this chapter has suggested, many of the efforts of NWMs have been weakened by a failure to engage with internal state accountability systems — for instance, by auditing government expenditure to see that funds earmarked for gender equality programmes are actually spent properly.

The future for advocacy administration such as the NWMs reviewed here lies in developing strategies which tackle obstacles to gender equality in all three arenas: civil society, politics and the state. Most importantly, if states are to be held accountable for gender equality, then gender equality advocates have to 'engender' national accountability systems: both 'vertical' mechanisms based on political engagement and 'horizontal' mechanisms such as financial auditing, administrative rules and procedures, legal processes, and so on. Much has already been achieved in the political arena in many countries, though the emphasis remains on increasing women's representation, as opposed to accountability to female constituencies. But when it comes to public sector accountability systems, the experience of NWMs shows us that the work of making states accountable for gender equality has only just begun.

## Notes

1 This chapter is an edited version of the monograph: 'The Politics of Integrating Gender to State Development Processes: Trends, Opportunities and Constraints in Bangladesh, Chile, Jamaica, Mali, Morocco, and Uganda' UNRISD Occasional Paper No. 1, 1995, Geneva, also published in *Missionaries and Mandarins: Feminist Engagements with Development Institutions* (eds: Carol Miller and Shahra Razavi), London: IT Publications. The original paper was based on data up to 1994 and investigated women's machinery in seven countries. Because of space constraints, Mali and Uganda have been left out here. Efforts have been made to update the data for this paper, but there will be places where the information is out of date, and for this the author apologizes. My thanks to Shahra Razavi for permission to reprint.

2 The primary data on which this chapter is based are drawn from interviews commissioned by the UN Research Institute for Social

Development in 1994–95. The interviews were held with members of state bureaucracies, representatives of non-governmental organizations, members of women's organizations and academics, almost all of whom in one way or another were involved in promoting improved state attention to women's needs and interests in development. The interview data are rich in subjective assessments of official policy efforts, but perhaps because of this there is considerable unevenness in the details provided on formal policy measures and their impact. My thanks to the writers of these country reports: Nadira Barkallil, Lalla Ben Barka, Mohsena Islam, Joy Kwesiga, Christine Mariott, Molly Pollack and Tran Thi Van Anh.

# 4

# National women's machineries: structures and spaces

NÜKET KARDAM AND SELMA ACUNER

## Introduction

This chapter will focus on the 'lessons learned' by national machineries in mainstreaming gender issues, drawing from our experience of the Turkish national women's machinery (NWM) as well as other published case studies. As we enter the twenty-first century, we have seen a number of institutional changes for gender equality. National machineries have been established, restructured, streamlined and upgraded in an effort to promote gender equality and increase NWMs' capacities where they already existed. The majority of United Nations member states now have national machineries, a number of them having been established in the 1980s and 1990s. The concept of 'national machinery' includes many different bureaucratic units, ranging from ministries to desks, departments or directorates. Some may be located within the President's or Prime Minister's office; others may be a portfolio within a state ministry or local administration; yet others may be ministries in their own right. The mandates, responsibilities and resources of these machineries vary as well. There are some characteristics that national machineries seem to share. These are: (1) they are all bureaucratic bodies whose mandate includes, in one form or another, changing institutions towards greater gender equality; and (2) they are usually relatively weak compared with other state institutions in terms of resources and political clout. In fact, one of the major recent debates in the literature centres on the marginality and lack of effectiveness of NWMs. This debate acquires greater importance as development agencies stress 'good governance' and the need to strengthen public sector management, transparency and accountability.

We would like to consider the following question here: what role can NWMs play in promoting and institutionalizing gender equality? We will begin our discussion by examining mainstreaming and institutionalization as a goal. We will then focus on the opportunities and constraints that NWMs face within the contexts in which they work, dividing them into political, organizational and cognitive contexts. Finally, we will discuss some strategies for NWMs that emerge from this analysis as well as those that incorporate NWMs but go beyond them to include other political actors.

## Gender mainstreaming and institutionalization

While in the 1970s and 1980s Women in Development advocates talked of 'integrating women into development', in the 1990s the emphasis was on the institutionalization of gender issues in development policy and planning. This shift in emphasis stemmed from the recognition that institutions were already 'gendered', typically placing women in sex-typed services and targeting women's reproductive or social functions. It is clear that without changing institutions to reflect and represent women's interests, the goal of gender equality cannot be attained. 'Mainstreaming gender' is a cognitive, organizational and a political process which requires shifts in organizational cultures and ways of thinking, as well as in the goals, structures and resource allocations of governments (see Staudt, chapter 2 in this volume). Mainstreaming requires changes at different levels within these institutions, in agenda setting, policy making, planning, implementation and evaluation. Instruments for the mainstreaming effort include new staffing and budgeting practices, training programmes, policy procedures, guidelines and incentive structures.

Mainstreaming is a worthy goal but it is a long-term goal that may never be attained in its entirety. It is more useful to think of 'mainstreaming a gender perspective' as the process of assessing the implications for women and men in any planned action including legislation, policies and programmes in any area and at all levels. It is a strategy for making sure that women and men benefit equally in all political, economic and societal spheres and that inequality is not perpetuated, but reduced. What role can NWMs play in attaining this goal and what constraints have they faced? What can we learn from their experiences and how can these constraints be overcome or at least understood more clearly? After a decade or more of attempts to institutional- ize gender, there is a growing volume of data on and analy- sis of gender issues worldwide. By 1985, over 90 per cent of countries had established an institutional body or system for promoting the status of women. However, NWMs have often proved to be weak, vulnerable to changing political fortunes and under-resourced.

At the heart of the mandate of NWMs lies the promo- tion of gender accountability. We define gender account- ability as responsiveness to the structure of relationships between women and men and the interests of the former at two different levels: the political and organizational. The end goal of the mainstreaming process described above is to achieve accountability for gender policy. How is this made possible? We see policy outcomes as the result of two fac- tors: those pertaining to existing structural constraints and those to available strategies and options. Taking this ap- proach, a number of insights regarding the effectiveness of NWMs can be reached. The constraints posed by concep- tual, political and organizational factors shape, define and limit the choices open to actors, in this case to NWMs. This does not mean that there are no choices available but that the choices are circumscribed by the structural con- straints. A clear understanding of these constraints will lead to expanded choice and more effective outcomes.

## The political context

If politics means, according to one well-known definition (Lasswell, 1951), who gets what, when and how, or the dis- tribution of power in terms of both resources and influence, the politics of international agencies as well as politics at the national level are of utmost importance for gender policy outcomes. Given the time constraints, resource constraints and competing issues that demand attention from international and national bureaucrats, the question becomes: why should one pay attention to gender issues at all? Overall, international attention to gender equality, a politically committed and stable government, and a strong civil society should all encourage gender accountability and the work of the NWM. We now turn to each of these factors.

*International linkages: global discourse and donor assistance for gender equality*

At the international level the rise of women's movements since the late 1970s have pressurized development agencies and governments to discuss gender issues and find ways to promote gender equality. NWMs are mainly the result of this pressure and that is also paradoxically what constitutes their weakness. More recently the global discourse on democratization and human rights has further encouraged the institutionalization of gender equality. International social movements such as the women's movement are generally more successful in bringing new issues on the agenda rather than in institutionalization because they are on the outside rather than the inside. Many NWMs have been established because governments have been pressured in international forums and to avoid embarrassment they have made symbolic commitments, usually not backed by realistic resource allocations. This has meant that NWMs and many women's non-governmental organizations (NGOs) have turned to international donor agencies for funding. But the reliance on donor funding has also proved to be a double-edged sword.

The objectives of international donors may conflict with the objectives of the recipients, in this case bureaucracies that receive funding for gender-related projects. While the donors attempt to ensure appropriate performance, the recipients wish to maximize their autonomy and resources. Sometimes, the very existence of international donor support may reduce local commitment or interest or lead to the perception that gender-related activities are 'foreign imports'. For example, Turkish NWM projects and programmes are supported by international donor agencies such as the United Nations Development Programme and the World Bank. Many Turkish NGOs receive funding from the European Commission and bilateral donors of Northern Europe and Canada. These donors have the ability to shape project objectives and activities. NGOs may seek projects that do not fit their goals and objectives just because funding is available. Even when there is a seeming fit between project objectives and broader recipient and donor goals, effective performance cannot be guaranteed because such a fit does not reveal whether the project is a priority for the recipient or not. If it is not considered a priority (this means that either the project objective specifically fits into policy priorities of recipient bureaucracies and/or is supported by top officials in relevant recipient bureaucracies), the project may serve implicit or unofficial priorities instead of official ones. In order to capture resources, bureaucracies may accept unwanted projects.

Once the resources are secured, there is a tendency to abandon implementation and turn to the competition for the next round of resources. This means that the incentives for effective performance are vastly reduced. In the case of projects for women, governments may accept funds for such projects but may not necessarily have the interest or the will to implement them. The identification of programmes to implement may be more influenced by the types of initiative that donors are willing to fund than by a coherent strategy that links implementation and policy advocacy functions. Given that formulating a coherent gender equality policy and strategy is at the heart of NWM effectiveness and is generally considered an area of weakness, the donor-driven projects may in fact further encourage this weakness, rather than allow NWMs to formulate self-driven coherent strategies.

Public administration and development literatures demonstrate how many instances of ineffective public sector management stem from conflicting objectives of stakeholders. In the case of NWMs, conflicting objectives of donors and recipients raise special concerns, partly because NWMs are generally so dependent on donor funding. What strategies may be recommended to NWMs? NWMs have to tread a fine line between international agencies and their own governments. Being associated too closely with foreign funding limits the opportunities for the 'national owner-ship' of gender issues and may lead to alienation from the NWM's national constituency. Given that international donors are valuable allies, we would argue for NWMs to formulate their own strategies carefully and diversify their funding sources as much as possible so that they are able to face international donors on an equal footing. These activ-ities also require the identification and employment of national technical human resources.

Activities at the international level do provide legitimacy and support to NWMs. International women's conventions and platforms for action to promote women's equality le-gitimize national efforts. For example, one of the mandates of the Turkish NWM is to act as the link between interna-tional platforms and Turkish society, to represent Turkey on these platforms and to make sure that the conventions signed by the Turkish government are adhered to and im-plemented. There is evidence of the positive influence of international norms from several countries. According to Sawer (1995), even in Western industrialized countries such as Canada, Australia and New Zealand, international pres-sure has been used by feminist bureaucrats to press home policy change at the domestic level. In Turkey paragraph 4.1 of the Convention on the Elimination of All Forms of Discrimination against Women (which provides the grounds for legitimizing 'temporary special measures aimed at ac-celerating *de facto* equality between women and men') was taken as the basis of efforts to bring an Equal Status Act to the political agenda. This initiative came from Ka-Der, a Turkish NGO that supports and trains women candidates and the Turkish NWM supported it. Such linkages should be explored further.

*Symbolic political commitment to gender equality*

Gender equality is generally not perceived as a priority area by politicians and is easily manipulated for their own inter-ests. Furthermore, the few resources accorded to gender equality are in proportion with the small political clout of women's groups. In many countries the main problem is the lack of ideological leadership. There is no stable polit-ical perspective that incorporates and owns gender equality policies. For example, in Turkey support for gender equality depends very much on the socio-political context of the times, and such support moves from centre-right to centre-left parties depending on political expediency. Under such circumstances, NWMs find themselves in a politically precarious position.

These constraints can and have been turned into opportunities in several cases. As Goetz (1995) has pointed out and is also true in the Turkish case, the weaker NWMs have built partnerships with civil society, including women's organizations and other stakeholders as visible demonstration of the organization's commitment to mainstream for equality. In countries where the state tradition is strong, these first steps towards alliances with civil society constitute important ones towards building democracy. NWMs, in order to be effective, have to have a broad base of support and respond to demands from society. In this way, they can build legitimacy and get political commitment.

*Political instability*

The instability of government and frequent changes of government, including the Minister for Women's Affairs, have made NWMs dependent on political fortunes in many countries. What does political instability imply for NWMs? Instability leads to job insecurity, an atmosphere of uncertainty. Inevitably, lack of motivation and ineffective performance follow when it is not clear how long one's job is going to continue. In order not to depend on the top administrative level, which tends to change with governments, it may be a useful strategy to build in-house technical capacity.

Times of instability are also times of transition and do not necessarily signify negative outcomes. As some case studies, such as those of Brazil, Chile and Turkey, have demonstrated, times of transition towards more democratic rule have opened up space for gender policy. Alvarez (1990) argues that in transitional regimes from authoritarianism to democracy, gender-specific demands may stand a greater chance of being met if women's mobilization is seen as necessary to consolidate the regime and achieve larger developmental goals. Goetz's research also shows that in countries undergoing a period of transition, such as Uganda and Chile, some political space to promote women's issues is likely to present itself (Goetz, chapter 3 of this volume). This is not just the case in developing countries. For example, Sawer discusses how women's machineries in Australia and Canada were assisted by a political opportunity structure which included both reforming governments eager to expand the policy agenda and the economic prosperity of the 1970s (Sawer, chapter 12 of this volume and 1995). Many observers see the Turkish women's movement as the first democratic movement to emerge after the military coup of 12 September 1980. Most agree that the emergence of the women's movement was due to an atmosphere of indifference to women's activities, or perhaps an assumption that it would not create any danger for politicians. In short, NWMs have to be politically astute and ready to seize opportunities when they arise, and even times of instability may be turned to advantage.

*The gap between civil society and the state*

Lack of trust between governments and women's NGOs hampers open communication and opportunities for reaching a consensus. In authoritarian systems, women's NGOs may not be ready for dialogue on equal terms, being used to taking directives from the state. In Turkey, there is a lack of communication between different women's groups: they compete for the same pool of funds rather than collaborating. Many NGOs do not trust the government yet still want the resources and services it provides. So there is a 'love–hate' relationship between NGOs and the state and among NGOs. States may have a tendency to co-opt NGOs rather than treat them as equal partners, while NGOs may also lose their autonomy and become a part of the state bureaucracy in their eagerness to receive funds and favours. While NWMs need to see NGOs as allies and partners, NGOs also need to remind themselves of their function as pressure groups.

In Chile, some civil society organizations saw the NWM as an arm of a state which did not represent their interests. In Guatemala, the NWM, whose programmes focused on home economics, had little relevance for more radical women's organizations addressing peace, human rights and economic issues (Byrne and Koch Laier, 1998). However, there are also examples of constructive collaboration. In the Philippines, government agencies have a long history of cooperation with NGOs on gender, facilitated through an alliance of some 300 national women's NGOs and umbrella organizations, as well as government personnel (Honculada and Ofreno, chapter 6 of this volume). In Belize, the Department of Women's Affairs and the NGO 'Women Against Violence' together carried out a consultation, lobbied the government and eventually succeeded in getting a law passed against domestic violence (Byrne and Koch Laier, 1998). In Turkey women's NGOs are partners to the activities of the NWM through their participation in four commissions on health, education, employment and law. It is obvious that collaboration between NWMs and NGOs have both constructive and problematic sides that need to be carefully considered.

The gap between state and civil society can only be bridged through democratic governance. Political accountability is integrally tied to the concept of democratic governance, since without it the latter would be a contradiction in terms. Democratic governance requires both a high degree of accountability of the state and a democratic civil society, as represented in community associations, interest groups and political parties, to influence the processes, regulations and policies and hold the office bearers of the state to account. For civil society to exist, the state must be receptive to possible sources of opposition and recognize the rights of its population actively to participate in all spheres of life. There must be a political culture conducive to political action and participation in NGOs should be encouraged in order to promote citizen involvement and help create a political culture and the social capital necessary to sustain democracy. Turning to Turkey, as this process has begun and gained strength Turkish women's NGOs have appeared and voiced their concerns. The media cover gender issues on a regular basis and most recently the changes to civil law to remove discriminatory articles against women has been on the public agenda. Ka-Der, whose objectives to increase women's political participation created a media event by its establishment, succeeded in building alliances with the media and staying on the public agenda.

The relationship between the state and civil society is reflected in the relationship between bureaucrats in the NWM and women's NGOs in society. If the state tradition is strong and the gap is wide, we also see a general indifference or a 'looking down' on the NGO sector by bureaucrats. This presents a very important constraint to NWMs' effectiveness. But the opportunity is there to find ways to promote open communication between different stakeholders. Several donor projects in Turkey promote collaboration between different government bureaucracies and women's NGOs, with the NWM acting as the focal point. Yet it has also been found to be quite difficult to allow equal access to women's NGOs of different ideological persuasions; those that follow the official state position on women are more likely to receive greater support. It is clear that NWMs' role needs to be considered within the democratization process itself as to a great extent it determines their interaction with other stakeholders.

**The organizational context: public sector management**

Gender policy and practice takes place within institutions. It is of utmost importance to pay attention to specific organizations' objectives, goals and procedures in order to understand how they encourage or impede gender mainstreaming. The more recent attention to effective public sector management and streamlining the public sector presents both opportunities and challenges to NWMs. Resource allocation towards gender equality is mainly achieved through institutional mechanisms of the state. New bureaucracies such as NWMs have been established just at the same time as state bureaucracies are being asked to scale down and become more efficient and effective.

*Procedural differences among stakeholders and bureaucratic rigidity*

Procedures that are control oriented tend to hinder flexibility and response to unforeseen circumstances — qualities that are especially needed in new areas such as gender policy. Control-oriented procedures discourage frequent consultations between stakeholders and may lead to mis-understandings and resentments. For NWMs, control-oriented procedures may mean that a lot of energy and effort goes to the project proposal and report writing, rather than implementation and policy advocacy activities.

Bureaucracies are generally rule bound and top down, but over-centralization leads to rigidity and resistance to change. Procedural differences are even more important if the organizations involved operate in different cultural and economic contexts. What this means for project teams is that they are accountable to several masters; that is, they have to work with at least two different organizations with quite different procedures. Furthermore, in a typically hier-archical bureaucracy, staff at the lower levels are usually reticent in voicing positions in opposition to their bosses for fear of losing their jobs. This leads to bureaucratic rigid-ity, a lack of creativity and flexibility. Bureaucracies in general are not open to agendas which challenge accus-tomed organizational patterns and this is a special concern for NWMs working in a new area.

Yet within these constraints, NWMs need to find ways to promote change by acting as advocates for gender equal-ity and find strategies to promote change. This requires presenting new information/facts to policy makers to con-vince them why a new policy should be formulated. With-out the conscious effort of some people, a new issue will not be accepted. What is required is the formulation of gender issues in ways that gain acceptance and fit in with the larger goals of government, with national development policy and plans. For example, Waylen (in Goetz, 1997) has argued that the National Service for Women, the Chilean women's bureau established in 1990, succeeded because it consciously sought to achieve outcomes which fitted with the agenda of the government; that is, measures associated with poverty alleviation rather than those which threat-ened to alter gender relations directly. It is also necessary to define gender issues in one's own language and devise one's own methodology; otherwise the theory and practice of gen-der equality are bound to remain a foreign import. Gender issues have to be embedded in one's own national context.

It is very hard to be an agent of change if one's priority is to keep one's position; career aspirations often compete with the commitment to gender equality. The paradox that NWMs face is the following: NWMs are state institutions in the business of altering those very institutions. This requires working inside the state but sometimes against the state. This means that NWM staff have to acquire a dual identity: they can't be just bureaucrats; they have to bring in the goals of the women's movement that are outside the state and make them palatable within the state.

*Weak bureaucratic position and unclear mandate*

Overall, NWMs are still not equipped to alter the incentive structures governing individual bureaucrats or departments. According to Goetz, they usually cannot offer material or status rewards, they cannot provide useful technical support, and they lack the powers of ultimate sanction over policy and programme proposals that fail to incorporate gender-sensitive perspectives (Goetz, 1995:52).

There is usually ambiguity regarding the role of NWMs: are they coordinating, resource-allocating or policy-making bodies? Should they be building human resources on gender issues? Should they promote internal policy advocacy and build alliances with other state bureaucracies? How can one bureaucracy undertake all these tasks? Should the role of the NWM be a resource for policy dialogue on gender equality, a place for establishing common ground for joint efforts among all sectoral counterparts and pertinent actors such as advocacy groups, women's movements, women's NGOs, public officials, political parties and the media?

The central mandate of NWMs should be preparing, monitoring and assisting in the implementation and monitoring of policies in line with the demands of civil society. To this end, collaboration with women's NGOs is of utmost importance, without which NWMs cannot be effective and legitimate. NWMs will have to work closely with gender specialists or gender units of other bureaucracies, building networks and alliances, and sharing good practices related to mainstreaming a gender perspective in all substantive programming areas, as well as with the media and the private sector. NWMs will need consciously to find and cultivate groups in society who are allies, to whom they can provide resources and who are able to pressure the government on behalf of the NWM.

## Weak monitoring systems

Gender sensitivity requires an accountability structure that provides appropriate motivation, based on incentives such as pay or promotion to monitor performance. If there is a failure to relate incentives to performance on a fair and compulsory basis in regard to women's empowerment, public institutions will simply not be responsive. Bureaucrats will be attracted to gender programmes only if they believe that there are opportunities to be tapped; once funds and other incentives dry up they are likely to fall back on traditional gender discriminatory practices (Bangura, 1996:31).

Policies should be further elaborated by action plans or strategies which clearly describe goals, tasks and accountability for gender equality mainstreaming at all organizational levels. Gender training and other similar activities should be employed in order to develop clear and salient procedures, guidelines, monitoring and evaluation mechanisms so that the question of 'how to mainstream gender' is addressed and understood.

There is, however, a previous step that needs to be completed before mainstreaming can occur. Legal tools for gender equality have to be in place and administrative bodies that are entrusted with the task of mainstreaming, such as ombudspersons or equal opportunity commissions, have to be in place.

## Gender budgeting practices

All national bureaucracies implementing policies and programmes and disbursing budgets should publicly report on their performance and national and international civil society organizations should be empowered to monitor this performance. There should be systematic gender analysis of budget allocations at all levels, with special emphasis on the reallocation and effective utilization of resources. Good practices in gendered budgeting should be shared. Specific time-bound targets for the achievement of gender equality should be set and monitored. Overall, means to transfer gender equality rhetoric to substantial policy need to be found and by that we mean redistributive policies which are lacking in many developing and developed countries alike.

## Cognitive context

NWMs generally face an environment in which gender issues are considered sensitive and contested. There are conflicting ideas on what the role of women in society ought to be and conflicting perceptions of the causes underlying gender inequality. There are no clear and salient solutions in this issue area. Furthermore, what women can and cannot do strikes at the core of societal rules and, in many developing countries, these rules are not necessarily agreed upon.

In order to promote a new policy, a gap between reality and the desired state has to be seen. Furthermore, reasons for the existence of such a gap need to be elaborated so that, based on these reasons, one can devise ways to overcome them. There is a wide diversity of views regarding why there is a gap between what exists and what the ideal state of gender relations, of development and of gender relations in development should be, as well as how this gap should be overcome. Gender and development combines two broad theoretical issues: women's and men's social, economic and political roles within society and the nature of development itself. As is well known, international development agencies states, and various groups within developing countries differ on the definition of both of these issues. The international women's movement itself has not been able to reach an agreement, except in broad terms of promoting gender justice and overcoming discrimination against women (Kardam, 1991). This is mostly because the definitions had to be left broad and ambiguous in order to elicit cooperation from different actors. Unfortunately, this state of affairs leaves a great deal of responsibility to domestic actors to define, interpret, and come to an agreement on what gender equality is and what to do about it.

Looking briefly at gender relations, most would agree that the power relations between women and men are unequal and that what women do is generally undervalued, but the reasons why this is the case and the policy recommendations that stem from these reasons differ vastly. If the reasons for unequal gender relations are seen as being caused by exploitative economic relations, as socialist feminists view them, then policy recommendations would include the different treatment of women from different socio-economic backgrounds. Thus, for example, different policies for urban middle-class women, urban factory workers, domestic workers or peasant women in rural areas would be devised. On the other hand, if the crux of the issue is seen as the lack of opportunity for women within male-defined institutions, then policies are targeted to establishing space for women and rewriting laws to promote women's interests.

The discourse on development, like the discourse on gender relations, also presents a vast and colourful array of definitions and policies that flow from these definitions. Since the issue is not gender relations *per se*, but gender relations in development, gender policy and practice has been justified and interpreted differently depending on the development policy that a government follows. When efficiency and economic growth are emphasized, the economic contributions of women to development are brought on to the agenda. Policy recommendations then include ways to improve their contribution to national development through programmes and projects in training, education and employment of women. It is suggested that patriarchal norms, principles and institutions be dismantled to the extent that they interfere with women's contributions to economic growth. When equity, basic human needs and welfare issues dominate the discourse, the discussion turns to women in poverty and lacking in basic human needs. Recommended programmes then include increasing literacy, providing loans for small-scale enterprises for women, providing upgraded technology to reduce hours of work, and the like. More recently, with the introduction of the term 'empowerment' into development, women's empowerment has come on to the agenda. Women's empowerment includes achieving control over one's life through expanded choices. The policy recommendations that would flow from this view would deal with, for example, ways of resolving conflicts between women's reproductive and productive roles, child care and men's share in the maintenance of the family, as well as women's overall participation in the redefinition of gender relations and the meaning of development itself.

*Strategies for NWMs*

In countries such as Turkey, where there is a wide diversity of ideological positions and conflict between secular and Islamic positions on women, NWMs may face a difficult situation, depending on which political party is governing. Political parties and women's groups represent many diverse views on the reasons for gender inequality. How can the NWM prevent this diversity from turning into a 'cacophony'? One way that governments deal with diversity of views is to cater to the politically important groups separately, if necessary. In Turkey, two separate bureaucracies have been established within the State Ministry for Women's Affairs, one that deals with the status and problems of women and the other with the family. However, because they were located under one roof — namely the same ministry using the same resources and personnel — they engaged in efforts to gain control over the other's operations. Furthermore, different ministers in charge of the State Ministry for Women's Affairs showed favouritism towards one or the other of these bureaucracies. Experience shows that units established with similar mandates need to be given autonomy from each other so that they can compete fairly.

A second strategy is for the NWMs to identify the different stakeholders on gender policy (such as women's NGOs, research centres on gender, local governments, international donors, ministries and the private sector) and to ask them each to present their views in terms of both the causes of gender inequality and the solutions they propose. Overall, one of the major challenges that NWMs face is to formulate a coherent gender equality policy through valuing differences, synthesizing diverse views and, sometimes, recognizing indifference. Such a policy requires an awareness of the cognitive context, an awareness of both the national and international gender discourses, and development policies, including economics and budgeting.

## Conclusions

NWMs face some formidable challenges. They are expected to provide leadership as the focal point for follow-up to the

Beijing Platform for Action and are indeed expected to be a public sector institution, as well as a set of policies. They need to be catalysts for action by other government ministries and the agency that builds the capacity of other government ministries. To undertake this capacity-building function in other institutions, as well as of itself, is a formidable task for which sophisticated political and bureaucratic skills are required. Furthermore, NWMs are expected to work with international donors, develop coherent strategies, and manage the process of policy advocacy and relations with other institutions, while delivering programmes directly to the public! These expectations are too high even for the most efficient bureaucracies. The function of catalyst offers few political rewards. This is a long-term process in which the achievements are slow and incremental and where it is generally difficult to demonstrate progress. Thus this ministry or NWM is not often the most attractive assignment for politicians or experienced bureaucrats. On top of this, the actual and perceived weaknesses of the NWMs have meant that some donor agencies are reluctant to work with them. We have asked NWMs to be an 'ideal, non-existent bureaucracy' and have punished them for not living up to their task!

We would argue that NWMs should have an achievable agenda. First, NWMs need to be involved in a redefinition of gender issues in alliance with international donors, women's NGOs and their own governments that is appropriate to their own contexts. Second, they need to clarify their position, develop coherent strategies and engage in incremental steps, such as the development of procedures, guidelines and support gender training programmes. Third, they need to cultivate political allies. Leadership is a matter of entrepreneurship; it involves the combination of imagination in inventing institutional options and skill in brokering the interests of numerous actors to line up support for such options. In order to do this, one needs to be aware of the structural constraints discussed above, so that options and strategies can be devised *within* these constraints.

While it is important to understand the role of the NWMs, we cannot just focus on them without understanding the role of other political actors. Gender accountability requires broader conditions that include: (1) a political commitment to gender equality, including by political parties; (2) constitutional guarantees to gender equality; (3) a political culture that institutionalizes democratic and participatory values; and (4) the existence of gender-sensitive and knowledgeable women and men in decision-making positions. Perhaps we need to revisit the conventional understanding of the notion of national machinery. Case studies on the experience of national machineries suggest that policy processes are complex and multi-layered, not linear and predefined. As such they require multiple interventions by different actors. At a recent expert group meeting which examined case studies from the Dominican Republic, Romania and South Africa, it was concluded that successful gender mainstreaming is unlikely to take place in countries where this responsibility is located in a single governmental body. For example, the South African case showed that it is possible to institutionalize a variety of structures, instruments and mechanisms to serve the purpose of gender mainstreaming at the state level (United Nations International Research and Training Institute for the Advancement of Women (INSTRAW), 2000). These may include gender equality commissions made up of representatives of political parties, NGOs and government departments, women's advisory committees in legislatures, monitoring bodies to measure the implementation of national plans of action, special units in ministries, ombudspersons for gender equality and family courts. As United Nations reports show these have already been established in some countries (INSTRAW, 2000; UNDP, 1995). It is thus time to insist that states should move beyond the symbolic commitment to gender equality which has often translated into the establishment of NWMs. NWMs should be provided with the required clout and resources to monitor state practice and simultaneously mechanisms should be set up so that NWMs' work can also be systematically monitored.

# Part III
# Case studies

# 5

## The role of the women's movement in institutionalizing a gender focus in public policy: the Ecuadorian experience

SILVIA VEGA UGALDE[1]

### Introduction

The institutionalization of a gender focus in state policy is a long, complex process. It presupposes intervention in a variety of areas and further presupposes the active presence in society of actors who campaign, promote and lobby in order that the gender dimension becomes visible in political and social relations. In this chapter I present the experience of the Coordinadora Politica de Mujeres Ecuatorianas — CPME (Ecuadorian Women's Political Coordinating Organization), one of whose strategies is to work with members of Ecuador's women's movement for a gender focus in public policy.

CPME was founded in February 1996 at a National Women's Conference in which more than 800 representatives from 21 provinces participated. That Congress, the first of its kind in the country, was preceded by wide-ranging discussion throughout the country of an Ecuadorian Women's Political Agenda. This process of consensus formation led to the strengthening of the organization and the creation of closer ties among women's groups. Congress participants voted in favour of the Political Agenda as the founding document of CPME and, in a secret ballot, elected a group of fourteen national leaders. CPME's reason for being is to implement the Women's Political Agenda, a document that includes an analysis of the situation of women in Ecuador and a series of proposals for change intended to bring about social and gender equity. The Political Agenda contains sixteen chapters in which the general proposals and those related to specific interest groups are synthesized.

Why does CPME use the word 'political' to refer to the Agenda and the organization formed to realize its goals? This is because CPME is working to bring women's issues into the public sphere in order that they be dealt with as political issues on the national level — as issues appearing on the agendas of elected representatives. Further, CPME uses this word because it defines its actions as political. However, CPME is not a branch of any political party but is instead an organization made up of women from a wide variety of backgrounds who hold varying political and ideological beliefs and have had a range of organizing experiences.

The creation of the Political Agenda required a significant effort by members of the women's movement to develop an ability to analyse and think systematically about women's problems in the national context, as well as the ability to offer proposals while, at the same time, building an organization that would be capable of generating opinion, making its presence felt and negotiating from a position of strength. The development of the Political Agenda also led women's organizations, especially a number of non-governmental organizations (NGOs) in existence since the 1980s when they began accumulating knowledge and experience, to realize that the moment had come to work together in a permanent fashion in CPME. Previously, women had coordinated efforts on specific issues, and had even attempted to build a national organization in the midst of preparations for the Fourth World Conference on Women (Beijing 1995). However, that effort failed because it did not provide for the coming together of a significant and representative contingent of women's organizations.[2]

### The national political context

CPME was formed at a time when the state body responsible for women's issues was in transition. The Direccion Nacional de la Mujer, DINAMU (National Office for Women), was one entity among many within the Ministry of Social Welfare. It had a weak political presence and a limited budget, and was dependent, in administrative and financial terms, on the Ministry. The marked political instability that has characterized Ecuador's recent history was also evident in DINAMU, especially between 1992 and 1994, as a result of which a series of directors were unable to develop long-term policies. Beginning in the 1990s, women's organizations, together with several directors of DINAMU, proposed the creation of a Women's Institute as a state body charged with the institutionalization of a gender focus in public policy. At that time a number of studies were undertaken for this purpose, but the political will to put the ideas developed into practice did not exist.

When the administration of Abdala Bucaram took office in 1996, an individual with no ties to the women's movement was named Director of DINAMU. The Director's goal was to use the office to implement small, traditional welfare projects which could have only a limited impact. Bucaram was forced to step down by a wave of protest from citizens and members of Congress after six months in office. The interim government inaugurated in February 1997, indebted to the social movements that had participated in the downfall of Bucaram, signed an executive decree creating the Consejo Nacional de las Mujeres, CONAMU (National Women's Council), in October 1997.

CONAMU is situated in the President's Office, and is charged with institutionalizing a gender focus in public policy across all state sectors. It functions through a board of Directors[3] with three representatives of national women's organizations. CONAMU's President is appointed by the President of the Republic. During its first months, CONAMU concentrated on putting in place its administrative and financial organization and on strengthening its institutional base as national political structures stabilized, with the interim government giving way to a democratically elected constitutional government. CONAMU's Executive and its technical team have maintained the organization's stability during this period of uncertainty.

The National Constitutional Assembly met between December 1997 and May 1998. During this time CPME, CONAMU and other women's organizations developed an active presence, lobbying delegates for the inclusion of a number of constitutional reforms dealing with women. CPME's strategies for influencing public policy varied depending on the specific political circumstances and the changes taking place in state's women's machinery devoted to gender issues, first DINAMU and then CONAMU. In the following sections I examine the role of CPME and CONAMU in three different periods: (1) February 1996 to November 1997 — influencing public policy; (2) November 1997 to May 1998 — influencing constitutional provisions of the new constitution; and (3) September 1998 to the present — focusing on the social and political fabric rather than the state.

## Lobbying the state/influencing public policy

### The Bipartite Technical Commissions: the first phase

In 1996, CPME developed a strategy of engagement with the state based upon 'Comisiones Tecnicas Bipartitas (CTBs– Bipartite Technical Commissions). These were implemented during the short-lived administration of Bucaram (August 1996 to February 1997) and during the interim government. CPME conceived of the CTBs as bodies made up of state technicians (Ministry officials, congressional consultants, and so on) and representatives of CPME, whose role would be twofold: as technicians in their area of expertise and as political representatives of CPME. The purpose of the CTBs was to develop goals for different social sectors for a specific period, taking as a starting point the Women's Political Agenda on the one hand and, on the other, to assess proposals submitted by ministries and other state entities. Initially, the CTBs negotiated these goals and, when agreements were achieved, provided follow-up and oversight to ensure that goals were achieved. Representatives of CPME and the CTBs were required to coordinate their activities with other CTBs and to keep all those involved informed of their actions so that the members of the women's movement could respond effectively, through lobbying or social mobilization, to policy changes that might affect compliance with the agreements reached between CPME and the CTBs.

Fifty women technicians were added to work on a volunteer basis for around fifteen months on the implementation of this strategy. After the start of the CPME–CTB partnership, the Gender Equity Fund of the Canadian International Development Agency provided a grant to support this process which, for the most part, has been carried out in an enthusiastic and militant fashion by women from CPME. This was a recognition of the significance of the Women's Political Agenda and to the plural character of CPME which has generated confidence in a collective effort not subject to co-optation by particular interests.

To commemorate the first anniversary of the Fourth World Conference on Women, in 1996 CPME organized a nationwide event entitled 'From Words to Actions', in which a Public Commitment was signed by representatives of the state for the functioning of the CTBs. Signatories to this agreement included the President of Congress, the Prime Minister, the Minister of Foreign Relations, the Minister of Industry, Commerce and Crafts, and the Minister of Agriculture.

## CTBs: Assessing the first phase

Given the short period of time that the administration was in office, and the political upheaval that characterized those six months, the CTBs barely had time to begin working. Nevertheless, their usefulness was apparent in the following respects: first, the creation of a CTB in the Ministry of Government was decisive in halting the direction in which the six Women's Commissaries existing at the time were being pushed. Given the populist character of the government, the Commissaries, along with all public appointments, were being handed out as political favours to friends of the administration, in spite of regulations that required the participation of non-governmental counterparts. The pressure that CPME exerted through the CTB, and public criticism from the women's movement, mitigated this tendency. Second, CPME achieved an official presence on a number of congressional commissions: Budget, Public Management and Women.[4] For example, during those months members on the Budget Commission concentrated primarily on ensuring that the funds for existing and planned Women's Commissaries were not eliminated. Also, the Commission established in the Ministry of Agriculture was able to work with new administration appointments to strengthen the Office for Rural Women. The CTB was initially asked to promote a process of training in gender issues for ministry employees. However, this was something CPME could not involve itself in. Progress was made in new initiatives in law in the interest of gender equity. A new law governing water resources, an important issue for rural men and women, was formulated and the Bill was sent to Congress for debate. Third, in the congressional Commission for Public Management, members began working on the decentralization and social participation law. CPME was actively involved in the months-long discussions, which involved fourteen workshops providing a forum for public consultation and debate with other actors interested in local development. The resulting law includes a number of CPME's suggestions though it still contains, generally speaking, many gaps and is not entirely satisfactory. Fourth, the relationship established with the Ministry of Foreign Relations was fruitful as it provided for close collaboration on the inclusion of gender issues in documents prepared for the Hemisphere Summit that took place in Santa Cruz, Bolivia in December 1996. As a member of the Political Coalition of Andean Women,[5] CPME worked to include in all Summit documents related to 'sustainable development' concrete statements on gender equity. The success of this effort is apparent in the Final Declaration of the Summit. The Foreign Office of Ecuador proved very willing to work with us on this matter.

*CTBs November 1997 to May 1998: extending lobbying through participation*

When the Bucaram government was forced to step down, CPME proposed the re-launching of the CTBs to the new authorities. While the presidential government was replaced after the elections, there was greater continuity of personnel in Congress, in spite of the fact that the President of the legislature moved to the executive branch after being named Interim President. The BTCs became more flexible during this period in order to bring together a greater range of actors, as new ways of dealing with the state were developed and because at that point the National Constitutional Assembly was gradually becoming the focus of political attention. One new way of dealing with the state was participation in processes and objectives arising within various state entities and taking place within a fixed time period. For example, during this period the nation's planning body and the National Security Council launched 'Strategy 2025', a long-term planning proposal for development in Ecuador, and invited CPME and CONAMU — which had only recently been created — to work on the gender focus for this strategy. This was a task that CPME and CONAMU delegates accepted. The Legislative Commission on Women, Children and the Family worked with a number of women's organizations to develop a draft of penal code reforms, and these organizations were present during the discussions leading to approval of the reforms. The most important among these reforms were inclusion of sexual harassment as a criminal offence and more severe penalties for rape. Similarly, the Ministry of Health asked CPME and CONAMU, together with the Gender and Health Coordinating Committee, a group of NGOs working in this area, for comments on the gender focus of the *Health Procedures Manual*, used by Ministry personnel providing health services to the public.

The two organizations also participated in getting representation for women within other bodies, such as the National Education Council and the Inter-institutional Forestry Committee of Ecuador. While the law does not require that women be represented on the National Education Council, the Minister, recognizing the importance of a gender focus in education, invited CPME to participate. CPME worked on the design of policies for the training of educators and also coordinated with CONAMU the training of a group of women as gender trainers within the Ministry of Education's teacher-training programme.

Participation in the Inter-institutional Forestry Committee of Ecuador took place when CPME realized that the Forestry Plan of Ecuador did not take into account the interests of all actors involved in the use of forest resources. Together with representatives of indigenous communities, the timber industry, and environmental organizations, CPME pointed out the need for women to be represented on the committee. This demand was not understood initially, but was gradually proved legitimate and CPME was charged with developing one of the programmes constituting the

'Forestry Plan: Participatory Forestry Development with Rural Populations'. At present, with the Ministry of the Environment and the forestry sector having undergone an institutional reorganization process, CPME continues to be called upon for consultations.

## Assessing strategies, reviewing processes: post-1998

CPME has drawn a number of conclusions based on its first attempts to work with the state in order to lobby for public policy with a gender focus. First, in order for the women's movement to plan a strategy that will have an impact on the state, it is indispensable to develop a process for defining proposals that deal with the major problems affecting women and the country. In Ecuador, this was achieved with the development of a Women's Political Agenda which provided guidelines for action. Second, together with this programmatic basis, it is also necessary to develop the political ability to anticipate and judge key opportunities and possibilities for effective political impact. Apprenticeship in how to combine negotiation, pressure and censure takes time, but it is important in safeguarding the autonomy of the women's social movement *vis-à-vis* the state and thus avoiding co-optation by the state, as has occurred in some other Latin American countries. CPME's experience in testing various strategies for working together with state sectors under the Bucaram government was valuable, as was the simultaneous active commitment in publicly censuring and opposing government actions harmful to the dignity of women and to citizens in general that took place during that administration. Third, given the weak institutional presence of a gender focus in Ecuador, a problem complicated by the political and institutional instability that has characterized the country in recent years, it was exhausting for a women's organization to maintain a permanent and global presence in state bodies, especially as every appointment of a new minister meant a new beginning of the lobbying process. Thus CPME was probably more effective in achieving concrete results due to participating in processes that were fixed in respect to time limit, objectives and area of action. In the experience of CPME, invitations for participation in processes of this type have generally involved consultations over documents and policies, for example, Strategy 2025, the penal code reforms and the *Health Procedures Manual* — but CPME has not been able to do follow-up in these matters, which suggests a serious weakness from the point of view of its ability to measure the extent to which participation in processes of this type has led to real improvements in the situation of women. Fourth, given the limited knowledge and assimilation of the gender focus among political authorities in general, individuals, personal contacts and friendships with government officials have been almost decisive in identifying points of entry and support for initiatives proposed. The presence of special offices and individuals charged with gender issues within ministries is useful in this sense in order to have reliable counterparts within state entities. It is thus effective to create 'alliances' with mid-level state personnel who are, in general, more open and more stable than appointed and/or elected officials at the top of the political machinery. Requirements included in international cooperation agreements also aid in pressuring state entities dependent on financing through such agreements. Finally, while state entities specializing in gender, such as CONAMU in Ecuador, have a more specific technical function in their relationships with the rest of the state, the role of the women's movement is that of proposing, pressuring, negotiating, overseeing, criticizing and demanding explanations; that is, a specifically political role. Nevertheless, the political role requires technical skills in order to be effective, just as technical advisory roles require political clarity and astuteness. The two are important as they contribute to empowering the women's social movement through being effective in lobbying the state for change and also in keeping feminist state bodies and NGOs in tune with the women's movement. An absence of this dialectical relationship would lead to a weakening of the women's movement and increase the threat of co-optation of women's national machineries. A greater clarification as to CONAMU's role and those to be assumed by the women's social movement is still required in order to avoid conflicts and negative duplication of efforts. The subject of the autonomy of the movement *vis-à-vis* specialized state entities continues to be a topic for discussion in Ecuador.


## Constitutional reforms and the creation of a state office

The popular movement that led to the overthrow of President Bucaram not only rejected a series of policies and a style of government thought by the citizenry to be ineffective and an insult to the dignity of the country, but also expressed the desire for deeper changes. A range of social movements proposed a new Constitution and established the parameters for the changes it would include. Political elites tried to twist the popular will and to limit as far as possible the reach of the Constitutional Assembly, which began work in December 1997 (one month after the creation of the National Women's Council).

The election of Assembly representatives took place through a new electoral system which considerably restricted the participation of minorities, and in which a law requiring quotas for women was only partially applied.[6] Women accounted for 10 per cent of Assembly representatives. CPME came up with the slogan 'Women in the Assembly with their own voice' and actively supported women candidates. During the campaign, CPME held workshops in provinces for the discussion of proposals to be presented to the Constitutional Assembly, and worked with CONAMU and other women's organizations for a number of months in preparing a single document (the new Constitution of Ecuador) that was presented in conjunction with a women's march.

CONAMU and women's organizations were helped by consultants — in the case of CONAMU — and lobbyists — on the part of the women's movement — activities which bore fruit, specifically the inclusion of a number of important rights. These included rights to:
1 *personal integrity*, that is the eradication of physical, psychological and sexual violence, and moral coercion;
2 *freedom and responsibility* in making decisions regarding sexual behaviour;

3 *personal freedom* to decide the number of children a couple will have;
4 *equality under the law*, ending discrimination based on sex, health status, age and sexual preference;
5 *equality of rights and opportunities* for men and women in access to resources for production and economic decision making in the administration of the conjugal relationship and of property;
6 *recognition of unpaid domestic work* as productive labour;
7 *equitable participation* of women and men as candidates in the popular election process.

The new Constitution also states that 'The state will formulate and execute policies to achieve equality of opportunities for women and men, through a special entity which will function as determined by the law, will incorporate the gender focus as well as plans and programmes, and will offer technical assistance for its obligatory implementation in the public sector' (Article 41). It is believed that this Article will result in greater stability for CONAMU which, up to now, has existed as a result of an executive decree that could be rescinded at any time.

The consolidation of CONAMU as a state machinery for women which is an autonomous institution was a victory for women's organizations which had been fighting for this goal for a number of years. However, some confusion has probably been created as a result, both in CONAMU and in the women's movement, regarding its character and role. It is thought that the women who work as officials in CONAMU are part of the women's social movement, that they have the same objectives and that it is necessary for CONAMU and the movement to work together when approaching other state bodies, for example. However, the question remains: does the women's movement require a stage within the state or does it need to affirm its identity as a movement in order to question the state on an equal footing? Do convictions and love for the cause of women that state bureaucrats (femocrats) may profess to hold automatically make them 'part' of a social movement which has its own dynamic, interests and roles, or is the identification a source of confusion when dealing with other state officials and in their dealings with one another (see Sawer, chapter 12 of this volume)? Do agreements on specific issues that may come about among specialized state bodies and the women's movement relieve the state of the responsibility to give an accounting of its activities to a citizen's movement? Does the lack of differentiation between the two work in favour of or hold back citizen efforts in demanding a full accounting from the national state machinery for women?

These are some of the new questions which have arisen in the course of the women's movement's engagement with the state. Often, members of the women's movement want to preserve their identity as actors on the cultural and social stages, as critics who question existing social relations without, as a result, losing the ability to negotiate and achieve concrete goals in the political arena. These are also, no doubt, questions that should be asked by those working in national machineries for women, who should not be looking at the women's movement as an instrument to be used, or a workforce in implementing their strategies, but rather in a broader sense as necessarily independent actors in social processes (see Rai, chapter 1 of this volume). This is a debate that remains open in Ecuador, and in which both sides have expressed a willingness to talk.

## Towards enforcement of rights won by women

With the new Constitution that was completed and approved in August 1998, women in Ecuador have embarked on a new phase in which we must put into practice the rights won in that Constitution. This is, without a doubt, a 'long march' that begins with disseminating among women, public institutions and society in general information about these rights, and that also includes the creation of mechanisms for demanding that the said rights are respected.

With the re-inauguration of institutional stability in the political realm as a result of the election of a new President and legislators, a new effort has been assumed by various organizations in the women's movement and the legislative Commission on Women, Children, Youth, the Elderly and the Family, an entity which is now a Permanent

Legislative Commission. Rights specified in the Constitution must have concrete status as laws or legal reforms, a task that is being carried out by this Commission made up of congresswomen from, or with ties to, the women's movement.[7] Without underestimating the progress that might be made in this fashion, and the effectiveness of the said Commission, I believe it is necessary for the women's movement to question the dynamic that is created when an initiative arises from the state rather than from civil society. Experience demonstrates that there is greater mobilization, greater public visibility, greater impact on public opinion and a greater degree of participation by women when such an initiative arises from below, from civil society, and thus the results will be longer lasting and more sustainable.

CPME's current concern is that of learning from our cumulative experience of dealing with the state and continuing to work together with existing state bodies, but without losing the political initiative that will maintain the social vitality of the change process proposed by feminists.

CPME held its Second National Political Congress in September 1998. At that event, a strategy oriented more towards the social and political fabric than towards the state apparatus as such was proposed. CONAMU now exists with its specific role within the state, but CPME has identified multiple gaps in gender vision in the political realm and in society, beginning with large numbers of women who do not know their rights. Its new strategy does not underestimate the importance of ties with state institutions, but focuses on creating those ties on a new basis or with a different emphasis: not so much to integrate the gender focus into public policies (which process, in many cases, is understood in a technical or instrumental sense) but to crystallize the rights of women and men in relations among citizens, in the political culture, in social practices, in everyday life.

## Notes

1 I write this chapter in my individual capacity. However, I have based my observations and analysis on my experience as a national leader of the Ecuadorian Women's Political Coordinating Organization.

2 The panorama of the women's movement has been changing towards a greater diversity of views.

3 Currently, the National Office for Planning, the Secretary of State and the Social Front.

4 The presence of CPME on this stage created a permanent channel for communications with Congress. Today, a significant number of legislative commissions sends their Bills to CPME for our comments.

5 The Political Coalition of Andean Women (PAM) was formed in June 1996 as a forum for national women's organizations from Andean countries. The purpose of the Coalition is to exercise influence on behalf of women in the subregional integration process and to exchange experiences in follow-up on PAM's compliance in our countries.

6 In the three provinces with the greatest number of voters, the quota for women was a minimum of 20 per cent.

7 The Legislative Commission has signed an agreement with CONAMU which provides for technical assistance and financial support.

# 6

## The National Commission on the Role of Filipino Women, the women's movement and gender mainstreaming in the Philippines[1]

JURGETTE HONCULADA[2] AND
ROSALINDA PINEDA OFRENEO[3]

### Introduction

The Philippine experience shows that a vibrant women's movement plays a critical role *vis-à-vis* a national women's machinery — lobbying for its creation, providing leadership and direction, pioneering new initiatives such as gender training that are key components of gender mainstreaming, and serving as a gadfly when government fails to deliver.

The National Commission on the Role of Filipino Women (NCRFW) has had a long and chequered history, often interwoven with the twists and turns of Philippine feminism. Placed directly under the Office of the President, it was founded during the Marcos period of dictatorship (1975–86), strengthened during the Aquino era of restored but still limited democracy (1986–92) and further expanded during the Ramos regime which placed both globalization and gender mainstreaming onto the agenda (1992–98).

Twice has the women's movement played midwife to the NCRFW: at its creation in 1975 and at its rebirth in 1986. The NCRFW's deepest impulses reflect this fact: its leadership is largely drawn from academia and women's non-governmental organizations (NGOs) and its major themes resonate with issues raised by the women's

movement. The first decade of Balikatan[4] organizing of
local communities created a nationwide women's movement, albeit in the direction of income generation and
micro-enterprise. The second decade's theme of gender
mainstreaming was compelled by the small but steady gains
of women's NGOs in gender awareness raising, advocacy
and institution building.

Thus the functions of the Commission now include
coordinating 'the preparation of Philippine development
plans for women as well as their monitoring, assessment and
updating'; serving as a 'clearinghouse and data base for
information relating to women'; conducting reviews of existing legislation, policy studies and gender awareness-raising
programmes; monitoring and assessing the implementation
of laws and policies on women, including international
commitments such as the Beijing Platform for Action; and
implementing pilot projects 'for the delivery of services for
women as a basis for policy formation and programme recommendation'. The NCRFW has a Board of Commissioners to
set its policies, programmes and campaigns. It is led by an
Executive Director assisted by a Deputy Executive Director
and the Chiefs of five functional divisions: policy analysis;
information resources; monitoring and evaluation; technical services; and administration and finance.

## Two streams of feminism

The NCRFW's leadership has emanated from the Philippine women's movement, and from two streams in particular: liberal and left-of-centre feminism. Liberal feminism in
the country emerged in the early 1900s, gaining force and
visibility in the 1920s with the nationwide campaign for
suffrage. Spearheaded by the National Federation of Women's
Clubs, then the biggest coalition of women's organizations,
the campaign mobilized all major women's groups to a
resounding victory in the 1937 plebiscite that recognized,
for the first time in Asia, women's right to vote. Through
the next two decades this 'first wave'[5] of feminism sought
its goals in equal laws and equal opportunities. This wave
was spearheaded by professional groups and a number of

welfare-oriented socio-civic women's organizations which later became the Civic Assembly of Women in the Philippines (CAWP), predecessor of the National Council of Women in the Philippines.

The CAWP's lobbying efforts for the creation of a national women's machinery date back to the late 1960s. But it would take the added leverage of 1975 as International Women's Year for President Ferdinand Marcos to redeem a half-forgotten pledge and decree the birth of the NCRFW. Unknowingly the NCRFW had two fairy godmothers: first-wave feminists and the international women's movement.

The 'second wave' of feminism in the country would gestate in the late 1960s and 1970s, aware of the emergence of the Western women's liberation movements while affirming its roots in the historic struggles for nationhood. Such emergence was palpable in a much-publicized protest against the 1969 Miss Philippines beauty contest by the then left-identified women's organization Makibaka, an acronym for Malayang Kilusan ng Bagong Kababaihan (Free Movement of New Filipino Women). But this nascent feminist group had to yield to the exigencies of underground resistance to a dictatorship in the early 1970s. In the 1980s second-wave feminists would largely come from mixed groups such as political formations, people's movements and women-only NGOs. All were critical of martial law and some of the more politically minded shared a socialist perspective. This created a tension with women's groups that had made peace with the establishment or kept their silence vis-à-vis martial law.

In the great divide between those for and against martial law, the NCRFW was perceived by second-wave feminists to be an ally of government. This was so for a number of reasons: Imelda Marcos chaired the NCRFW Board of Commissioners and local politicians' wives headed Balikatan councils; and as part of the government structure, it was assumed that the Commission would be pro-government. Yet a third reason stemmed from the fact that the CAWP, the NCRFW's major partner, was seen to have come to terms with martial law.

Many groups within the second wave of the women's movement which emerged at the height of the Marcos dictatorship sought to balance class and gender issues, exemplified by two autonomous women's organizations, PILIPINA and KALAYAAN, founded in 1981 and 1982, respectively. PILIPINA affirmed that 'the struggle for social transformation would have to be waged along gender lines' and not just in terms of 'class and property relations'. KALAYAAN viewed itself as 'autonomous but not separate [from]' and 'distinct but not integrated [with]' the national democratic movement, refusing to sacrifice women's liberation for some 'higher goal' of national liberation, according to former NCRFW Commissioner Fe Mangahas.[6]

A third organization, GABRIELA, was founded in 1984 as a broad coalition to rally various women's groups against the Marcos dictatorship. Part of a larger political formation, GABRIELA has disavowed working directly with government, and that includes the NCRFW. Organized in 1975, the KaBaPa (Katipunan ng Bagong Pilipina or Association of the New Filipina) also belongs to a larger political group and has roots in the peasant movement. Infusion of gender concerns came in the 1980s.

### Broad unities and deep fissures

For the Philippine women's movement (or movements, which some claim as being more accurate), the decade of the 1980s revealed broad unities as well as deep fissures. On 28 October 1983 various sections of the women's movement set their differences aside to march in full force against the dictatorship. This shining moment of feminist sisterhood would be repeated in the 1986 campaign for gender equality provisions in the new Constitution that was being drafted by a Constitutional Commission. The Commission was appointed by then President Aquino after she had been catapulted to power on the strength of the EDSA revolt against the Marcos dictatorship. Four organizations and coalitions initially met to consolidate their proposals: the Concerned Women of the Philippines, Women's Caucus, GABRIELA and Lakas ng Kababaihan spearheaded by PILIPINA, with Lakas serving as initial convenor and secretariat.

Five provisions were encompassing and prescient here: seeking women's fundamental equality with men in all spheres of life; affording protection to working women, including a concern for child care, and ensuring equal work and pay; recognizing the economic value of housework; safeguarding women's choice of career and property rights; and mandating women's equal representation in policy making at all levels.

The month-long process of consultations also prefigured the vibrant Governmental organization (GO)–NGO partnership that would be foundational for the NCRFW's rebirth and new growth in its second decade. Leticia Shahani, by then Deputy Minister of Foreign Affairs, formally convened the consultations with the NCRFW as host. Lakas ng Kababaihan Chair (and later NCRFW Board Commissioner) Teresita Quintos-Deles coordinated the NGO side. Shahani was concerned that the progressive women's groups enter the process, while Quintos-Deles sought the engagement of other streams of the women's movement. This effectively took care of the entire spectrum of women's organizations.

On a stirring Women's Day of Unity in July 1986, presided over by the outgoing Executive Director of the NCRFW, Leticia de Guzman, the final document was signed by 2,000 representatives of 200 women's organizations as well as school and government delegations. Crossing 'social and ideological boundaries', the gathering was also graced by suffragists of the 1920s and 1930s. Quintos-Deles observed that the entire process was 'imbued with intellectual alertness, emotional honesty, moral commitment, and a political maturity that all Filipino women can be proud of' (Honculada and Ofreneo, 1998:5). The document was formally presented to Constitutional Commission President and eminent jurist Cecilia Munoz-Palma by female members of the Constitutional Commission.

This test case of gender solidarity in the post-dictatorship period showed that a broad unity between 'first and second wave' feminism, within the more left-inclined women's groups and, finally, unity between women in the NGO community and those in the bureaucracy was essential for a high-stakes campaign to succeed. Yet it also became clear that sections of the women's movement continued to have different perspectives towards working with the government.

One perspective was that of critical opposition on the premise that the Aquino administration would not be fundamentally different from its predecessor. Another position was that of critical collaboration with progressive forces within government, to be able to espouse pioneering initiatives such as peace and an enlarged women's agenda.

With the NCRFW's doors open to the wide array of women's organizations, the new Board of Commissioners in 1986 included women's advocates, feminists and women professionals representing the private sector. The deepest hues of purple, the symbolic colour of feminism, now scintillated in the NCRFW.

The two global Women's Conferences in Mexico in 1975 and Nairobi in 1985 gave the then NCRFW Executive Director Remmy Rikken her first intimation of gender mainstreaming. But NCRFW staff and other women in government had to be converted to the vision. The presence and leadership of brash, young (and not-so-young) women activists at the 1987 consultations and other NCRFW meetings was edifying, if not electrifying. Women bureaucrats had a taste of what 'movement' meant, its dynamism and refreshing spontaneity. But the learning went both ways. Women activists realized that bureaucracy was not a faceless, genderless mass and that feminism could make inroads there. Indeed, feminism *had* to make inroads there.

Gender training was pioneered by the women's movement. Ging Deles says that the Harvard tools of gender analysis 'became exciting only because there were practitioners interacting with the technology. It was these practitioners sans technology who first realized the implications and possible impact of having technologies to measure or to communicate what you're trying to say.' It was also the women activists who first expressed the need to move from 'heart' to 'hard' data. Ging put it plainly: 'We [women NGOs] created the motivation, the environment to make it necessary to go technical.' And so the consultations provided the bare bones on which gender mainstreaming would grow. These gatherings would set into motion a process that would produce two historic volumes: the *Philippine Development Plan for Women (1989–1992)* (NCRFW, 1989) and the *Philippine Plan for Gender-Responsive Development 1995–2025* (NCRFW, 1995a).

## The GO–NGO partnership

One high point of the GO–NGO partnership nurtured early on by the NCRFW was the annual GO–NGO congress starting in 1989. Drawing in participants from far and wide, the congress had both a serious and carnival side to it, with lectures, workshops, joint planning, poetry reading and singing, as well as movie screenings, folk art displays, and sales of posters, brochures and the like. Not a few top women bureaucrats point to the first congress as a turning point in their lives when they really got to 'talk women' with other women.

The GO–NGO collaboration is also credited with two executive proclamations issued in 1989: declaring the first week of March as Women's Week, with 8 March as International Women's Day and, later, March as Women's Role in History Month. In 1990 8 March became a special holiday by legislative action. Only in the Philippines does the celebration of International Women's Day fill an entire month: at least a hundred activities are held yearly in Metro Manila and the provinces, engaging both NGO women and their sisters in government. These activities include marches and rallies of left-wing-oriented women's groups, founding anniversaries of other women's organizations, film festivals, art exhibits, symposia and public forums, testimonies on violence against women, and the like. This prolonged observance has highlighted women's culture and aided in the full flowering of women's advocacy.

## Cory Aquino's term: the best and worst of times

Patricia 'Tatti' Licuanan, who served as NCRFW Board Chair for most of Cory Aquino's presidency, describes this period as the 'best of times [and] worst of times'. Why the ambivalence, if not seeming contradiction? The times were favourable, she says, because the national leadership was 'deeply committed to reform' and was 'comfortable with NGOs and GOs eager to work with them'. Though Cory Aquino was not a feminist she was 'instinctively supportive' of women's causes.

But it was also the worst of times for women's problems, which could easily be sidelined with an economy in near-shambles. Moreover, as Licuanan observed, GO and NGO 'working styles seemed incompatible' and NGO participation and partnership were difficult to concretize. A third reason was the NGOs' deep-seated suspicion and distrust of government. Licuanan wryly noted: 'Some of this destructive competition . . . characterized the women's movement as well.' She also observed that 'having a woman President did not always work to the benefit of women' because her situation, if not success, became generic for all women. A woman President also raised undue expectations about what could be done for women (Honculada and Ofreneo, 1998).

Nevertheless, gender mainstreaming and its evolving technology was part of Cory Aquino's legacy to the incoming administration of Fidel Ramos. Towards the end of her term, the initiative for gender mainstreaming lay with government structures. But the role of NGO women's groups remained critical, especially when gender mainstreaming started moving out to pilot regions and local government units.

Ugnayan ng Kababaihan sa Pulitika or UKP had drafted a ten-point women's agenda with demands related to peace, the environment, agriculture, work, business and industry, health, social services, education, culture and media, violence against women and political participation. Among the presidential candidates, only Fidel Ramos signed the agenda, an auspicious beginning. UKP included women NGOs and women from academe and government. Among its leaders was Imelda 'Mely' Nicolas, who would become NCRFW Board Chair in the Ramos administration (1992–98). A military man, who initially provoked women's fears with the scarce representation of women in his first Cabinet, Ramos proved a staunch ally of the NCRFW. Issuing a number of executive orders that sought to deepen the bases and broaden the scope of gender mainstreaming, Ramos increased the frequency of presidential meetings with the NCRFW from twice yearly to quarterly.

A notable accomplishment during Ramos' term was the allocation of a 5 per cent budget for gender and development. At last, the government seemed to be putting at least some of its money 'where its mouth is', in the words of the then NCRFW Chairperson Imelda Nicolas. It was time to stop just talking about gender and start providing substance to the rhetoric by giving it a budget. After all, gender advocacy and commitment to women's empowerment would sound hollow if they were not accompanied by provision of resources for the implementation of programmes and projects on the ground. As succinctly put in *The Women's Budget* (NCRFW, 1995), 'the most reliable measure of government's political will to respond to women's concerns is . . . how much it spends on them.' The then Senator Leticia Ramos Shahani (sister of the President) also served as an important catalyst, insisting on a minimum allocation of 5 per cent for gender and development, despite arguments that such a small share would again reinforce women's marginalization in terms of access to, and control of, resources. On the other hand, beginning with a specific amount, no matter how minimal, would be better than vague rhetoric about an 'amorphous thing' called a Gender and Development (GAD) budget devoid of clear and attainable targets.

## The NCRFW and global feminism

The GO–NGO partnership proved a winning combination in three major undertakings during Ramos' term: the United Nations Fourth World Conference on Women in Beijing, the Asia-Pacific Economic Cooperation Forum (APEC) and the Social Reform Agenda.

The NCRFW was at the forefront of three years of preparations of Philippine GO and NGO women for the global women's conference and NGO forum in Beijing. As at Nairobi the NGO women's forum raised cutting-edge issues, with the crystallized debates finding their way into official conference sessions and the final document, the Beijing Platform for Action. Those preparations were both a labour of love and an exercise in discipline, engaging women NGOs in a three-tiered process: drawing the agenda from the regions via networks and major organizations; thence meeting at a national conference to come to a consensus; and, later, sharing their agenda with counterpart organizations in the Asia-Pacific region. The NGO consensus document was further pared down to three major issues to be championed by the official Philippine delegation to Beijing: migrant women workers, rural women and violence against women, particularly trafficking in women.

It is a tribute to Filipino women that one of their own chaired the tumultuous United Nations Women's Conference in 1985, and again in 1995, to produce a consensus document that rang true for most, if not all, of the world's women. Leticia Shahani served as Secretary-General of the World Conference in Nairobi in 1985; Tatti Licuanan, as Chair of the main committee in Beijing in 1995, won the 'battle of the brackets'[7] with grace and firmness, with one journalist describing her, as an 'iron bladder'. It is no surprise therefore that Tatti Licuanan succeeded Letty Shahani as NCRFW Chair when Shahani ran for the Senate in 1986. Another Filipina feminist, Irene Santiago, served as Executive Director to the NGO women's forum in Huairou outside Beijing which boasted 35,000 participants.

The total commitment of major sections of the Philippine women's movement to the Beijing Fourth World Conference on Women and its preparatory process was bolstered by executive support. In the midst of the frenzy at Beijing, the Philippine delegation was cheered by news that President Ramos had issued an executive order approving the Philippine Plan for Gender-Responsive Development. The Plan would, in fact, be the 'main mechanism to implement the platform for action in the country' (NCRFW, 1998a:14).

The NCRFW's intense gender advocacy permeates its international engagements, an advocacy rooted in the women's movement. The APEC forum was founded in 1989 to promote open trade and economic cooperation in the Asia-Pacific region. The NCRFW has played a leading role in raising the issue of gender within APEC by commissioning policy research papers on APEC's priority areas of cooperation from a gender perspective.[8] Most of these papers were forthright about the expected negative effects of globalization on the majority of women. These were presented at the Senior Women Leaders' Network, which the NCRFW is supporting. For their part, women's groups sponsored a series of forums to probe the perils and promises of increasing globalization in the Asia-Pacific sphere. The NCRFW has likewise been charged with the task of monitoring government compliance with the Beijing commitments.

## Gender advocacy and the social reform agenda

The Social Reform Agenda (SRA), espoused by the Ramos government to alleviate poverty and institute social reforms, has its origins in the peace and NGO movements in the country. As one of the basic sectors represented in the Social Reform Council, women have sought to raise the gender issue *vis-à-vis* the SRA framework and its sectoral programmes. Council meetings chaired by the President have been venues for gender advocacy in legislation and executive policy.

The issue of violence against women is instructive. The anti-sexual harassment Bill and expanded anti-rape Bill were produced through years of gender awareness raising, broad-based women's mobilization and coalition building on the issue of violence against women. Women workers consistently raised the issue of workplace-related harassment. Yet the Bills languished in the halls of a male-dominated Congress, saved from a natural death by a combination of factors, not least of which was the strategic support of women bureaucrats, the NCRFW and the President. For instance, last minute strategizing by women's NGOs led by Sentro ng Alternatibong Lingap Panlegal (the Alternative Legal Assistance Centre) and PILIPINA rescued the anti-sexual harassment Bill from the freezer; and unrelenting advocacy by the women's coalition Sama-samang Inisyatiba ng Kababaihan sa Pagbabago ng Batas at Lipunan (the Joint Women's Initiative in Changing Law and Society) was key to the passage of the anti-rape Bill.

## Gains

In spite of the current rough sailing (see below), two key gains have marked the decade 1989–98 and have refused to sink in the murky waters of the present: deepening the discourse on gender and starting to redirect the mainstream in terms of logic and resources. The first meant learning to read and write anew. The women's movement may be credited with raising gender to the level of public discourse but sustaining the discourse apart from massive mobilizations and sharp confrontations with a macho Congress is beyond the capacity of even the most fervent gender advocates. Learning to read anew meant spotting the issues simmering beneath the surface of mundane reality: rank discrimination, a paralysing double burden, a punishing double standard, opportunities squandered, families in pain, communities in stagnation. This new literacy meant, for a growing number of bureaucrats (and non-bureaucrats), a new numeracy and learning to write afresh: counting women and making women count, in their labour in production and reproduction, and factoring the female population into projects, policies and activities. Not as mere recipients, clientele or passive objects but as active subjects, making the decisions that impinged daily on their lives.

In the concrete, the gains appear modest. However, aggregately the infrastructure for gender mainstreaming is being built slowly, stone by stone. First comes the human resource base, the NCRFW staff and their counterparts in the agencies, that has become a 'community of people' with a passion for their work, trust and confidence in each other, and the dedication and commitment to see gender mainstreaming through. A second gain is the knowledge resource base, the tools and mechanisms, many of which have been crafted in good old trial-and-error fashion. Integral to this is the conceptual framework, the GAD framework, that was not ready to hand in 1989, but emerged from the hit and miss of GAD focal point building in many line agencies. Another gain is the expanded sisterhood, with women in government staking out their claims as much for themselves as for the whole bureaucracy, networking among each other and with women in the GO–NGO community for mutual growth and inspiration and a common agenda. These websites of sisterhood are crucial to both sides: for NGO women to comprehend and critique the gender mainstreaming process; and for women in the bureaucracy to locate their issues within the broader macro-realities with which the majority of women grapple, such as globalization. There has also been an increase in male advocates and champions of gender issues in government. Gender mainstreaming would not have gone as far as it has in pilot agencies and regions without their staunch support.

The international women's movement and international development agencies have played crucial roles at each stage of the NCRFW's history. In processes that continue to affirm the NCRFW's autonomy, they have shared resources, helped to clarify directions and provided inspiration.

Finally, the 5 per cent GAD budget is an ingenious way of securing funds for GAD activities, projects and programmes in a situation of scarce resources. Regular compliance reports are the basis for the National Economic Development Authority's monitoring of agency performance. A similar call has been issued by the Department of Budget and Management to local government units.

## Challenges

While the gains have been many, they are not irreversible. Bureaucracy has existed for decades without a gender perspective (or with a biased one) — why change? Thus many GAD reports are surreal, not real. Reporting for compliance means equating anything female with gender. One critic archly inquired whether enumerating male, then female, carabaos constituted sex-disaggregated data in agriculture. This is like the claim that a project is gender responsive on the strength of listing male and female beneficiaries. Bureaucratic culture could very well ignore the requirements for a GAD budget and GAD reports (see Staudt, chapter 2 of this volume). But in today's world, it is easier to keep the form without the substance. Thus the GAD budget has become an end in itself, rather than a means to an end — women's empowerment. Many dangers ensue from a bureaucracy with petrified ways of thinking and doing: outright opposition and hostility towards women's movements and groups, marginalization of GAD focal points, death by starvation (no funds), lip service and compliance simply on paper.

When coupled with macro-economic constraints that require severe fiscal cutbacks, the danger is potent, if not
fatal (see Kwesiga and Sawer, chapters 10 and 12 of this
volume). Gains, painstakingly built since the 1980s, could
be reversed. The economic crisis that hit Southeast Asian
economies in late 1997 has adversely affected many sectors
of the economy. The government has had to reduce budgets
drastically. Viewed as a fad or 'flavour of the month', the
GAD budget is deemed expendable and among the first to
go (see also Jezerska and Kwesiga, chapters 8 and 10 of this
volume). In fact, in 1998 69 agencies reported a 2.69 billion
pesos allocation for GAD, a mere 0.49 per cent of the total
appropriations worth 546.7 billion pesos.

If the NCRFW loses steam because of factors beyond its
control, gender mainstreaming will all the more become
rarefied rhetoric convenient to disarm women and humour
the funding agencies. The GAD budget will either remain
on display, funding all sorts of initiatives involving women
but not empowering them, or be revoked as so much gender
claptrap.

In the final analysis, the litmus test of gender mainstreaming in government does not lie within government
itself, but in whether and how gender advocacy is able to
transform relationships between women and men in the
country's towns and villages, farms and workplaces, upland
and coastal communities. Women's groups existing auto-
nomously or within larger political and civil society formations need to conjoin with the NCRFW and women in
the Philippine bureaucracy in this Herculean effort.

## Notes

1 This chapter is based on *Transforming the Mainstream: Building a
Gender-Responsive Bureaucracy in the Philippines*, written by the
authors and published by the UNIFEM East and Southeast Asia Pacific
Regional Office, which documents the gender mainstreaming experiences of the National Commission on the Role of Filipino Women from
1975 to mid 1998.

2 Women's Secretary, National Federation of Labour; and Vice Chairperson of PILIPINA and the Women's Action Network for Development.

3 PhD and Professor, Department of Women and Development Studies,
College of Social Work and Community Development, University of the
Philippines, Diliman, Quezon City.

4 Balikatan sa Kaunlaran or BSK, the nationwide organizing of rural women's councils for socio-economic uplift under the aegis of the NCRFW.

5 Some prefer the terms 'first wave' and 'second wave' feminists as more neutral, if not more inclusive, and less subject to polemics. While first-wave feminists were invariably liberal, second-wave feminists encompassed the liberal and left-of-centre. The terms 'nationalist feminism' or 'Third World feminism' have also been used for the latter substream.

6 From a 25 March 1998 interview with Mangahas, who was also a founder of *Kalayaan*.

7 Contentious points in official United Nations documents are bracketed and the effort to produce consensus in Beijing was Herculean, with the deletion of over 400 pairs of brackets.

8 Numbering seven, the policy papers are collectively entitled 'Gender Analysis of Selected Philippine Concerns under APEC'.

# 7

# National machinery for gender equality in Sweden and other Nordic countries

BIRGITTA ÅSESKOG

## Introduction

In this chapter I want to describe the 'Nordic model' of national machinery for gender equality. I want to show the similarities between the countries, but also the differences. The official Nordic cooperation on gender equality, conducted by the Nordic Council of Ministers, is based on the development of pilot projects and reports on priority areas. It provides excellent opportunities to develop new methods and strategies and is a forum for the exchange of experience. This cooperation is of great importance for progress in all countries in the equality policy area.

I argue that the development of a Nordic mainstreaming strategy is an important next step in the efforts to promote gender equality in this region. I conclude this chapter with a focus on the specific case of Sweden.[1] Norway was the first Nordic country to start systematic work to mainstream a gender perspective in all policy fields (early in the 1980s). The other countries have recently started to develop their mainstreaming strategies. In 1996 the Nordic Council of Ministers decided to launch a three-year project (1997–99) in order to develop methods and tools for the integration of a gender perspective into labour market policy and youth policy in the Nordic countries.

## Nordic cooperation and a 'Nordic model' of gender equality

The Nordic countries have strong cultural, historical and linguistic ties, as well as firmly rooted democratic traditions. This has enabled them to succeed in developing a pattern of close, constructive cooperation in various areas. Official Nordic cooperation involves the five Nordic countries of Denmark, Finland, Iceland, Norway and Sweden, as well as the autonomous territories of the Faeroe Islands, Greenland and Åland, with a total of 23 million inhabitants. The Parliaments cooperate in the Nordic Council and the governments cooperate in the Nordic Council of Ministers. The cooperation is not supranational but based on voluntary equal cooperation between independent nations. Several Nordic institutions and project activities are funded from a Nordic budget. As a result of the significant levels of cultural homogeneity of the countries and cooperation between their governments, the Nordic countries have achieved more or less uniform legislation in some areas. One of these areas is gender equality, where the countries have agreed on certain standards and adopted common goals.

### Cooperation programme for gender equality, 1995–2000

Cooperation on gender equality among the Nordic countries is based on projects and reports commissioned by the Nordic Council of Ministers. In the build-up to the Beijing Conference on Women, the Council launched an initiative called 'Cooperation programme in the equality area 1995–2000'. The main goal of the initiative was to promote the further development of a united Nordic approach to the issue and a common Nordic platform within the framework of broader European and international cooperation. It emphasized that gender equality aspects must be implemented in all areas of society and in the areas covered by the Nordic Council of Ministers' own programmes and projects (the implementation of a mainstreaming strategy). The activities have focused on:

- promotion of equal access for women and men to the political and economic decision-making processes;

- promotion of equal economic status and influence for women and men. Particular emphasis will be placed on steps to promote equal pay;
- promotion of gender equality in the labour market;
- improved opportunities for both women and men to combine parenthood with a job;
- measures to influence European and international developments in the field of gender equality;
- development of methods of promoting active steps to achieve gender equality.

*Common policy framework*

Equality between women and men is a crucial part of the Nordic welfare state model. In an international perspective the Nordic countries enjoy a very high standard of living. Moreover, they have made considerable progress in their efforts to promote equality between women and men since the 1980s. The political view prevails that society can progress in a more democratic direction only when the competence, knowledge, experience and values of both women and men are acknowledged and allowed to influence and enrich developments in all spheres of society. Although there are some differences between the systems of the different countries, the similarities are such as to create a 'Nordic model' of gender equality. The Nordic model is based on the assumption that women and men have the same rights, obligations and opportunities in all essential areas of life. This broad concept of equality in turn imposes demands on the fundamental structure of society and its various functions.

Economic independence is the foundation of the Nordic gender equality policy. An important aspect is, therefore, to enable both women and men to reconcile economic activities with parenthood. This is reflected in the labour force participation rate, which, for both women and men, is one of the highest in the world. From the age of twenty until retirement, between 72 and 83 per cent of women and 81 and 92 per cent of men work in the labour market in the five countries (Nordic Council of Ministers, 1994). But even though women represent a large part of the labour market, there are considerable differences between men's and women's positions there. Women work part time to a larger extent than men; women are mainly employed in the public sector in care- and service-related jobs, men in private enterprises; and women have non-managerial jobs, whereas men form the majority of managers and bosses. There are also differences in earnings between women and men (between 11 and 12 per cent in industry) although the differences have decreased since the 1980s. The sex-segregated labour market is one of the explanations for the wage gap between women and men. Sex segregation is more of a problem than direct wage discrimination since the wages are low in those workplaces and positions in which women work — and higher where men work (Nyberg, 1997). Altogether, the differences between women and men in terms of working hours, occupation and job levels result in lower incomes for women compared with men.

In parallel with women's rising participation rate in working and public life, the Nordic countries have developed public child-care facilities and other forms of family support such as parental leave programmes and support for single parents (mostly mothers). The support combines general economic cash support with various kinds of service and assistance for the families. There are parental leave programmes, including wage compensation after the birth of the child, in all the countries. It is well recognized that the distribution of the workload between women and men in the family, in working life and in society must be changed, and that the active involvement of men is necessary if gender equality is to become reality. Therefore, a variety of initiatives have been launched to improve the everyday life of families with children and to give fathers in particular the opportunity to take active responsibility for their children. For example, in Norway and Sweden provisions on leave for men only have been introduced, which stipulate that four weeks of the joint parental leave can be taken by the father only.

Issues concerning men and equality have accounted for much of the policy work on equality between women and men in the Nordic countries since the 1980s. All the countries have had, for shorter or longer periods, so-called 'ideas groups' on issues concerning the male role, functioning as advisory committees to the Ministers for Equality Affairs. In 1995, a Nordic conference on 'Nordic men' was held in

Stockholm at the initiative of the Nordic Ministers for Equality Affairs. A conference report was compiled by the Nordic Council of Ministers, and was available at the United Nations (UN) Fourth World Conference on Women in Beijing. The report paints a broad picture of current changes in men's view of masculinity, new family patterns, the role of the father, the caring professions, and men and violence. The positive experiences arising from the Conference have led, among other things, to the adoption of a three-year action plan on men and equality (1997–2000). The plan covers such things as themes for seminars, cooperative projects, network building and research projects.

## Equality legislation and national machineries

Shared power between women and men is another corner-stone of the gender equality policy. Nordic women have had the same political rights as men since the beginning of the twentieth century. They gained the right to vote between 1906 and 1919 and the right to be elected between 1907 and 1922. However, women do not yet participate in political life on equal terms with men, although their representation on political bodies is higher than in any other part of the world. In Norway and Sweden about 40 per cent of Members of Parliament are women, in Denmark and Finland about 35 per cent and in Iceland 25 per cent. Sweden has the highest proportion of women at ministerial level — eleven of the twenty ministers are women. Norway has had a woman Prime Minister — Gro Harlem Brundtland — for many years and Vigdis Finnbogadóttir was President of Iceland from 1980 to 1996.

The preparation of decision making is an essential part of exercising influence. Laws that have important policy implications are generally prepared by state commissions, committees, advisory boards or similar preparatory bodies. The Nordic countries have applied partly divergent strategies to increase women's representation on these decision-making bodies. The countries have different opinions on the merits of quota systems as an instrument for achieving greater gender equality regarding the composition of decision-making bodies. In Denmark, Norway and Finland legislation has proved effective in increasing the percentage of women appointed to public bodies, while in Sweden strong political will, clear goal setting and strategic administrative procedures have given good results. Other strategies which are playing an increasingly important role in all countries are new forms of cooperation between women; for example, cooperation across party boundaries and the setting up of loosely structured (informal) women's networks.

Although non-governmental organizations (NGOs) are not considered part of the national machinery for gender equality, women's organizations are nevertheless a vital factor in influencing attitudes and awareness of gender issues. They also have an important role as pressure groups for the development of equality policy in the Nordic countries. Cooperation between the governments and the NGOs is very close. Governments give financial support to women's organizations and representatives of NGOs are included in official national delegations to international forums.

Despite similar principles and goals, the Nordic countries have chosen somewhat different ways of establishing gender equality by law. The systems of law enforcement and organizational structures also differ to some extent. In Norway, Sweden and Finland, a Gender Equality Ombuds person ensures that the relevant Act on gender equality is duly complied with, while other bodies (e.g., councils) draft policy on this issue and related matters. In Iceland, a Gender Equality Council is responsible for both drafting the policy and the implementation of the relevant legislation. The details of the structures vary: despite apparent identity, no two systems are completely alike. All the Nordic countries, however, share the defining feature that work on gender equality is overseen by public offices connected to, and set up by, the central authorities. The gender equality legislation is also in accordance with that of the European Union and with other international conventions such as the UN Convention on the Elimination of All Forms of Discrimination against Women.

While the emphasis of legal provision for gender equality is similar, the details vary. In Denmark, for example, the national machinery is under reconstruction. In 1999, the Prime Minister appointed a Minister for Gender Equality, who has overall responsibility for the government's policy on gender equality. As one of her first tasks the Minister introduced a new organization of the work with gender equality in Denmark. The gender mainstreaming strategy is consolidated as official Danish policy. All ministers have within their remit a responsibility to promote gender equality. The underlying state institutions and organizations will every second year report to the relevant minister on efforts to promote gender equality and all ministers of the government will then report to the Minister for Gender Equality. Each year the minister is under an obligation to deliver a review on the previous year's progress and action plan for the coming year's work to Parliament. Each minister is responsible for pursuing a balanced representation of women and men in public boards and committees, and the ministers have the right to leave seats empty should nominating parties, without an adequate explanation, fail to suggest both women and men for the seats in question.

If the legal provision is varied within the Nordic region, so are the national machineries overseeing the process of initiating policy and implementation of the laws. Denmark, for example, has three laws on equal opportunities:

- *The Equal Treatment Act (1976)*. Equality in the labour market and with regard to vocational and professional training (women and men may not be discriminated against on the grounds of gender).
- *The Equal Pay Act (1985)*. Men and women are entitled to equal pay for the same work or for work of equal value.
- *The Act on Equality between Women and Men (2000)*. Establishes the principle of gender equality, the possibility of using preferential treatment, the national machinery, and rules concerning the participation of women and men in public committees and boards.

In Finland the 1987 Act on Equality between Women and Men has three goals: the prevention of sex discrimination; the promotion of equality between women and men; and the improvement of women's status, especially in working life. Temporary positive action based on equality action plans is permitted. Since 1995 the Act has included a quota provision: in official committees and councils the proportion of representatives of either sex should not be below 40 per cent.

In Iceland the first Act on the Equal Status and Equal Rights of Women and Men came into force in 1976 (revised in 1991). It aimed at establishing equal rights and equal status of women and men in every sphere and prohibiting any form of gender discrimination. In May 2000, a new Act on the Equal Status and Equal Rights of Women and Men was passed. A new Centre for Gender Equality has been established which is in charge of administering the new Act, as well as providing counselling and education in the field of gender equality for governmental and municipal authorities, institutions, companies, individuals and NGOs.

In Norway the Equal Opportunity Act took effect in 1979 and applies to all parts of society. The Act promotes equality between the sexes and aims particularly at improving the status of women. Public authorities have to change conditions in order to achieve equality within all spheres of society. Women and men need to have the same opportunities for education, employment and equal pay for work of equal value. The Act prohibits any form of discrimination, but stipulates that positive action for improving equal status is not contrary to the law. The Act has been supplemented by collective agreements in most parts of the labour market.

In Sweden, the Equal Opportunity Act has been in effect since 1992. It supersedes the 1980 legislation on equal opportunities. The Act is restricted to working life and its main purpose is to promote equal rights for women and men with respect to employment, working conditions and opportunities for personal development at work. The Act aims to improve conditions for women in working life. It has two main parts: rules prohibiting an employer from discriminating against a person because of gender; and rules requiring an employer to take active steps to promote equality in the workplace. Employers are to make it easier for both women and men to combine parenthood and work. Similarly, employers are to counteract differences in pay and other conditions between women and men who perform equal work or work of equal value. Steps must also be taken to ensure that no employee is subjected to sexual harassment. Employers with ten or more employees must present an annual plan for the promotion of equality at the place of work, including a survey of pay differentials between their female and male employees and a report on measures taken.

### Gender mainstreaming: a step towards gender equality

Gender equality work in the Nordic countries is currently going through a very important and exciting phase. Mainstreaming strategies are developed and used as a complement to more traditional equality strategies. The adoption of the Platform for Action by the Fourth World Conference on Women in Beijing in 1995 has been of great importance for that development. Governments have agreed to 'promote an active and visible policy of mainstreaming a gender perspective into all policies and programmes, so that, before decisions are taken, an analysis is made of the effect on women and men respectively' (PfA: 79, 123, 164) in important policy fields. The challenge for the governments of the Nordic countries is now to implement this agreement.

In the 1970s and 1980s equality policies were introduced at national level. Institutional mechanisms such as Equal Status Councils, Gender Equality Acts and Equality Ombuds persons were established. As Drude Dahlerup (1988: 8) has commented on this phase of the equality work:

> These new agencies constitute the first institutionalization of the equality policy, which was previously conducted solely as pressure group politics by voluntary associations. Although their resources and influence are limited, these new agencies exemplify the mobilization of institutional resources for improving women's position. Also in the regional labour market authorities, in the public administration and in large firms and trade unions, staff are now being hired with equality policies as their area of responsibility.

In the 1950s, feminists would not have dreamt of a situation in which people would actually get paid for work on equality between women and men.

Now, these institutional mechanisms are well established and recognized as an important part of the democratic system. This recognition is crucial for the next stage in attaining gender parity. While the emphasis on equality legislation in the 1970s and 1980s was an important step towards addressing gender issues in public life, it has also become clear that by themselves these measures were not enough to tackle the issue.

Along with measures taken to ensure formal equality through legislation, implementing measures are needed. It has become more and more obvious that awareness-raising campaigns, pilot projects and different ways of making up for deficiencies by introducing supplementary measures (e.g., the improvement of women's skills and competence) are not enough. New strategies and methods must be developed, aimed at changing the societal structures which still maintain sex segregation (e.g., the unequal power relationship between the sexes, the sex-segregated labour market and the gender-based distribution of family responsibilities). Much of the equality-promoting work has so far been organized as projects outside ordinary policy processes, often financed by special funds for a limited time. It has been sidelined and not really affected societal structures. A Swedish researcher, Gertrud Åström, has described this sidelining as an 'impressive equality annex, where activities can take place, leaving the rest of the political house largely undisturbed' (Åstrom, 1994:2).

A shift of strategies from targeted equality policy to gender mainstreaming is a step towards the goal — de facto gender equality. Gender mainstreaming addresses the problem of sidelining directly. It aims at taking gender equality issues into the mainstream of society, into ordinary policy-making processes in all areas. It involves the reorganization of policy processes because it moves the attention of gender equality policies to everyday policy processes and to the activities of the actors ordinarily involved in policy shaping. Making gender issues visible and integrated into the mainstream of society will lead to changes in gender-biased societal structures. But prerequisites for successful gender mainstreaming are a strong political will at the highest level and a national machinery with the mandate, tools and resources to exert influence on the policy process at all levels. However, it is important to underline that a national machinery has a catalytic role in facilitating and supporting the mainstreaming process. It should work to ensure that the highest levels of government and administration take responsibility for equality-promoting work within their fields of responsibility. The case of the national machinery of Sweden illustrates the strengths as well as areas of concern that face national machineries in the Nordic region.

## Gender mainstreaming in Sweden: national, regional and local levels

A national machinery for the advancement of women has been in place at central governmental level since the early 1970s. Also since the 1970s, a Cabinet minister has held overall responsibility for the government's policy for gender equality. However, since there is a conviction in Sweden that a policy for equality cannot be developed independently of other policy areas, each minister in the Swedish government is responsible for promoting, analysing, evaluating and following up the work for equality in his or her field of responsibility. From 1994 onwards the Prime Minister has declared in the annual statement of government policy that the gender equality perspective should be taken into account in the preparatory proceedings of all decisions by the Cabinet. This written statement is an important legitimate base for the implementation of mainstreaming methods. It is often referred to in the dialogue on gender issues between the Division for Gender Equality, located in the Ministry of Industry, Employment and Communications, and the other ministries.

Another important tool for mainstreaming is the requirement that all government committees of inquiry have to analyse and discuss their proposals from a gender perspective. The gender impact — whether direct or indirect — of proposed changes in the labour market, in the economy, in the welfare system, in education should be described. If the committee or the special commissioner considers it impossible or unnecessary to do this, the reason must be stated. Training courses are offered to all special commissioners and their secretaries in order to help them fulfil the requirements.

The Division for Gender Equality has overall responsibility for developing tools and mechanisms for mainstreaming and for supporting and pushing through the work for equality at national and regional levels. The Division also reviews proposals for government Bills and other government decisions emanating from various ministries. This is to ensure that a gender perspective has been taken into account and to monitor the work towards fulfilling the target of an even distribution of women and men in committees and state boards. It is important to note, however, that the Division's role is to promote, encourage and support initiatives/activities to promote gender equality. The actual work of ensuring that the gender impact is considered in the administrative proceedings, for example in planning processes and budgeting, rests with the staff of each ministry/division.

At regional level the County Administrative Boards, which are government authorities, are responsible for mainstreaming the gender perspective in all policy fields. The Boards have employed gender experts to start, support and monitor the process of mainstreaming a gender perspective in ordinary policy processes in all relevant areas. A medium-term strategic plan (1997–2000) for the equality-promoting work has been designed by each Board and submitted to the government.

In order to stimulate the development of a mainstreaming approach to gender equality work in the municipalities, the government allocated funds in 1995 to the Swedish Association of Local Authorities. A two-year programme was launched with the aim of examining how a committee or board can work systematically for gender equality in its own field of operation. The 3R method, the main purpose of which is to systematize a gender equality analysis, was tried out in the programme (see Appendix at end of chpater).

The cornerstones of the mainstreaming strategy therefore are:

- *Responsibility at the highest level.* Strategies and tools are needed to make it clear that overall responsibility for the implementation of gender mainstreaming rests with the highest level of government and public administration.
- *Making gender visible.* To this end, statistics disaggregated by sex are indispensable. The government has therefore given instructions to Statistics Sweden to

present all official statistics, to be disaggregated by sex. The same goes for public authorities which produce statistics in their fields or which are request statistics from Statistics Sweden.

- *Increasing the knowledge on issues related to gender equality.* A mainstreaming strategy implies that not only gender experts but also other staff will deal with equality issues as part of their daily work. In order to do this they need knowledge. What is most important is that the top-level management has sufficient knowledge to fulfil its duty to mainstream a gender perspective in its field of responsibility. Awareness raising and training seminars on gender equality for top-level management were first arranged by the Equality Affairs Division in 1994. Most of the ministers, state secretaries, political advisers, special commissioners and press secretaries in the Cabinet Offices have already attended. The training is now being extended to all top managers of the public sector. The main aim of the training is to provide basic facts on the situation of women and men respectively in Swedish society and to discuss equality issues in relation to the national goal for equality.

- *Developing methods and tools.* Although each ministry is responsible for the development of methods and tools for the integration of a gender perspective in their field of responsibility, the Equality Affairs Division has an overall responsibility to encourage and support the development. To this end a 'flying expert' on gender issues has been engaged to help some of the ministries develop tools and routines which ensure the integration of a gender perspective in policy processes (such as gender statistics, training courses, checklists and follow-up procedures). An analytical tool to check gender relevance and assess the different effects on women and men of policy proposals has been developed and distributed to the ministries.

  In order to stimulate the development of tools for gender mainstreaming, a Working Group Chaired by the State Secretary for Equality Affairs and with representatives from central, regional and local levels was set up in January 1998. The focus of the Working Group is on developing methods and models that facilitate the implementation of the gender perspective in policy and administrative processes, which means turning knowledge into practice. The purpose of many of the methods developed hitherto has been to facilitate gender impact analysis in a certain area of policy making.

Another Working Group has been assigned to develop ways of incorporating a gender equality perspective into all parts of the budget process. This group includes representatives of the Ministries of Finance, Education and Industry, Employment and Communications and of experts from the National Institute for Working Life, Statistics Sweden and Linköping University.

- *Monitoring and follow-up.* The State Secretary for Equality Affairs meets regularly with her colleagues from other ministries to discuss, *inter alia*, gender impact analyses and promotion and evaluation of measures undertaken. In order to supply Parliament with information on the development of the mainstreaming process in the government, all ministries had to review and report on their equality work (from 1994 to 1996) to the Minister for Equality Affairs.

In 1997 an assessment was carried out on the effects of the special terms of reference (1994), which stated that all government committees of inquiry should analyse and discuss their proposals from a gender perspective. The assessment showed that 33 per cent of a total of 193 committees of inquiry had discussed their results from a gender perspective, although very few of them had presented a comprehensive gender analysis.

The Swedish National Audit Office has been directed to scrutinize how the gender equality aspect is reflected in the government's administrative control of the various national agencies and in their reports back to the government.

The mainstreaming process has only just begun in Sweden and it is not possible to evaluate effects on policy processes in general. My experience, however, is that the mainstreaming strategy has raised awareness in society of the relevance of gender in all policy making. There is also a growing awareness of the need to analyse both proposals and the distribution of resources from a gender perspective. A growing number of men are actively involved in gender equality policy making since gender issues are integrated into the ordinary work of the ministries. A growing number of mainstreaming tools and methods have also been developed by ministries; for example, a manual on gender equality in development cooperation (Ministry for Foreign Affairs), an action programme for the development of mainstreaming procedures (Ministry of Health and Social Affairs), a commission on gender mainstreaming (Ministry of Industry, Employment and Communications) and a Bill to Parliament on gender equality at the universities (Ministry of Education and Science).

However, many politicians and officials at the ministries still lack knowledge on gender issues. It can be hard to understand what it means (in a concrete way) to take a gender perspective into account in their normal work. A common misunderstanding is that equality-promoting work deals only with personnel policy, for example by setting up targets for the recruitment of women, training of women leaders, and so on.

The arrangement of seminars on gender issues and the further development of educational tools are therefore important. Equally important is the development of analytical and monitoring tools. Implementing a mainstreaming strategy is a long-term procedure.

## Conclusions

I have described a 'Nordic model' of gender equality policy and national machinery which to a certain extent has been successful. *De jure* equality between women and men has been achieved in all countries. Although much remains to be done, a continued positive development towards *de facto* equality is under way. It is important to realize that this 'model' is based on a long democratic tradition in all the Nordic countries and that people in general have confidence in the political system.

Institutional mechanisms for gender equality, equality legislation and the implementation of measures to promote equality neither can nor should be structured in the same way in all countries. Differences in political and bureaucratic systems, cultural differences and so on must be taken into account in order to choose efficient structures. However, information on different ways of organizing national machineries and exchange of experience is one way of stimulating the further development of work to promote gender equality in all countries.

## Appendix: 3R for mainstreaming at local level[2]
GERTRUD ÅSTRÖM

The JÄMKOM ('Gender Equality in the Municipalities') project has, within the framework of the Programme Group of the Swedish Association of Local Authorities (SALA), developed and tested a method, the 3R method, for incorporating gender equality considerations into the work of local authorities. The strategy on which the project is based is 'mainstreaming'; that is, the idea that gender equality is not regarded as a separate issue, but is observed and given concrete expression in the everyday activities of the authority.

*The project*

During the spring of 1996, work began with the formulation of the ideas behind the 3R method. An invitation then went out to all local government committees and boards in Sweden to take part in testing the method. In early autumn of the same year a selection of the committees and boards was made on the basis of certain criteria: geographical distribution; variation in size and political composition of the municipal councils; committees and boards from different fields; previous experience of working with change and development within their field of operations; and, ideally, previous experience of work with gender equality. Of these criteria, variation in political composition of the councils was not achieved.

The following municipalities and committees/boards were selected: Haparanda, Social Services Committee and Child and Youth Welfare Services Committee; Skellefteå, Leisure and Recreation Committee; Södertälje, Town Planning Committee; Köping, Social Services Committee and Education

Committee; Växjö, Cultural Amenities and Recreation Committee, and Municipal Executive Board; Göteborg, Recreation Committee.

In September and October 1996, the ideas behind the project were presented at an introductory meeting with the relevant senior officials from the local authorities; that is, the municipal commissioners, the chairpersons of the committees and boards, and administrative heads. The conditions for participating in the project were set out in a contract detailing reciprocal commitments, such as the requirement that the committees/boards apply JÄMKOM methods at a minimum of five meetings during the project period, and that they would receive SEK 40,000 to cover the extra costs incurred. A timetable was presented. It was made clear that the tests should be conducted using the usual staff, and that the committees/boards were at liberty to limit the JÄMKOM work to certain areas of their activities.

At the first JÄMKOM meetings held by the committees/boards, the background to the project was presented. SALA's work for gender equality and the 3R method were presented and a talk was given on Sweden's gender equality policy and gender theory. All members of the committees/boards and the officials involved were given two JÄMKOM compendia to help them with the project. The first compendium contained factual and background information, whereas the second was a work file in which the different phases of the project were set out, from inventory, through statement of objectives, to final assessment of the project.

Each committee/board appointed a local project leader. It was they who drew up a local project plan and tested the 3R method in their respective towns, together with other colleagues and politicians and in close collaboration with project officials at SALA. The results of the 3R tests have always been discussed at a meeting of the committee/board.

The local authorities project ended in mid summer 1997, and the various committees/boards presented reports of their work in autumn of that year. Specific training courses were developed by SALA on the basis of the project. Several municipalities have trained their officials in order to start implementing the 3R method.

## 3R

The 3R method is based on a systematization of Swedish experience of work on gender equality, and has also been inspired by other methods used in gender and action research. 3R stands for Representation, Resources and Realia. Representation and Resources are quantitative variables, whereas Realia is qualitative. The idea behind the method is that a systematic review of men's and women's representation in different places and positions within the committee's/board's field of operations, and of the distribution and utilization of resources, would trigger discussions about why the products the municipality produces — goods, services and situations — are as they are, who gets what and under what conditions. How do the activities of the local authorities work for the people who live there?

The tests that have been carried out by the councils/boards have shown that the method really does work in that way. The surveys and analyses that have been carried out have led to the rethinking of gender equality in the committees'/boards' spheres of operations, including the writing of specific gender equality objectives into their guidelines. Some have also decided to include gender equality in their budgets, to collect new and continuous information in the form of statistics and different types of customer surveys, and to monitor actively the impact of the different measures. The 3R method has been adopted, and some municipalities have decided to spread the method to other committees and administrative authorities.

### Representation

The first part of the methodology deals with looking at how women and men are represented in the committee's/board's field of operations. The simplest way is to begin with the composition of the committee/board itself and then to go on to the administration. The existing organization is studied and the positions in the hierarchy occupied by women and men are mapped out. From this initial plan, the study of representation can move on to other committees, working groups, permanent reference groups, *ad hoc* reference groups, and the committees of associations and organizations within the field of operations and with which the board/committee and administration have dealings. How are women and men represented among those who contact a committee/board to raise an issue?

The different committees/boards have carried out different studies, but common to all has been that politicians and local government officials have kept 'contact lists'. For at least two weeks they systematically noted down all the contacts they had in their work. They recorded whether the person concerned was male or female and acting as a private citizen or as a representative of an interest organization. This was done in order to raise awareness of the distribution of representation among those with whom the politicians and officials come into contact and from whom they receive information. The contact lists led to lively discussions, including why some politicians reported that they had had no contacts at all, and the differences between the number of contacts recorded by paid and unpaid politicians. 'How representative are the representatives?' was one question that was raised.

Resources

The resources analysed by the 3R test are money, time and space. The main idea was that the results obtained under the Representation section could be supplemented by statistics concerning the distribution of resources. One example of this is that certain committees/boards have constructed 'salary trees' showing the total number of women and men and their position on the salary scale. One committee studied the gender distribution among artists exhibiting at the local art gallery, and the information was completed under the resources section of the test by recording how much money was paid to the female and male artists respectively. The amount of funding distributed to different cases, subject areas and organizations has also been studied.

All the committees/boards have timed some of their meetings. Some decided that it should be done without the members knowing exactly when, while one chose to use a chess clock on one occasion. Besides recording how much women and men talked at the meetings, more detailed analyses of the measurements were carried out. Often the distinction made was between politicians and officials, and chairperson and other members. One finding that gave rise to interesting discussions was that officials often talked more than politicians at committee/board meetings.

One study of how the 'space' resource could be measured was carried out at a day nursery, with the staff themselves observing how girls and boys made use of a particular demarcated area.

## Realia

Realia is qualitative, and is about the norms and values expressed in the structure that produces the local authority activity — that is, committees and boards, administrative authorities and work places — and the products that are produced — that is, goods, services and situations. Who recognize themselves in it? Whose needs are served?

Some committees/boards have looked at the Realia by studying, together with staff, such things as morning assembly at day nurseries and classroom situations. Others have visited different establishments for which they are responsible. The politicians have formed multi-party groups and gone to places such as sports centres and made note of such things as lighting, hair-dryers and sauna space. They have also interviewed employees about the amount of attention they give to girls and boys, women and men. One committee working with meetings between the administration, politicians and employees has decided that gender equality is to be a regular annual theme for a meeting when the results of the previous year's decisions and measures are to be followed up. The politicians who have been involved in different studies have expressed themselves as satisfied. Some have said that they have received greater insight into their field of operations and that they better understand what gender equality really means and how they can specifically work for it.

The town planning committee that took part in JÄMKOM has used 'mental maps' to help build up an understanding of how different categories of citizens feel about a particular urban renewal area. This involved groups not to be found among the normal reference groups in the committee's field of operations.

## Notes

1 I have worked for the government of Sweden at the Equality Affairs Division as a principal administrative officer since 1990.

2 This Appendix is based on the 1998 report, *Gender Mainstreaming: Conceptual Framework, Methodology and Presentation of Good Practices*, Final Report of Activities of the Group of Specialists on Mainstreaming (E-S-MG). Copenhagen, Council of Europe.

# 8

# Gender awareness and the national machineries in the countries of Central and Eastern Europe

ZUZANA JEZERSKA

## Introduction: the basic problem of identification and terminology

The countries of Central and Eastern Europe (CEE) saw fundamental changes to their political and social systems towards the end of the twentieth century. The processes of change affected most aspects of the social and political lives of the citizens of these countries. However, men and women experienced differently the burdens and gains of change. Furthermore, the processes of change took place in the context of globalization, which impacted upon the economic restructuring of CEE countries, as well as making demands upon their political structures to democratize. The state structure had to deal with these varied pressures. The Platform for Action of the United Nations' (UN's) Fourth World Conference on Women (Beijing, 1995) focuses on state structures for implementing gender mainstreaming (see Staudt, chapter 2 of this volume) under the chapter on national machineries for women. The chapter on national machineries seems to be often overlooked by both governmental bodies and the non-governmental organization (NGO) community in Central and Eastern Europe. There are several reasons for this: the domination of renewed traditional values in politics; transitional and at times unstable democratic/pluralist state structures; and the lack of active participation of women in political life.

Moreover, the definition of 'national machinery for the advancement of women' is very vague. It can vary from NGO status to a very strong mandate within the government.

National machineries can be regarded as instruments for gender mainstreaming, as well as for the implementation of policies in other critical areas (see Kardam and Acuner, chapter 4 of this volume), though the UN Division for the Advancement of Women (DAW) consultation document (1998) cautions against burdening national machineries for women with taking on the role of implementation. Such definitional confusion is not a problem of this region exclusively, as other case studies in this volume indicate. This confusion is often reflected in the debates on women's national machineries. For example, should/can an institution, organization or ministry play the role of a national machinery for women only when it includes the word 'women' in its name? There are also issues regarding the discrepancy between form and content, proclaimed mandate and real contribution of the institutions deemed to represent women's interests at the national and global levels. Therefore, in the CEE region, we not only need gender awareness but awareness of the role and importance of national machineries for the advancement of women *per se*.

## Historical and political background

The region of the CEE countries lived through perhaps one of the most controversial and differential processes of societal development in modern European history in the twentieth century. The First World War (1914–18) represented the culmination, and in fact the violent solution of a long period of political and social convulsion in the lives of the various social and ethnic groups inhabiting the region, especially those in the area of Central Europe. After the war, the Austro-Hungarian Empire disintegrated into new or newly shaped republics and states. Countries such as Czechoslovakia, Poland, Yugoslavia, Romania and even Austria and Hungary were re-created on the map of Europe. The free progress of new countries did not last too long. After the Second World War (1939–45), just about twenty years later, the strategic territory of Central Europe was again reshaped by the new superpowers. The Eastern part of it fell under the influence of the Soviet Union, except Yugoslavia and Albania, which achieved a measure of autonomy after breaking with Stalin's regime. The Soviet Union itself was the 'empire' of countries of very different cultural, societal and historical backgrounds.

The Soviet era brought about drastic changes to the history of Central and Eastern Europe. The political order and societal relations were authoritarian and not rooted in the historical experience of the region, thus resulting in dictatorships that mostly had little support within the populations. Socialist countries covered more than half of Europe and part of Central Asia in geographical terms. It is obvious, indeed, that the social, economic and cultural differences between these countries, though they were unified in the region by the power of collaborating Communist Parties, were significant. However, not all parts of this huge territory suffered in the same ways. The situation was much more complicated and is still waiting to be comprehensively analysed. In the period of political transformation starting in 1989, it emerged that substantial societal differences between individual countries persisted under the surface of uniform socialism and that serious problems among the countries had been suppressed and/or overlooked during the Soviet era.

## CEE countries and 'a policy for women'

The unique territorial and historical features of the region presented particular gender dynamics for women. At the time of Soviet domination, the countries and their inhabitants were driven to adjust to the antithetical political and social structures not in a time frame of centuries, but of decades. Therefore, the social behaviour and societal consciousness of the population, which is in fact a matter of very slow evolution, developed controversial forms. Women as traditional carriers of responsibility for a basic social nucleus — the family — were perhaps the most affected by these socio-economic changes. Right after the Second World War, especially in the countries most wounded by the war (e.g. Russia, East Germany) women frequently replaced men in rebuilding post-war society. They often replaced men physically — working hard on the reconstruction of buildings and infrastructure — and they have been respected partners in the villages as well. However, as part of the Marxist understanding of gender relations, women's participation in the labour force as a means for women's emancipation came to be the basis of 'women's policy' in most of the region. This was a radical transformation of gender relations in most of the countries of the region, as it was only in a few countries, such as Czechoslovakia and Slovenia, that women made up more than 30 per cent of the work force before the Second World War. Later, when society was more stable, women in socialist countries gained some important advantages, especially in social fields such as the length of maternity leave, financial contribution during pregnancy and pre-school kindergarten. Health care was free of charge and progressive state provisions were also represented by other special treatments, for example preventive health examinations for women and children. The currently often-discussed abortion issue was a part of the health policy, but the state's policies on populations took precedence over women's rights (Davin, 1992; Siemienska, 1998). The official image of women changed rapidly from a pretty 'hausfrau' in the pre-war period to a worker and fighter for the socialist future together with men. Equality for all citizens (except those who were enemies of the regime) was enshrined in the Constitutions. Primary education was compulsory, illiteracy was disappearing and higher/university education was free of charge and open to everybody, especially those who were 'more equal' with the 'proper' (i.e. working class) family backgrounds. Women's level of higher education (with university and/or completed secondary education) ranked at 40 to 60 per cent in the region and rates concerning economic activity of women were also high as duty to work was also enshrined in the Constitutions. As far as societal consciousness was concerned, in most countries of the region, the persistence of traditionally rooted gender insensitivity framed by historical, religious and patriarchal order was confronted with the high educational and economic involvement of women. This, too, created a unique environment for most of the women in the countries of Central and Eastern Europe.

In a political sense, women were officially equal with men under the communist system. For example, 'the greatest number of women in the unicameral parliament [in Poland] under the Communist regime was 23 per cent, 1980–85', far higher than in many Western democracies (Siemienska, 1998:137). But it is difficult to speak about equality in a society where the ruling political party is the only ideological, economic and political power. Women were mostly organized in one association, frequently called the 'union of women', chaired by members of the Communist Party. While sometimes they were able to influence political decisions, decisions were not always made for the advancement of women and had to be in line with the Party. More often, 'women's associations just played a role of illusory state feminists' (Lokar, 2000).

## Governmental policy towards women after the fall of the 'Iron Curtain'

The situation of women in the 1990s has been changing as fast as the 'new democracies' are transforming their economic and political systems. The similarities among countries of the region that were imposed by the logic of the state-centric system under the communist regimes are fast disappearing and specific indicators of the 'subregions within the region' are becoming more and more obvious. CEE countries are struggling with their problems individually, as well as in cooperation with other regional or global networks. European countries are now partners again — sometimes for good, sometimes for bad.

The governments of most CEE countries addressed issues concerning women in pre-Beijing Conference activities in close cooperation with the UN. There were exceptions, such as Poland, where the Government Plenipotentiary for Women was established in 1986 as a reaction to the World Conference to Review and Appraise the Achievements of the United Nations Decade for Women: Equality, Development and Peace, held in Nairobi in 1985. Not having been active participants in previous Conferences concerning women's issues, the UN Fourth World Conference on Women in Beijing represented the CEE countries' admission to dialogue and the policy process, which had started in 1975 at the global level. The Beijing Declaration and the Platform for Action stressed the need for continuing international cooperation with, and assistance to, countries with economies in transition. The Platform noted that 'In countries that are undergoing fundamental political, economic and social transformation, the skills of women, if better utilized, could constitute a major contribution to the economic life of their respective countries' (PfA: paragraph 159). Moreover, the regional activities of the Council of Europe focused on human rights issues; hence the issues concerning equality between women and men created a platform for starting discussion on the situation of women in the former socialist countries.

In the process of democratic reforms, the governments in the region formally recognized the importance of empowering both women and men to become partners in order to correct gender disparities inherited from the past and to promote gender equality. Nevertheless, having gained their independence a relatively short time ago, these countries have to find their individual way of economic transformation at the same time as they create new social structures. This process, contrary to the history of most Western European countries, is occurring under the pressures of time and political circumstances, which have consequences for the policy-making and implementational strategies and structures that are instituted. Furthermore, due to the diversity of countries in the region, now unencumbered by the artificial uniformity imposed by the power of the previous regime, and where the post-1989 changes have sometimes resulted in bitter civil wars, the enthusiastic anticipation of change has turned to complicated reality. And in this reality of conflicting priorities, the governments of the CEE countries do not have a very clear and classified policy for gender equality. Moreover, considerations of security and economic restructuring have been prioritized in policy-making processes, to the detriment of issues of equal opportunities and equal rights for women and men.

## Global institutions and the gender agenda in CEE countries: relations with the UN

The situation of women in the countries in transition was analysed at the UN regional seminar, 'Impact of Economic and Political Reform on the Status of Women in Eastern Europe', organized by DAW, which was held on 8–12 April 1991 in Vienna. The high-level Regional Preparatory Meeting of the Fourth World Conference on Women organized by the Economic Commission for Europe in Vienna, 17–21 October 1994, adopted the Regional Platform for Action. However, at that stage CEE countries were newcomers and were not experienced in women- and/or gender-related policy. A year after the Beijing Conference, on 12–14 September 1996, the regional Conference of Senior Governmental Experts was organized by the United Nations Development Programme's Regional Office in Bucharest. It focused on the 'Implementation of the Platform for Action Adopted by the 1995 Fourth World Conference on Women in Beijing, in Central and Eastern Europe'. As Angela King, then Director of DAW, emphasized in her opening statement, the Conference 'should [contribute] to increasing awareness among public policy makers, and to strengthening the institutional capacity of national machineries and other institutions in the region and activities of non-governmental organizations, and the other actors of the civil society as well'. The Conference in Bucharest was of utmost importance, because it evaluated the progress made in the CEE countries and defined eleven priority objectives relevant to women's status in the region. These were:

- institutionalizing national machineries;
- facilitating equal participation of women in decision making;
- improving the economic and labour market situation of women;
- improving women's health, including reproductive health and family planning services;
- eliminating violence against women;
- reducing the effects of environmental degradation on women and improving women's role in environmental management;

- reducing the social costs of transition;
- improving the situation of rural women;
- addressing the effects of armed conflicts on women, including the problems of displaced and refugee women;
- alleviating women's poverty, including the problems of minority groups of women, such as Roma women;
- utilizing the mass media for eliminating gender stereotypes and conducting gender training.

Discussion on national machineries emphasized the need to strengthen their institutional capacity, and urged the governments of the countries of the region to consider the following measures towards this goal:

- strengthening the mechanisms for the representation of women's issues within governmental structures and linking these mechanisms with the overall process of administrative reform;
- establishing national machineries at the highest level, such as the Office of the President or Prime Minister, in compliance with both the Economic Commission for Europe (ECE) and Beijing Platform for Action;
- developing inter-ministerial/interdepartmental cooperation with a view to achieving an integrated policy based on comparative gender analyses, as well as on evaluation of the effectiveness of such analyses for the purpose for determining the appropriate political, economic, social and legal frameworks for the improvement of women's living and working conditions;
- introducing the dimension of equality of opportunity as a permanent indicator in the analyses and evaluations of overall governmental activities;
- allotting material resources with a view to supporting, substantiating and distributing studies made in the field, and training experts and establishing institutions for studies and research in this area;
- addressing the need for consultative mechanisms aimed at fostering cooperation with parliamentarians;
- establishing coordination mechanisms among NGOs at the national level;
- supporting dialogue and bilateral and multilateral cooperation with all social partners.

Both the ECE Regional Preparatory Meeting in Vienna and the Beijing Conference thus gave an impetus to the

development of the national machineries for the advancement of women in the CEE countries, and encouraged the
governments to establish women's entities on different
levels acting as national machineries for the advancement
of women. Before the Beijing Conference only a few countries in the region realized the importance of establishing the
institutional mechanisms for the advancement of women:
they were Poland (1986), Russia (1993), Albania (1992) and
Slovakia (1991). However, all of them had an unclear and
limited mandate and were directly dependent on their host
ministry. With the participation of the CEE governments
in the UN-sponsored conferences and initiatives, there has
been 'further development, in some countries, of existing
institutional mechanisms for gender equality and creation
of new ones; wider acceptance of the mainstreaming
approach; growing awareness that gender equality and
women's rights constitute a "common good" for human-
ity; awareness of the need for both traditional women's policies and gender mainstreaming policies' (UN/ECE, 1999a).

Since the Beijing Conference, some CEE countries have
initiated some legislative reforms benefiting women and
others have completed national plans for action, and/or have
established national committees for women (or equality),
and/or national ombuds person offices. Activities have also
increased at local government level.

## Current situation of national machineries for the advancement of women in the CEE countries: case studies

As has been mentioned previously, the environment of
individual countries in the region differs quite a lot. Therefore, there is no common clue or model of and for the
successful development and advancement of the national
machinery in the region. Nevertheless, there are some
positive examples and experiences as well as common
obstacles and visions for future possible improvement.

A survey of the national machineries for women in the
CEE countries reveals some important features of the
processes affecting the establishment and functioning of

national machineries for women (table 4). First, in the majority of CEE countries national machineries are located within the Ministry of Social Affairs and/or Labour. Often they have been set up by the order of a government or council of ministers (Albania, Bulgaria, Czech Republic, Hungary, Macedonia, Poland, Romania and Slovakia). In Russia and Ukraine, for example, they have been set up by presidential decree.

Second, in many countries the processes of economic and political transition have a direct bearing upon the life and functioning of the machineries. In some cases this takes the form of reconstituting and reconfiguring the name, size, membership and the site of the national machinery (see also Kwesiga, chapter 10 of this volume). So, for example, in Albania in 1992, the Women and Family Section was set up within the Ministry of Labour, Emigration and Social Affairs. Two years later it was upgraded to the Department of Women and Family and within the next two years it became the State Secretariat of Women attached to the Ministry of Culture, Youth and Women. In March 1997, the national machinery stepped backwards and was transferred to the Department for Women and Family in the same Ministry. In November 1997, it moved again to the Ministry of Labour and Social Affairs and in July 1998 by the decision of the Council of Ministers it was appointed the Committee on Women and Family, reporting directly to the Office of the Deputy Prime Minister (Katro-Beluli, personal interview, 1999). Finally, in March 2001 the name was changed to the Commission for Equal Opportunities.

Third, changes in government, in this period of transition, can have a disproportionate impact on the structures and powers of national machineries. In Poland, for example, there is no national machinery existing at present. In 1986, the Governmental Plenipotentiary for Women was created. It existed until 1991, when its name was changed to the Plenipotentiary for Women and Family. In 1995, it was renamed again as the Plenipotentiary for Family and Women. This functioned until October 1997, when the new right-wing government closed it down. In its place the Plenipotentiary for the Family was established in November 1997 (Lohmann, personal interview, 1999). Similarly, in Moldova we find that a governmental crisis in December 1999

**Table 4** National machinery in the CEE countries, June 2001

| Country | Name | Year of establishment | Host/location | Membership |
|---|---|---|---|---|
| Albania | Commission for Equal Opportunities (named 1 March 2001) | 1992 (transformations in 1994, 1996, 1997 and 1998) | Ministry of Labour | 8–9 employees |
| Belarus | The Family and Gender Issues Department National Council on Gender Policy | 2000 | Subdivision of the Ministry of Social Welfare | Representatives of National Assembly, Council of Ministers, NGOs, scientists and local authorities (23 persons) |
| Bulgaria | None at present | | | |
| Croatia | Committee for Gender Equality (renamed in 2000) | 1996 | Ministry of Labour and Social Welfare | One representative from each ministry (in Council 5 NGO representatives) |
| Czech Republic | Division for Equality between Men and Women | 1998 | Ministry of Labour and Social Affairs | 3 employees |
| Estonia | Bureau of Equality | 1996 | Ministry of Social Affairs | |

**Table 4** (*continued*)

| Country | Name | Year of establishment | Host/location | Membership |
|---|---|---|---|---|
| Hungary | Secretariat for the Representation of Women | 1996 | Ministry of Family and Social Affairs | |
| Latvia | Focal Point for the Coordination of Gender Equality Related Issues | 1999 | Ministry of Welfare | |
| Lithuania | Inter-ministerial Commission for Equal Opportunities for Women and Men | | | |
| Macedonia | Unit for Gender Equality | 1997 | Ministry of Labour and Social Policy | 1 person |
| Moldova | Department of Family Policy and Equal Opportunities | | Ministry of Labour, Social Protection and Family | |
| Poland | None at present (only Plenipotentiary for the Family) | | | |
| Romania | Direction for Equality of Chances | 1995 | | |

| Country | Institution | Year | Responsible body | Composition / Notes |
|---|---|---|---|---|
| | Consultative Interdepartmental Commission for Equality of Chances between Women and Men | 1999 | | Deputy Head of State Government — Chair, members are appointed by the state government |
| Russia | Commission for the Advancement of Women | 1997 | Government of Russian Federation | Representatives of ministries, NGOs and experts |
| Slovakia | Coordination Committee for Women's Issues | 1996 | Ministry of Labour, Social Affairs and Family | |
| | Department for Equal Opportunities | 1999 | | 2 employees |
| Slovenia | Office for Equal Opportunities (renamed in 2001) | 1992 | Government of the Republic of Slovenia | |
| Ukraine | Committee for Women's Affairs, Motherhood and Childhood | 1996 | Ministry of Family and Youth | |
| | Sector for Women's Affairs, Family, Mother and Child Protection | 1993 | Attached to Cabinet of Ministers | |

Sources: UNDP RBEC/RSC, Bratistava, Slovakia, June 2001. National Machinery, Action Plans and Gender Mainstreaming in the Council of Europe. Regional Report on Institutional Mechanisms for the Advancement of Women in the Countries of Central and Eastern Europe, Warsaw: Karat Coalition Press, 2000.

resulted in the abandoning of some strong structures of gender equality that included: the Equal Opportunities Subcommittee (within the Committee on Human Rights), established in 1998; the Committee on Women's Issues (February 1999), a consultative and coordinating body for the government; gender focal points within all ministries (starting in April 1999); and the Committee on Women and Family Issues (May 1999), instituted in order to assist the President of Moldova. The future of the national machinery is now unstable and unclear (Budrug-Lungu, personal interview, 2000).

Fourth, some of the CEE countries have experienced civil and ethnic conflict and war, and are yet to engage with issues of special structures for furthering women's position. Thus, 'Four years after the Dayton Peace Agreement where no one woman participated, Bosnia and Herzegovina is in a process of social, economic and political reconstruction as well as of establishing new legislative frameworks, but without giving any significant attention to issues of gender equality' (Helic, personal interview, 2000, League of Women in the Bosnia and Herzegovina Federation). This has been the experience of women in many countries where women's participation in political or military movements has not been reflected in the processes of institution building and where independent statehood has seen the marginalization of women in the political system (Jayawardena, 1989; Anthias and Yuval-Davis, 1990). Fifth, the processes and the dominant political discourses of transition also affect the shaping of national machineries. In the Czech Republic, for example, the government officially proclaimed the equality of all citizens and, therefore, excluded the existence of any further discrimination and other forms of inequality (Novakova, personal interview, 1999).

Sixth, the motivation to gain access to the European Union (EU), in the context of the Union's strong commitment to structures of gender equality, has been important to many transitional democracies in the CEE region. Thus the Czech Republic started the process of establishing the national machinery for the advancement of women at the beginning of 1998, in part motivated by the seriousness with which the EU regarded institutional mechanisms for the advancement of women. Wanting to be part of the EU was thus an important impetus for the establishment of the Czech national machinery (Simerska, personal interview, 2000).

Finally, while the external impetus to institute national machineries has been strong — both from the UN as well as the EU — in some countries the women's movements have had a considerable role to play in formation of national machineries. In Slovenia the Commission for Equality was the second to be established (in 1990) in CEE countries. It was the consequence of a genuine women's political movement separated from the communists. Starting in 1986, there is evidence of free and open political discussion on women in politics, and women and peace, violence, ecology and freedom of sexual orientation. In 1992, when the political orientation of the country shifted to the centre-left, the Governmental Office for Women's Policy was established. After the elections in 1996 women lost half of their representation in Parliament. Today, the Governmental Office for Women's Policy (renamed office for Equal Opportunities in February 2001) is very active in advocating for women's issues, but without a clear mandate and without real support from the Commission for Equality in Parliament, which is still formally in existence. These changes in the life cycle of national machineries due to political and economic pressures within the government and country point to the fragility of the machineries if they are not supported by strong women's movements from within civil society (Lokar, 2000).

Here one would also point to the trajectory of women's engagement with politics. Jaquette and Wolchik make the point that the politics of women's equality was associated with the ideological positions of the communist regimes and 'not with women's understanding of their own interests' (1998b:8). They also point out that in the CEE countries, women lacked experience in organizing in their own interests. Finally, they argue that international pressures, while helpful to evoke a state response, were not always supportive of gender politics: 'some of the most outspoken women in the region have complained of heavy-handed attempts on the part of Western feminists to pressure women in the region to conform to their views' (Jacquette and Wolchik, 1998b:9).

There are thus many reasons for the rather patchy growth of women's national machineries. Some are political/ideological shifts in political discourses, as well as the pressures of governmental and party hierarchies on the one hand, and those of global and European institutions on the other. Other issues for the marginalization of women's machineries are to do with the lack of sustainability of governmental planning in many CEE countries, lack of mechanisms to hold governments to account and to monitor progress in the field, and 'in some parts of the region, insufficient understanding of the political significance of gender equality issues as issues of democracy and human rights' (UNIFEM, 1999). However, what is lacking most is political will: the motivation of political leaders, both women and men, in decision-making positions to raise gender awareness, to disseminate information, to encourage gender-sensitive communication, and to insist upon mainstreaming gender issues in development strategies and policy planning.

## Looking ahead: national machineries in CEE countries in the twenty-first century

Since December 1999, there has been significant progress in analysing, mapping and evaluating the situation of national machineries in the countries of Central and Eastern Europe. This is due to the increasing collaboration of national, regional and international networks at both official and NGO levels. The support of the international and/or European community, as well as the increasing strength of women's movements and groups within civil society, has also raised the awareness of governments in this regard. We have a saying in Slovakia: 'The road to hell is paved with good intentions.' Even an excellent idea is lost when it is not implemented well. In the current environment of the CEE countries, the following tasks of governmental structures should be given attention in order to build upon the recent advances made in mainstreaming gender in the policy-making and implementational structures of government. First, introducing and disseminating, to the widest possible population (not excluding official bodies), the idea of gender mainstreaming as an integral part of the progressive development of society as a whole. Second, understanding the importance of raising gender awareness at all social and territorial levels. Third, providing a gender approach in all forms of education and training. Fourth, stimulating and encouraging the mass media to produce and disseminate information on national and international activities in the field of gender issues. Fifth, constructing procedures for regular and open communication, within official bodies as well as from the bottom up and vice versa, in a sustainable manner. It is also important to formulate methodologies for monitoring processes of implementation of governmental policies on mainstreaming; to set up the indicators of progress made to date; to utilize feedback; and to set up other relevant controlling mechanisms. All this has to be done on a very transparent basis. Finally, the region of 'conflicting priorities' should not be isolated at any cost during the critical time of transformation. International, intergovernmental and regional institutions should be encouraged

> to provide financial and technical assistance in support of institutional mechanisms and the development and implementation of tools for gender equality; and for countries in the region where financial support from donors is substantially decreasing, set up a technical assistance fund managed by an international or UN organization, where governments and NGOs could apply to obtain specialized technical expertise. (UNIFEM, 1999).

## 9

# The government of the United Kingdom: the Women's National Commission[1]

WENDY STOKES

## Introduction

There have been two significant stages in the creation of national machineries for women within government in the United Kingdom. The first phase was in the 1960s and 1970s, when anti-discrimination and equal pay legislation was accompanied by the creation of the Equal Opportunities Commissions (EOC) in England, Scotland and Wales, and the UK-wide Women's National Commission (WNC). The governments of the 1980s and 1990s established a Minister for Women and a Cabinet Committee on Women, and gradual integration into the European Union (EU) has entailed the absorption of a considerable amount of regulation favourable to women. However, the second significant phase in the creation of the national machinery only came after the 1997 general election, when the new Labour government established a Minister for Women at Cabinet level, supported by a more junior Minister for Women and a Women's Unit (WU).[2]

## Political background

The mainstream of UK politics, parties and government since the 1960s has been characterized by a reluctance to engage directly with gender (let alone feminist) issues. Both of the major parties (Conservative and Labour) as well as the third party (Liberal and more recently Liberal Democrat) have tended towards a liberal approach: an assumption that the adoption of policies which outlaw discrimination and open up access will eventually achieve a broad measure of equality across all socio-economic cleavages.

The 1960s was a period of relative optimism and prosperity in the UK. A post-Second World War politics of consensus between the parties was still in place and politicians responded to social change with a raft of liberal legislation: relaxing control on divorce, contraception, abortion, homosexuality and prostitution. This was also the period in which the UK attempted a corporatist approach to economic and industrial policy making.

Corporatism was a short-lived experiment in the UK which was largely abandoned in the 1970s as the oil crises translated into economic instability and industrial unrest. However, while it was in place a number of institutions were created for consultation between government, business and labour. Specific consideration of women's role in the economy did not figure large in the concerns of any of the three partners; nevertheless the WNC was founded in 1969 as a non-departmental public body with a small budget and the brief of bringing the informed opinion of women to bear on government policy. Its foundation was seen in terms of preparing for the forthcoming sex discrimination and equal pay legislation, and in keeping with United Nations (UN) policies, particularly the approaching the UN International Year of Women.[3]

The background to this and the changing role of the WNC within the present Labour government are the subject of the following sections.

## The 1997 Labour government

The establishment of the Ministers for Women and the WU by the incoming Labour government in 1997 marked not only a new phase in gender policy making, but also a new approach. By creating a Women's Unit and placing it alongside the WNC, the government made a commitment to mainstreaming gender equality. The WU was part of a new experiment in the creation of cross-cutting Units (along with the Social Exclusion Unit) forming a central element in what is referred to as 'joined-up government': ensuring that government policies address the whole problem rather than parts of it. Thus gender equality was entrenched as a component of joined-up government (Veitch, 1999).

## Gender policy background

The period of change from the 1960s to the 1970s in the UK has been well documented (Coote and Campbell, 1987; Rowbotham, 1990). Whether driven by the women's movement or by economic imperative, free contraception and abortion (if not on demand, at least without too much argument) were made available through the National Health Service in 1967; the WNC was established in 1969 under a remit 'to ensure by all possible means that the informed opinions of women are given their due weight in the deliberations of government' (see note 1); anti-discrimination and equal pay legislation was implemented in 1974; and the EOC was created at the same time to oversee the implementation of the Act, albeit with a reactive rather than proactive brief.

In the thirty years between the start of this process and the in-coming 1997 Labour government, women's lives in the UK changed considerably, although the extent to which such change was encouraged and supported by central government remains a topic for debate (Lovenduski and Randall, 1993). The sex discrimination and equal pay laws have been roundly criticized as weak tools which place an onus on the victim to press her case; the EOC, despite producing valuable and useful research, is not a campaigning body and lacks both the authority and the resources to initiate action. Individual women and women's pressure groups have found the EU and EU legislation to be stronger sources of support and justice, although the process of taking a claim through both national and international courts is a lengthy one. The EU position on equal pay for work of equal value, for example, went some way to plug the loopholes in the UK equal pay legislation, and EU regulation of the pay and conditions of part-time workers will (when it is fully implemented) compensate women for their disproportionate participation in part-time work in the UK.

The general trend of policy during the long period of Conservative government was based on a strong liberal position of choice and freedom: all citizens would benefit from the conditions of free choice; special treatment of any sort smacked of privilege and undermined liberty. Women, like men, would benefit from the freedom to make economic choices in an expanding economy, unencumbered by excessive taxation. Despite some high-profile initiatives, notably Greenham Common and the Miners' Wives, the 1980s was not a happy decade for the women's movement.

The women's movement had sprung up in the UK in the 1960s alongside parallel movements in the United States of America and other European countries (Bouchier, 1993). Driven by the realization that legal provision did not guarantee social, political and economic equality, the women's movement of the 1960s and 1970s aimed to change public consciousness and women's *de facto* position. By the 1980s certain measures had been achieved and in the process an awareness of the complexity of gender politics had evolved. On the one hand, there were challenges to the notion that 'sisterhood is universal' from groups of women who considered themselves marginalized in the women's movement as well as in the wider society; on the other, there was a shift on the part of some women away from the intentionally outsider ethos of the social movement into mainstream politics of parties and government (Coote and Patullo, 1990; Lovenduski and Randall, 1993).

From the late 1970s some women with a background in the women's movement took their concerns into political parties in the UK. Neither parties nor government were particularly hospitable (Loach, 1985). This is described in Loretta Loach's 1985 article in *Spare Rib*, in which she quotes Ann Petifor, founder of the Women's Action Group within the Labour Party, as saying, 'It is the resistance of labour men to the empowering of women of their own class which can only be described as brutal. We've struggled for six years along these lines; we've struggled to get more women into Parliament and each year the resistance from men gets worse and more frightening and women are damaged more and more by it' (1985:18). Similarly, in a 1986 article Sarah Perrigo described the discomfort she had experienced in the Leeds Labour Party. This generated tensions between women who had moved into the mainstream and those who pursued the autonomous route (Roelofs, 1989). Similar responses are documented in Australia and Scandinavian countries (Dominelli and Jonasdottir, 1988; Eisenstein, 1990; Lovenduski and Randall, 1993). In the UK the pursuit of women's interests remained alive in the unlikely space provided by local government (Campbell, 1984). While the Conservative Party dominated Westminster, the demoralized Labour Party focused on local government and used this as an arena in which to develop alternative policies and approaches (Gyford, 1985; Goss, 1988). Now largely written out of Labour Party history, what was referred to at the time as the 'New Urban Left' generated an approach which has been quietly adopted by the present government. A number of Labour-led local authorities adopted a novel system of creating new committees, each with a cross-departmental brief, to ensure that the interests of women, ethnic minorities and disabled people were taken into account in all decisions reached by mainstream committees.

The present mechanisms for gender equality in the Cabinet Office are (possibly unwittingly) heir to the innovations made by local government women's committees of the 1980s and 1990s. These included adopting a three-pronged approach to gender equality: supporting women's initiatives in the community; establishing equal opportunities practices within local authority employment; and ensuring that the broad range of local government policies addressed women's specific concerns and perspectives. Importantly, women's committees drew on outside expertise, and made themselves accountable to the community, through the mechanism of co-option: women from local women's organizations were co-opted on to the committees (Stokes, 1998).

In the post-1997 Government, while the new WU was given responsibility for policy coordination, promoting long-term institutional change within government, acting as a taskforce within government and undertaking research projects, its responsibilities did not include community involvement (Veitch, 1999). However, the WNC already possessed a remit to bring the informed opinions of women to bear on policy making.

## The WNC: history

From its creation until 1998 the WNC was a membership organization. It comprised member organizations serviced by civil servants. There were fifty member organizations and thirty-five associate member organizations, and the role of the civil servants was to present to government the views of the members. The Commission itself was composed of 'fifty women elected or appointed by national organizations with a large and active membership of women' (Cabinet Office, 1998:3). Member organizations, which included the women's sections of the major political parties, trades unions, religious groups, professional bodies and business women's organizations, provided the individual women who comprised the Commission and thus it was their interests which directed the Commission's activities. Associate member organizations were kept in touch with WNC business through regular bulletins, consultation exercises, conferences and seminars.

As a publicly funded body representing sectional interests the WNC was, and is, close to unique. However, its (in effect) ownership by fifty organizations limited its remit. By the 1990s it was little known outside of its membership and (when considered at all) generally regarded as a conservative, somewhat marginal body. It had a tendency towards consensus seeking that meant that consensus-sensitive issues were likely to be dropped, thus avoiding conflict but also avoiding engagement with important issues. This form of organization was neither as open, nor as democratic, as might be expected of an organization established to reflect the informed opinion of women in the community, yet many of its member organizations were opposed to change.

## New Labour and women

The 1997 Labour government came into power with a large electoral swing, a hefty majority of seats and a new generation of politicians, including an unprecedented number of women. Eighteen years in the political wilderness ensured that many of the Members of Parliament (MPs) in the new governing party were under fifty (some under thirty) and new to office; the size of the swing meant that some candidates who had not dreamed of being elected were (one stunned new MP noted on election night that he would have to resign from his job the following day); the abandoned women-only shortlist system and the size of the swing put nearly twice as many female MPs into Parliament than ever before.[4]

During the period of Opposition the Labour Party had, among other things, made commitments on gender equality. These included the notion of a Minister for Women (unfortunately announced in a pamphlet fronted by a white, suited, professional-looking woman wearing a wedding ring) and the document *Governing for Equality*, which contained a commitment to strengthen the WNC. A number of the new female MPs had come into Parliament from a background in local government, including experience with women's committees; those MPs that had come via women-only shortlists had a particular knowledge and concern for measures to enable women. The *image* of the party was woman friendly: less individualistic than the Conservatives, less men-in-smoke-filled-rooms than Old Labour. The change in image was partly because of the men who were there (younger, more gender aware) and partly because from the late 1970s women who were active on women's issues had been moving into the party (Perrigo, 1986). Moreover, the government had inherited from its predecessor obligations to the policies adopted at the 1995 UN Fourth World Conference on Women held at Beijing.

The new government's immediate response to the plethora of issues confronting it was not to act, but to refer problems to committees and commissions for consideration and to create the national machinery. The post of Minister for Women became Cabinet level and the post of Parliamentary Under-Secretary of State for Women was created; the WU was created to support the Minister for Women, but rather than re-allocate powers or create a new mechanism for consultation with external women's organizations, the WNC was to be reformed. Both the WU and the WNC were initially in the Department of Social

Security: the new WU placed there to serve the then Minister for Women, Harriet Harman.

## The WNC: process of change

A formal review of the WNC was launched in September 1997 and concluded in July 1998.[5] The terms of reference of the review were 'to examine the objectives, membership and the funding of the WNC in the light of the Government's need to ensure that there is an effective, independent channel of communication between women's organizations and Government for the twenty-first century. To assess costs and benefits. To develop, if appropriate, options for change'.

There were two parts to the review: the government's review and the WNC's own review. According to the government's Review Document:

> following the general election in 1997, the Prime Minister appointed two Ministers for Women. The mission of the Ministers for Women and their Women's Unit was to '*ensure that all women are treated equally with men and that their needs and concerns are properly understood and addressed by government*'. The Ministers for Women set themselves six priorities, including:
> - opening up a new dialogue with women and building a bond of trust between women and the government;
> - bringing women into the mainstream of government policy-making.
>
> The review of the WNC drew together these two proposals. (Cabinet Office, 1998:3).

The Government Review concluded that the WNC was a necessary and desirable organization, but that it should change. First, its membership should be opened up and expanded. Second, its independence should be protected and enhanced. Third, it should be more active, flexible, influential and acquire a higher public profile.

The WNC's own Review (derived from consultation between member organizations) made recommendations about the expansion of membership, to take account of the increased numbers of women's organizations springing up in the aftermath of the UN Beijing Fourth World Conference on Women, and organizational reform to take account of both devolution in the UK and membership of the EU; the Review also made recommendations about the WNC's mode of operation and relations with government. From the Review Document it appears that agreement was reached, by and large, between the government and WNC, with the notable exception of the WNC's suggestion that 'consideration should be given to the time and cost to members who take an active role in the WNC. Members should be able to give time and expertise to the WNC without having to consider the financial implications' (Cabinet Office, 1998:17). The rejection of these suggestions suggests that the government's commitment to using the expertise of women's organizations did not extend to paying for it; no small oversight in the light of the apparently ineradicable 25 per cent difference between the average male and female hourly wage.

The WNC was to continue as a non-departmental public body and expand its membership to include more organizations and even individuals. It would adopt a stronger process of operational planning and acquire press/publicity and research/information officers to raise its profile. Its central organizing committee would change in structure, becoming more representative and proactive. The general thrust of the Review and the measures adopted were that the WNC should become more active, more engaged with a wider (and expanding) range of women's organizations, and have more access to government as a legitimate representative of women's interests in policy making. Both the WNC and the WU moved to the Cabinet Office when the Women's brief was transferred to Baroness Jay, since she was the Leader of the House of Lords and a member of the Privy Council. Cabinet Office is the corporate headquarters of the British civil service; thus the WU and WNC moved to the heart of government.

## The WNC: structure

The WNC is wholly (although not generously) funded by government. As a non-departmental public body it is independent of government discipline and possesses considerable freedom, within the limitations of its remit and resources. Goals and strategy are directed by the WNC Chair, Baroness Christine Crawley, and a Steering Group of fifteen, whose appointment is governed by the Nolan Committee rules.[6] A clear goal of the regeneration of the WNC was to ensure that the new Steering Group would be made up of women who possessed gender expertise as well as board-level skills and could be seen to represent a constituency of women.

The WNC is staffed by civil servants 'on loan' from their home departments. Nuts-and-bolts issues such as budgets and staffing are managed by the civil service, while strategic direction is internal. Thus Susan Atkins, Director of the WU, is line manager to Janet Veitch, Director of the WNC, but with regard to strategic direction the civil servants are responsible to the Chair of the Steering Group of the WNC, at present Baroness Crawley. The WNC liaises with the WU, and through it with the Ministers for Women. It also liaises with both individual MPs and other government departments.

The new WNC is no longer tied into the interests of fifty women's organizations. Instead of a fixed number of members and associates it now has a growing number of partners (over two hundred at the end of 2000), including both large national organizations and small local ones (of particular importance since it is arguably the smaller organizations which require the information gathered and distributed by the WNC most, as well as the administrative resources that it can provide). This has facilitated the selection of a Steering Group of women who better meet the criteria of expertise, skills and representativeness, including at present the Director of the Fawcett Society (which conducts research and lobbies for women's increased participation in politics), the former Chair of the EOC in Northern Ireland, and the Chief Executive of the Family Planning Association. Partner organizations nominate a specific individual as the contact with the WNC and commit to a 'contract' whereby they agree to contribute to the information base and activities of the Commission rather than passively receiving briefings. The present Director recognizes that the WNC is the voice of its partners, but also regards itself as facilitating and coordinating the development of individual organizations and links between them as well as with government.

The independence of the WNC from the discipline of a government department and its integration with women's groups are its strengths; these therefore require protection. Its relations with the WU and the Ministers for Women pose questions about potential conflicts of interest. While the WU is part of the Cabinet Office, the WNC, despite being in residence, is not. The WNC is not just free to express independent views, but is *expected* to do so. Relations between the two bodies are intended to be complementary but contain the potential for conflict. At present relations are smooth, but this appears to be due to that most unpredictable element in politics — personalities — as much as to policies. The Labour government, having set these mechanisms in place, remains broadly in favour of their operations. The Director of the WU is supportive of the NGO agenda. The Director of the WNC, having moved there from the WU, is familiar with the personalities and the remit of both organizations.

## The WNC: policies and projects

The Steering Group approved a set of priorities for the WNC at its meeting in January 2000: the pay gap between women and men; the need to redesign work and welfare systems around the shapes of women's lives; establishing secure funding for women's refuge services; establishing a Parliamentary Committee on Equality; raising women's representation in decision making; and women's health and education issues (*WNC News*, 2000:1). These will shape the plans which the WNC presents to the government, exchanges between partners and discussions with the Ministers for Women. This is in addition to the responsibility for coordinating comments on the Beijing Process from women's organizations. This dates back to the 1995 Conference and has entailed annual responses; it was also concerned with input to the twenty-third special session of the General Assembly (Beijing +5), the meeting at which the progress of each participating nation was assessed.[7]

The activities of the WNC go in two directions: collecting and disseminating information among partners and facilitating their development through conferences and seminars; and briefing and informing MPs, which may include bringing in experts from partner organizations to speak to MPs. It is also taking on specific projects, either alone or in conjunction with the EOC or WU, for which its integration with women's organizations is both a resource and a mark of legitimacy. Recent projects include 'Future Female: A 21st Century Gender Perspective', and 'Women 2000', a report on the implementation of the Beijing Platform for Action in the UK (WNC, 1999).

The WNC receives copies of all consultation documents circulating in government and decides which to pass among partners for comment. Partners receive monthly newsletters which keep them up to date with parliamentary matters, relevant consultation documents, details of meetings and campaigns, and advertisements for public appointments. Partners are expected to express views on consultation documents and to pass on other relevant information. The WNC is able to reflect the views of the partners back to the government. This enables government to respond to informed opinion on its policies and may give advance warning on a controversial issue. One of the most disruptive issues in the early stages of this government (that occurred prior to the reconstitution of the WNC) was a change to the benefit system that was widely interpreted as a reduction in benefit to some lone parents. The WNC passed a resolution condemning the change and the then Chair, Valerie Evans, appeared on television condemning the change. Arguably, if the government had possessed the sort of information that the WNC now aims to provide, it might have altered its path.

## The WNC: partners and government

The WNC believes that the present government is willing to listen to arguments on behalf of women's interests, although partners think that it could do more for women. Recent analysis of the Chancellor's decisions on taxation and welfare benefits, for example, show that the system is tending towards benefiting children. This supports the general contention that the government, and in particular the Chancellor, is sympathetic to a gender agenda.

An active partner in the WNC, which provides a good example of how the organization can work with its members and how those members can work with the government, is the Women's Budget Group (WBG). The WNC supports this think-tank of academics and activists by providing a place to meet and administrative services for meetings. It also helps to organize meetings and arranges meetings with the Treasury. The WBG is able to bring information provided by partner organizations to bear on economic policy and the Treasury appears to be open to this source of information. According to the report *Women 2000*, '[s]ince the election of the Labour Government in 1997 the Treasury has actively consulted the WBG as part of the Government's policy of mainstreaming gender issues' (WNC, 1999:14). The WBG is recommending to the government the establishment of a Parliamentary Committee on Equality that would, among other things, oversee government work on gendering the Budget. It also recommends the publication by government of an annual budget for women that would include an analysis of expenditure on women and men as well as taking account of women's unpaid contribution to the economy (WNC, 1999:16).

## Women 2000

*Women 2000* is a good example of what the unusual positioning of the WNC enables it to do. The Beijing Conference of 1995 produced a Platform for Action on Women that all signatories, of which the UK was one, were obliged to pursue. In the follow-up to Beijing, and in preparation for Beijing +5, in June 2000 a questionnaire was sent to governments by the UN in order to assess the implementation of the Platform for Action. The UK government responded to the questionnaire. At this time the WNC put the government's responses out to partner organizations for their comments, and from these produced *Women 2000*. *Women 2000* is more than a summary of government responses and the reaction of women's organizations to those responses: in its second and third sections it considers and makes recommendations with regard to key financial and institutional mechanisms and reports in detail on progress against all the Critical Areas of Concern of the Platform for Action.

Each of the twelve Critical Areas of Concern of the Platform (Women and Poverty, Education and Training of Women, Women and Health, Violence against Women, Women and Armed Conflict, Women and the Economy, Women in Power and Decision Making, Institutional Mechanisms for the Advancement of Women, Human Rights of Women, Women and the Media, Women and the Environment and the Girl Child) is addressed twice in *Women 2000*. In the first section, the Platform for Action demands on the government are placed against the UK government response and the reaction from the women from partner organizations who responded through the WNC. For example, under the heading 'Violence':

*What the PfA says governments must do*:
- make sure women feel safe to report violence;
- provide well funded refuges;
- fund local campaigns against violence;
- train police, doctors, and judges to understand the effects of violence on women;
- support women's groups in stopping female genital mutilation;
- encourage the media to examine the effect of the images of women which they publish, and how this encourages violence.

*What our Government has done and is doing*:
- has developed the very first national strategy on violence against women;
- has made female genital mutilation illegal;
- has allocated £250 million to crime prevention;
- is funding awareness campaigns;
- has provided guidance to the police and to housing officials on helping women who have reported violence;
- is building up a database of local domestic violence services.

*What women are saying to us*:
- two women a week are murdered by their partners in this country: there must be secure core funding for refuge support services, help-lines, and counselling, so that services are available all over the country, and not just in some places; and are not dependent on Lottery funding;

- a legal duty on local councils to re-house women who leave their homes because of violence;
- better conviction rates for rape;
- a strong effort to stop female genital mutilation where it is still practised, and prosecute those who carry it out;
- the laws which can force mothers to allow violent and abusive fathers visiting rights to their children, who are often very afraid of them, must be changed;
- special protection from the police for refuge services and refuge workers.

In the third section the comments from partner organizations are presented under the same headings in the form of a summary of all that has been undertaken by government and non-governmental organizations, and recommendations for further development. In this section the consideration of violence runs to six pages, giving a general overview of the occurrence of violence and sexual abuse in the UK and then detailing the coordinated multi-agency approach at all levels of government to combating violence, as developed by the Women's Aid Federation, England in 1998. The report notes steps that have been taken and makes a range of far-reaching recommendations for changes in policy and legislation.

The document constitutes a valuable resource for organizations mobilizing around particular issues since it gives the position of the Platform for Action, government response, and both comments and recommendations from a range of women's organizations, which thereby possess legitimacy. It is an effective source of pressure on government but also a powerful tool *for* government, since it provides the legitimacy of 'the informed opinions of women' should government want to pursue any of the recommended courses of action.

## The WNC and the partners

Part of the legitimacy of the WNC derives from the broad range of its partners; however, the question arises as to what extent there can be a shared point of view among such divergent groups. Are the Union of Catholic Mothers, Stonewall (a gay rights group) and the Women's Engineering

Society ever likely to share an opinion? This is a common problem of representation and perhaps something of a red herring. There is no single, coherent women's viewpoint; the entire trajectory of feminism since the 1970s has demonstrated the range of women's perspectives. In an organization such as the WNC it is unlikely that all partner organizations will be interested in making a case on all issues; those organizations that do participate at a particular time may share a broad perspective while differing on details, or may differ radically. The role of the WNC, like that of the Trades Union Congress or Confederation of British Industry, is to present those views to government in their complexity, whether as a single report with the different opinions weighted, or as majority and minority reports. It is then up to the government to work with the range of women's concerns, rather than to simplify the issues.

The approach of the WNC is, in the broadest and most general sense, feminist. This is evident in its focus on strategic gender needs rather than practical gender needs. Focusing on strategy means taking the long view, and having some vision with regard to the sort of society being aimed at. Satisfying the criteria of strategic gender needs is more likely to entail changing the society in the direction of gender fairness than satisfying practical gender needs.

## Conclusion

With all advisory organizations, the most difficult and most important question is always whether or not they wield effective influence. The WNC is no exception. WNC officers maintain that MPs take up issues that are presented to them and respond to the briefings and information passed on to them. In *Women 2000* the WBG quotes two instances of success: 'modifications to the new Working Families Tax Credit, allowing households a choice in who claims the tax credit; and the insistence on the importance of independent taxation may have been a factor in influencing the decision not to tax child benefit' (WNC, 1999:15). In her discussion paper, *Institutional Mechanisms for Women within the UK Government*, Janet Veitch comments, 'There are mixed views on how effective these mechanisms are . . . There is a degree of consensus that the mechanisms are important and worthwhile' (Veitch, 1999:6).

As part of the civil service the WNC and its officers are bound by conventions of secrecy and therefore cannot broadcast their successes or failures. Confidential advice reflecting the opinions of women's organizations is provided to ministers, MPs and government. If information or advice is ignored, no one outside of government is any the wiser; if it is accepted, only an unusually humble government minister would give credit to an advisory body for a smart piece of policy design. There is a fine line between overt lobbying and behind-the-scenes manoeuvring and as a governmental body the WNC's remit is to collect and present the views of women, not to take a position or to promote those views. On the other hand, if government does not take account of the information and advice it is offered, the partner organizations have the data for themselves with which to mobilize external pressure on government.

The WNC has changed rapidly. Although the changes are to the advantage of both the organization and the promotion of women's opinions, there is a concern that the large number of new partners may not work efficiently at the outset because many of them will not know how to use the organization. It has tended to work very much on a personal level, with contacts in various organizations knowing each other and people in the WNC offices; this may change as a result of sheer numbers. Not all partners will be active, at least not on all issues. The efficacy of the networked organization will be constrained if contacts keep information to themselves; therefore some analysis will be required of both levels of participation and the penetration of ideas and information beyond the named contact in each partner organization.

The WNC operates at national and international levels, formally and informally. The experience of local government women's committees illuminated certain characteristics of cross-departmental bodies, which the WNC confirms. Formal placement in the wider organization matters, as do resources and the status of personnel, but these are overshadowed by informal factors. Support from significant figures in government matters, the access of personnel to influential people and important forums matters. These intangible facilities are invisible to the observer or researcher and in assessing the efficacy of an organization compound the problem already presented by civil service secrecy. At present the informal factors appear to be working for the WNC, but it is not hard to imagine that a change of government or even personnel could disrupt this. For this reason, if no other, stronger institutional support for gender equality is required. Therefore the WNC is 'calling for a select committee on equality to be set up, to complement the work of the Cabinet Committee and to scrutinize all legislation to ensure it is "mainstreamed". We would like to see a Public Service Agreement which dealt specifically with equality to ensure that all Departments set and meet equality targets' (Veitch, 1999:6).

The WNC is well placed within government and, at present, well supported by significant figures. Its new structure enhances its legitimacy as a voice for women in policy making and particularly with regard to the Platform for Action and the outcome document of the twenty-third special session of the General Assembly (Beijing +5). It is making the right sort of moves, but its efficacy will only become apparent in the longer term as the policies of this government translate into action. The real test will be whether its central position becomes entrenched and lasts beyond the 1997 government.

## Notes

1 I am indebted to Janet Veitch and Vicky Andreasson at the Women's National Commission for their valuable information and useful discussion. I hope I have not misrepresented their positions.

2 There had been a nominal post of Minister for Women under previous (Conservative) governments, but this responsibility had been held jointly with other posts and had never been given any real weight.

3 Thanks to Kath Davies of Engender and the Scottish Joint Action Group, partner groups in the WNC, for the information used here. The WNC does not figure in the Cabinet Diaries of the time, nor in the memoirs of Harold Wilson, then Prime Minister. It may owe its genesis to either Richard Crossman, who was responsible for the Department of Health and Social Security at the time, or to Barbara Castle, who had responsibility for equal pay.

4 For a period prior to the 1997 election the Labour Party operated a women-only shortlist system for the selection of candidates for safe seats. This was contested by two male Labour Party members and found to be in breach of sex discrimination law. Although the ruling is flawed (the position of MPs is not, after all, a job) Labour did not appeal. Constituencies could choose to reselect where a candidate had come from a women-only shortlist, but few chose to do so. The measure, although short lived, resulted in a far higher proportion of women candidates running for safe seats (and winning them) than usual.

5 The Government Review Group was made up of Joan Ruddock, MP; Minister for Women (Chair), Baroness Gould of Potternewton; and Anna Coote, Special Adviser to the Right Honourable Harriet Harman, Minister for Women; supported by WU officials.

6 Nolan refers to a government committee and report that laid down guidelines for transparency and accountability in the conduct of government, including the members of the governing bodies of public organizations.

7 Kath Davies of Engender and the Scottish Joint Action Group provided information on this.

# 10

## The national machinery for gender equality in Uganda: institutionalized gesture politics?

JOY C. KWESIGA

### Introduction

National machineries for the advancement of women are an accepted feature of many United Nations (UN) member states, having progressively gained ground during the 1975–85 UN Decade for Women and in subsequent UN Conferences on women which called for their strengthening. The Economic Commission for Africa (ECA) has observed that lack of appropriate structures officially mandated to implement the agenda for the advancement of women is 'a major explanation for failure to fully implement the 1985 Nairobi Forward Looking Strategies for the Advancement of Women' (African Centre for Women, 1995:3). As such, the Beijing Platform for Action gave prominence to the establishment of national machineries for women, which were defined as 'the central policy-coordinating unit inside government. Its main task is to support government-wide mainstreaming of a gender-equality perspective in all policy areas' (Platform for Action, para. 201. Report on Fourth World Conference on Women, 4–15 September 1995. UN). The *Report on the Fourth World Conference on Women* further notes that not only are these machineries 'diverse in form and uneven in their effectiveness, but in some cases some have declined' (para. 196). Indeed, 'institutional mechanisms for the Advancement of Women' is one of the Critical Areas of Concern in the Beijing Platform for Action.

This chapter focuses on Uganda as a case study. The analysis takes account of the checklist of the assumed ideal machinery, with the aim of assessing the strengths, weaknesses and successes of the national machinery in Uganda. Suggestions as to how the machinery can be rendered more effective are analysed. Lastly some global approaches that could enhance the effectiveness of such institutions are assessed.

## What constitutes the national machinery for gender equality in Uganda?

### Historical background

At the time of Uganda's political independence from Britain in 1962, women's issues were handled by the Ministry of Community Development, Culture and Sports. The situation pertained into the 1970s and early 1980s, although the Ministry's exact title changed from time to time. Specific attention to women was through the Department of Community Development, which worked through a network of Community Development Clubs, descending to grassroots levels. Through Community Centres, mainly at county and sometimes sub-county levels, women were trained in traditional women-related skills: basic hygiene, good nutrition, skills in production of better handicrafts and, sometimes, adult literacy. With the decline of the Ugandan economy and civil strife in the 1970s and early 1980s, the Community Centres lacked finances, became run down or were used for other purposes. However, since the late 1980s many Community Development Centres have been renovated and are in active use again (National Council of Women records).

The military government of Idi Amin (1971–79) banned all women's organizations. The UN requirement for member states to create national machineries for the advancement of women during the UN Women's Decade (1975–85) provided the opportunity for the regime to set up women's associations and to retain a strong hold on these associations. Through a Military Decree, the Uganda Council of Women (NCW) was created in 1978. The Council was charged with the duty of coordinating all women's activities in the country and all women's organizations were expected to be affiliated to this body. The NCW, a small department within the Ministry of Culture, Youth and Sports, ran on a very limited budget. It was not in a position to influence the planning process within the mainstream official system. Rather, the NCW geared its efforts towards working with grassroots women, utilizing the hierarchy of Community Development Clubs. Community Development Centres, under the jurisdiction of the Community Development Unit of the Ministry, provided venues for activities of the various Clubs. NCW Committees worked hand in hand with Community Development officials and any official mobilization of women by the Council used these channels. For example, at national functions to mark important days, women at district levels could be organized by a Community Development Officer (civil servant) and the NCW representative (woman volunteer).

The function of the NCW, primarily a government organ, was to coordinate women's organizations and groups, but it made little impact on changing the 'welfare approach' to solving women's issues. Its limited capacity can be illustrated by the fact that the UN Decade for Women left little effect on the Ugandan scene, compared with that of the neighbouring countries of Kenya and Tanzania.[1]

It is therefore no wonder that there is little trace of planning for women in any other ministry during this period. The various 'Five Year Development Plans' (1960–65, 1966–70, 1971–75, 1976–80) did not address women's issues. These documents focused on increasing economic production and production of 'manpower', but did not address gender issues. Women's issues were expected to fall specifically under one relatively low-status Ministry of Culture and Community Development (the title varied in subsequent years as explained below). The next phase of Ugandan institutional change, which also encompassed women's machineries, started with the ousting of Idi Amin and the coming to power of President Museveni. The women's machinery has thus been activated in the context not only of the democratization process, but also of economic reform under structural adjustment policies.

*Evolution of the contemporary machinery*

Most of the steps to make the national machinery effective have occurred during the regime of the National Resistance

Movement (NRM).[2] On 8 March 1988 (International Women's Day), the President of Uganda announced the creation of the Ministry of Women in Development (WID), a Ministry of its own, but housed in the Office of the President, under the guidance of a Minister of State. In 1992, under a general restructuring of government ministries, WID became part of the wider Ministry of Women in Development, Culture and Youth. In 1994, the Ministry was renamed the Ministry of Gender and Community Development (MGCD). Under yet further restructuring (June 1998) the Ministry was again renamed the Ministry of Gender, Labour and Social Development (MGLSD), with an expanded function, encompassing wider employment issues previously handled by a fully fledged Ministry of Labour, in addition to the tasks of the previous Ministry of Gender and Community Development.

## The structure and role of the machinery

The ever-changing structure of the Ministry is not only a destabilizing factor but it also changes the status of the gender component. This further complicates indicators that could be applied for its evaluation. Expansion of the ministry tends to downgrade the Machinery for Gender Equality, as demonstrated. Figure 2, which portrays the current structure, shows the many different units of the ministry, of which the official machinery is one part. The assumption of the government seems to be that if issues of social development are adequately addressed, then gender issues will have been considered.

One of the inhibiting factors in the gender mainstreaming process in Uganda derives from the mode of formation of the Ministry. In its initial years, the Ministry based its actions on presidential and ministerial pronouncements, as opposed to a clearly thought out plan. On 8 March 1988, when announcing the creation of the WID Ministry, President Y. K. Museveni stated: 'government policy aims at strengthening the position of women in the economy by raising the value and productivity of their labour and by giving them access to and control over productive resources'. The Minister of State for WID (J. Mpanga) then summarized the functions of the Ministry as follows:

**Figure 2** The Uganda Ministry of Gender, Labour and Social Development macro-structure

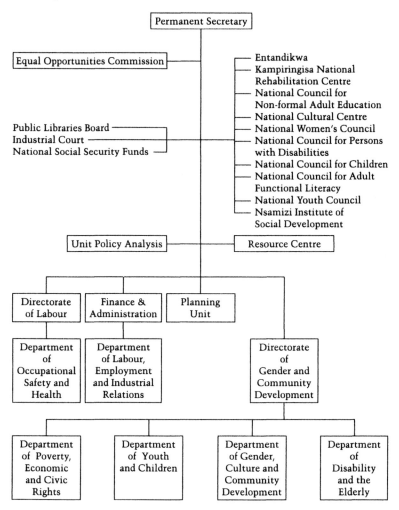

*Source*: Ministry of Gender, Labour and Social Development records (2000).

to coordinate with sectoral ministries and relevant [non-governmental organizations; NGOs], to ensure that women are accorded their rightful place in the national development process, to cooperate in the planning of projects and programmes to benefit women, to provide relevant and appropriate data and documentation for planning and policy purposes, to mobilize women to participate in and benefit from development

activities by improving their economic position, their skills
through education and training and their political and legal
status and awareness. (Ministry of WID records, 1989)

The Ministry has also projected itself as coordinator and/or
overseer of policy issues concerning women and other disadvantaged groups. This is especially so since the Ministry's
mandate goes beyond gender considerations, as illustrated
in Figure 2. This wider role is reflected in the Ministry's
mission statement: 'To empower communities, particularly
marginalized groups, to realize and harness their potential
for sustainable and gender responsive development'.

Working towards clarity regarding the machinery's mandate is therefore an ongoing process. The biggest step in
this process has been the publication of the *National Gender Policy* (NGP) (MGCD, 1997). Through this document,
the MGLSD is 'charged with the responsibility of spear-
heading and coordinating gender responsive development,
and in particular, ensuring the improvement of women's
status' (MGCD, 1997:7).[3] Its central role is to ensure that
the national development process is gender responsive,
including all national policies, reviews and other plans.
Activities include liaising with other actors to eliminate gender imbalance; the provision of technical support in gender
analysis and planning skills; conducting gender-sensitization
forums; the collection and dissemination of sex-disaggregated
data; and monitoring and evaluation of various interven-
tions/policy implementations (see Figure 2 for an overall
picture of the current functional units).[4]

Fulfilment of the national guidelines would go a long
way towards achieving gender equality, but the Ministry's
role remains amorphous and therefore not easy to fulfil
and, as we shall see later, strong barriers stand in the way.

## How effective is the machinery?

Two decades of utilizing national machineries in varied
countries has brought to the forefront what should be regarded as 'good practice'. It is against previous analyses at
national, regional and international levels that the MGLSD

will be assessed below. How does the Ugandan machinery rate against the recommended 'ideal'? Indicators for this assessment can be derived from various considerations.

*Political commitment*

Commitment to gender equality by top government leadership, including the head of government and Cabinet ministers, is arguably the most important issue affecting the functioning of the MGLSD. So far, the political leadership in Uganda has been positive on this issue. This is reflected in the official affirmative action programme, examples of which are:

1 *The District Woman Representative to Parliament provision*, which raised women Members of Parliament up to 18 per cent (1996–2001). (The number of districts is not static. In 1996, there were only forty-five administrative districts. In 2001 there are fifty-three districts due to further subdivision, and this will increase the actual numbers of women representatives when general elections take place again in 2001.) While women retain the right to contest parliamentary seats along with men, the district position is exclusively for women candidates only. In the 1996 general elections, seven women were elected to Parliament through constituency seats that are open to both men and women.

2 *The Constitutional requirement* for women to form at least one-third of local councils.[5]

3 *The position of Secretary for Women* at every local council level.

4 *Political appointments and recognition* of women's expertise that take account of the need for gender balance. At the top of this is a woman Vice-President, in position since 1994. Women form 20 per cent of High Court judges, 20 per cent of Permanent Secretaries (the top professional civil service position), and women are becoming more and more visible in the lower decision-making positions in the public sector. As a result of this recognition, women are also being elected to other offices, such as institutional directorships and academic leadership.

However, it is necessary to gauge whether this apparent commitment to gender equality has been effective in promoting women's interests, and whether the existence of the MGLSD reinforces this commitment.

### Adequate budgetary allocations

The apparent political commitment by the government top leadership is not always reflected in the amount of funds officially allocated to the MGLSD within the national annual budget. The Ministries of Finance and Economic Planning, Defence, Health, Agriculture, Education, Trade and Industry, and so on, receive proportionately much bigger amounts. Major activities of the MGLSD have so far been funded by international donors, including the Danish International Development Agency, the United Nations Children's Fund and the United Nations Development Programme. Thus the effectiveness of the Ministry is undermined by the constant threat of non-sustainability due to its weak financial base. This is a common complaint by ministers and other high-ranking officials of this Ministry. The catch therefore is that the government support described above, especially through the various affirmative action schemes, is not exemplified by relative financial support — an indicator of lip service.

### Trained human resources

To implement and sustain programmes in gender awareness, training, analysis, planning, monitoring and evaluation, trained personnel are essential. The MGLSD has therefore had a rigorous training programme where many of its staff have been enabled to undertake specialized gender-oriented courses. These range from certificate, diploma and degree awards, including graduate level. However, this achievement is transitory as the turnover, especially among elected officials, is high. Training is a constant requirement that the low level of government funding cannot sustain. This, coupled with the fact that individual staff have multiple responsibilities beyond gender considerations, creates barriers to success.

### High-profile government mechanism

The frequent relocation and renaming of the machinery throw doubt about the value attached to this machinery. More responsibilities are added to an already incoherent structure, but with no commensurate real authority. In her analysis of five such national machineries Goetz (1995 and chapter 3 of this volume) found this to be detrimental: 'Promoted to ministerial status under one regime, brought under the chief executive's wing in the President's office in the next, or shunted from one peripheral ministry to another . . . no WID/[Gender and Development] unit has been able to consolidate a place in the national bureaucracy' (1995:14). This is why it is often suggested that such machineries should be under the Office of the President or Prime Minister (South African Report 1996).

### A clear mandate

The Ugandan case is a good example of creating the machinery first and letting its role evolve. The varied restructuring it has undergone, the several attempts at streamlining its role are evidence of this. The Ministry is expected to perform wonders (judging from public comments), but these are beyond its remit, in resource as well as conceptual terms. It is expected to formulate policy, implement it and oversee other ministries and other actors, both at central and local government levels. Its mandate covers taking policy initiatives involving women's lives in both the public and private spheres, such as to eliminate domestic and other types of violence, change societal attitudes, and provide for legal literacy. As a result, the machinery is judged against unachievable goals. Any publicly voiced gender disparity is followed by the verdict — 'the Ministry has failed'. It is recognized that a clear, precise mandate is achievable in relative terms. Streamlining the current structure would lead to some positive changes.

### Meaningful structures

Focal Point Officers (FPOs) were appointed at various levels soon after the Ministry was created, to interact with and influence other government instruments. Unfortunately, this position is not officially sanctioned in the public service structures and therefore these FPOs have little or no authority and depend on their colleagues' good will. There is no agreed channel for interaction between the FPOs and the MGLSD that these contact persons represent. The level of communication will therefore depend on how proactive is the individual FPO. Many such officers are oblivious of what is going on in the MGLSD (personal interviews by the author with some FPOs).

At the district level a few Gender Officers have been appointed, and in some cases Community Development Officers (not necessarily trained in gender analysis) take up this task. Under the decentralized system, district committees appoint personnel according to their own priorities and Gender Officers may not be seen as a priority. The Ministry is therefore weak at the frontline, and it recognizes this (Ministry Plan 1996–2000:17 (b)).

## Multiplicity of functions

The MGLSD has many functions with neither adequate finances nor conceptual connectivity. For example, the Ministry is responsible for varied boards and councils. These include the National Women's Council, the Public Libraries Board, the National Council for Persons with Disabilities, the Industrial Court, the National Council for Children, the National Social Security Fund and many others, as Figure 2 illustrates. Some of the units seem displaced, such as the Entandikwa Unit, which coordinates national credit facilities programmes. In some cases, it is not clear that these units utilize the principle of collaboration/coordination. MGLSD has, for instance, an ongoing project on Functional Adult Literacy, but this is run independently of the Women's Programmes Unit, a sub-section of the Gender Directorate, despite the higher illiteracy rates among women and the fact that most of the participants are women. While the National Councils for Women and Youth are relevant to the Machinery's function, their actual roles are not so well articulated. Worse still, they are virtually unfunded by the state. Conflicting messages about them abound (personal interviews with many district officials, May and June 1998). Therefore not only is the mandate too enormous, but some units are created without being provided with the necessary instruments to perform.

## Mechanisms for research and dissemination

The MGLSD has collaborated with the Government Statistics Department in order to carry out research projects and to disseminate the outcome of these projects. In this connection, a publication, *Women and Men in Uganda: Facts and Figures 1998*, was produced and revised in 2001 (MGCD Statistics Department, 1988). The Ministry Resource Centre, which is open to the public, is growing too. While all this is commendable, constraints lie at the local level, where structures for collection and analysis are yet to be concretized. How can those directly concerned see the need for this kind of data collection and research and attend to this as a matter of course? This presents a gap yet to be filled.

*Mechanisms for monitoring and evaluation*

The foregoing discussion shows that, in its present form, the machinery cannot fully carry out monitoring and evaluation roles. It lacks strong frontline staff at the different policy and formulation and implementation levels, within the official structure. This is exacerbated by fragile lines of communication with vital Ministries such as Planning, Health, Agriculture and Education. Feedback about the performance of the Ministry or the needs of various connected institutions is received only when districts or ministries are approached. In addition, collaboration with civil society is at best very weak. Various pressure groups, such as networks of women's associations, perform this role too, but since these are not part of the official structure their activities are not enthusiastically embraced. In general it can safely be stated that the mass media (especially the print media) voluntarily perform part of the monitoring and evaluation role through various commentaries, features and articles that are published from time to time.

*Pressure points outside the government structure*

Parliament, NGOs and the wider civil society are necessary links to the official women's machinery. Some of the civil and political women's associations include the Parliamentary Women's Caucus and the National Association of Women's Organizations in Uganda (NAWOU) as the recognized umbrella body for civil society. NAWOU has 70 NGO member organizations and about 1000 community-based organizations (CBOs) on its register. The MGLSD can reach members through NAWOU and at times directly, although not all NGOs/CBOs are registered with NAWOU. However, this is not a two-way relationship. NGOs cannot easily summon or persuade the Ministry to enter into collaborative ventures and officials are unable to take up advocacy work without clearance from the top civil and political leadership.[6]

There are other policies and practices that limit the Ministry's effectiveness. These include a preference for working with individual consultants rather than with institutions. The opportunity to reach more potential partners is thus curtailed. The existing national and international base of 'experts' cannot be a substitute for a bottom-up transformation of society. Political commitment and dedication are often compromised by individual advancement.[7]

## What are the achievements of the Women's Ministry?

Despite the constraints presented above, the MGLSD has had some notable achievements. First, it has formulated a National Gender Policy aimed at providing policy makers, and other key actors in the development field, with references/guidelines for identifying and addressing gender concerns. Second, it has provided training skills in Gender Planning and Analysis for all stakeholders. To date the training has targeted Permanent Secretaries, Heads of Departments, District Technical Staff, Magistrates and State Attorneys. In addition five training manuals have been developed for the different target groups. Results of face-to-face interviews with twenty-five key civil servants testified that this training had made a change in the general outlook of these officials, towards gender and other forms of inequalities (Kwesiga, 1994). The capacity of mainstreaming civil service staff to address issues of gender and WID has increased as a result of this training. Experts provide technical support in government ministries and development agencies. Third, Development Plans for five sectors have been reviewed from a gender perspective. The MGLSD has initiated a programme aimed at making sector policies and plans gender responsive, and it has examined whether women and men participate and benefit equally from the development process.[8] Fourth, it has published extensive sex-disaggregated data which have been utilized by various stakeholders, including women's NGOs, to substantiate arguments on the disadvantaged position of women *vis-à-vis* that of men and to feed into the policy-making processes. Fifth, it has been able to insist on gender mainstreaming in national and district programmes and budgets. The Ministry works through planning mechanisms at national and district levels to support the integration of gender and develop indicators on how women and men are benefiting. This is very important under the new decentralized system. The initial project was aimed at covering all the forty-five districts for the period 1998/99. Sixth, it has been able to provide some legal education for women. A programme to sensitize women on their legal rights has been ongoing since 1993. The programme creates a community-based source of legal information and para-legal workers who assist women and children seeking redress. Finally, it has been effective in advocacy and awareness raising on gender issues. A lot of awareness has been created among the Ugandan public on gender issues. This is reflected in the level of discussion that goes on both in the media and other forums. Evidence of this is the public outcry at current attempts to marginalize the gender component of the restructured Ministry. For example, the Uganda Media Women's Association produced a special issue of its monthly newspaper, *The Other Voice*, on the topic in 1998. Several letters have appeared in the two main national daily newspapers (*The Monitor* and *The New Vision*). Similarly, voices have been raised about the omission of an Article on women and land ownership in the Land Act enacted by Parliament in July 1998. The visibility of the national machinery has stimulated interest in gender inequality and in some cases this has led to action.

The overall achievement of the existence of the Ministry is that it has *legitimized gender*. The gender variable is progressively forming part of public decisions. Appointments to posts can no longer ignore gender imbalance. When Chairs of government committees/agencies or commissions are instituted, for example, the Chair or Vice-Chair must be a woman. Other strong dividends are reflected in the various Articles in the new Constitution (1995) that provide a framework for gender-sensitive laws. The Ministry's work has strengthened and re-enforced other government affirmative action interventions, especially at the political level. Women councillors within the local government system are being trained and retrained, so that they can play an effective role in this field which they have only recently entered.

### Autonomy or mainstreaming? Dilemmas for a national machinery

The checklist against which the Ugandan case has been evaluated points to the dilemma that faces many national machineries for gender equality. Should they be separate entities or should they be 'mainstreamed'? As separate entities, such institutions can easily be isolated and marginalized. As part of the mainstream they tend to be too compartmentalized to be effective. Is there a middle way? Is there an ideal situation?

While a ministry sounds attractive and powerful, it has been demonstrated that without a clear mandate, adequate resources and political commitment to gender equality, a ministry for women cannot by itself be effective and sustainable. In addressing the economic pressures on the country, the Ugandan government will continue to restructure its organs from time to time as long as it adheres to the World Bank/International Monetary Fund restructuring conditionalities. Constraints in funding will persist. Any efforts at streamlining and reshaping within the current framework will not bring about long-term positive changes.

In the current situation, the machinery continues to be vulnerable. It is in danger of disappearing under the pretext of restructuring and the exaggerated reference to what women have achieved so far.

Although the MGLSD has helped to raise women's visibility and the public political sphere has recorded some success towards gender equality, it is important to note that the private sphere is still dominated by men. In any case, the need to ensure transformation at the individual level is still clear, whether those in charge are men or women. For even when official structures for the elimination of gender inequalities are put in place, it becomes imperative for the implementers to believe in them, for meaningful results.

Government ministries are under the charge of politicians whose turnover is high. This breeds discontinuity. A ministry, overloaded with so many councils and directorates, opens up more avenues for manipulation and mismanagement, and from reports gathered through interviews of staff by the author, this arrangement has enabled politicians to appoint relatives and friends who are not necessarily committed to gender equality to some key positions. There is evidence that efficiency is easily compromised under such circumstances. Because the MGLSD has many and varied responsibilities, at the time of writing the government had appointed six junior ministers (known as Ministers of State) to assist the senior Minister. This high number has inevitably led to disagreements and restrained working relations, as pointed out in several newspaper articles in 1999. Some new initiatives, such as the Equal Opportunities Commission, provided for under the new structure of the MGLSD are premature in that not enough ground work has been done to get them properly launched. In addition, these institutions are too expensive to run in relation to the meagre resources that are available to gender mainstreaming work. Without an extensive support in terms of legal education and gender-sensitive judicial structures, an Equal Opportunities Commission is likely to be ineffective.

One alternative to the Ministry, therefore, is to create a Commission for Gender Equality. Such Commissions already exist (Land, Education, Human Rights, Health and Communications) and others, including for Higher Education and Equal Opportunities, have been planned. A small Commission on Gender Equality, attached to a strong Office/Ministry (e.g. the President's Office or Ministry of Finance and Economic Planning) would possess the desired clout and have a manageable agenda. Such a Commission would be in a better position to raise its own funds. It would be able to phase its work and become more focused. This is because such a structure would be autonomous. It would face less bureaucratic bottlenecks. It would not be dealing with a conglomeration of units. It would consequently more easily reach its target groups through policy changes and data collection, analysis and dissemination, than is now the case, since the current units under the Ministry inhibit such developments. It would be more effectively run than a Ministry that will continue to be charged with multiple roles. The Head of the Commission and its members would have a specific term of office. They would have the opportunity to focus on a coherent agenda. I would argue that such a body would be able to avoid the limitations of bureaucracy and related bottlenecks that so often inhibit innovation.

The merits under this apparent 'isolationist' approach outweigh the disadvantages which are so glaring under the current Ministry structure that purports to 'mainstream' gender while in effect only scratching the surface. This arrangement would also eliminate the practice of creating a ministry where units do not fit within the wider Ministry framework, where any government unit that does not respond to the function of a particular Ministry is appended to the Ministry of Gender and Social Development. Although the Uganda Ministry is given a high-sounding title, it is not so well regarded within the political system, judging from the meagre financial support it receives.

## Beyond the national level

The Beijing Platform for Action and, particularly relevant to this case study, the African Platform for Action, have guidelines as to how to strengthen these machineries at international, subregional, regional and national levels. In addition, the following avenues can be further explored:

- *Strengthen networking among existing machineries at the various levels.* This is not a new strategy in itself but it has not been vigorously utilized. The South African visit to Uganda in 1996, and the questioning and exchange of ideas this involved, was a point of self-evaluation for the Ugandan machinery. Similarly, the UN Expert Group Meeting on National Machineries in Santiago, Chile in August 1998 provided a good opportunity to analyse and compare various machineries worldwide. In the case of Africa, the ECA and the Organization of African Unity can encourage regional networking. Subregional groupings such as the East African Cooperation Secretariat, the Southern African Development Community, and so on, could also work towards such goals.

- *Periodic research projects at different levels*, within national boundaries and beyond, will need to be carried out. This helps to 'actualize' issues and events on the ground and provide empirical evidence, which may lead to change.
- *Incentive schemes.* A specific fund for international recognition, either through competition for funding for successful innovations or prizes for 'good practice', may encourage ailing institutions to move ahead.
- *More effective ways in which donor funds can be utilized* without directing national agendas. Support should be for creating capacity and sustainability. For instance, training gender trainers for continuing transfer of women leaders would be money well spent.
- *Monitoring and evaluation* can be strengthened through periodic publications on progress made and constraints faced by the machineries, again reporting at different levels.

## Conclusion

National machineries for gender equality are still a necessity and governments should take some responsibility to ensure their success. Existing machineries that are considered to be declining need resuscitation. Experiences gathered from different contexts, such as in this volume, show that it is possible to work towards closing the identified loopholes.

The national machinery structure must have meaningful linkages with related organs of government, line ministries, local government structures and with publicly known channels of interaction. This is to avoid it being either too inclusive or too isolationist. A clear, mandated, well-structured and financially supported machinery should be able to outlive periodic restructuring and dependency on individual key actors. It can be likened to a well-thought-out system that operates efficiently, irrespective of the personalities involved. The expectation for such machineries is to transform women's lives, and without removing the obstacles on the way, such machineries can remain, but in name.

Also important is the contribution of the women's movement, on the local scene, through its varied tentacles — the executive, legislators, NGOs, CBOs, academicians and researchers, as well as individuals within these institutions. Pressure groups have an important role to play, which is not being adequately tapped in the case of Uganda. As this study emphasizes, the central issue of whether national machineries for gender equality should be separate entities or be mainstreamed within the government mechanism can be resolved according to national conditions. But until there is an effective political voice, either channel will not transform society in favour of women. The presence of gender-sensitive women and men in decision-making positions in various fields — political, civil service, religious institutions, local government, academic or the wider civil society — collectively contribute to this essential voice. This, in the end, can make effective and efficient either form of women's machinery. Signs of this development are beginning to appear in Uganda, through the mass media, publications, speeches of public figures and informal everyday conversation.

## Notes

1 The World Bank (1989c) report on the economic contribution of women in Kenya illustrates how well the Kenyan women became organized in the 1980s to form numerous women's groups. Even the large numbers of women who attended the 1985 UN World Conference to Review and Appraise the Achievements of the United Nations Decade for Women: Equality, Development and Peace in Nairobi from Kenya and Tanzania (compared with only the official delegation in Uganda) was evidence of better mobilization in those countries at the time. The women's networks formed in Kenya and Tanzania then, such as the African Women's Development and Communications Network, based in Nairobi, showed that here, women had started looking beyond national constituencies.

2 The NRM is the current ruling body. It came to power in 1986 after waging a five-year guerrilla war. The name refers to its revolutionary stand, when it was formed, to resist 'bad' government. Under the 'Movement' type of government, leaders are elected on the basis of individual

merit. The rationale for this 'no political party' system was to eliminate sectarianism created by political parties and reflected in tribe, religion and region, as opposed to 'issues' of development. Ugandans were given the chance to decide through referendum (2000), whether and when political parties could be reactivated. The Movement system was retained.

3 The NGP document outlines the following role for the MGLSD:

1 To ensure that the national development process is gender sensitive. This means that the national machinery plays a coordinating and facilitating role and functions as a catalyst in support of all relevant players for gender-sensitive development planning.

2 To ensure that all policy formulation and reviews, action plans and other major national planning exercises apply a gender-sensitive planning approach.

3 To liaise with other actors in identifying and drawing attention to key gender concerns and related needs, for example property ownership, land tenure, credit and legal rights, as well as relevant options for addressing them, such as constitutional guarantees, law reform and literacy campaigns. The national machinery, together with other actors, plays an advocacy role in the promotion of gender equality.

4 To provide technical guidance and back-up support to other institutions. This shall include the promotion of gender analysis and planning skills among all relevant sections of society, in order to build their capacity to identify, analyse and implement gender-sensitive programme interventions.

5 To liaise with relevant agencies and coordinate the collection and dissemination of sex-disaggregated data necessary for national development planning.

6 To promote social mobilization for the purpose of creating gender awareness, and thus foster positive attitudinal and behavioural changes necessary for the establishment and maintenance of gender equality. The national machinery, together with other actors, plays an advocacy role in this regard.

7 In liaison with other key actors, to monitor the progress made towards achieving gender-sensitive national development targets.

4 The Directorate for Gender specifies its role under the following units (source: Ministry of Gender internal chart):

1 Department of Gender
   • ensures mainstreaming of gender;
   • policy reviews/formulation;
   • gender statistics/Research;
   • gender sensitization.

2 Legal Department
   • watchdog on laws, bills;
   • legal research;
   • legal education;
   • legal advice.

3 Department of Women's Programmes
   • promotion of women's status;
   • designing programmes for women;
   • training on all aspects, especially skills development;
   • literacy programmes for women;
   • income generation activities.

4 Women's Councils
   • autonomous body;
   • mobilize women into unified body for developmental purposes.

5 Local councils/committees are socio-political institutions. Every community is organized into a council along the lines of local government, ascending the hierarchy through village, parish, sub-county, county and district levels. These are usually designated LC I, LC II, LC III, LC IV and LC V, respectively. At the village level, members elect an Executive Committee comprising a Chairperson, Vice-Chairperson, Secretary of the Committee, and Secretaries for Information, Security, Mass Mobilization, Youth and Women. Up to 1995, these were known as Resistance Councils, having been devised by the NRM during the guerrilla war period.

6 For example, in the Christmas period of 1997 women's groups get together to publicize and protest against the handling of the case of a woman who was allegedly murdered by her husband. At the cremation, Ministry officials could not join other women in making protest statements or clarifying the Ministry's, stand because they had not been sanctioned by their Permanent Secretary.

7 For example, there are quite a number of national women's NGOs that would enhance the work of the Ministry, through closer collaborative efforts, than has been the case hitherto. The Uganda Women Lawyers' Association, the Uganda Women's Finance and Credit Trust and Action for Development (a multi-issues women's rights organization) could all be effectively utilized. The Uganda Women's Network was very active on women and land rights in relation to the 1998 Land Act, which is fully acceptable to women. Others could enrich the Ministry from an international point of view, such as Akina Mama wa Afrika's Leadership Institute or the Uganda Chapter of the Council for the Economic Empowerment of Women in Africa, based in Kampala. There are also other non-women-specific NGOs, such as the Development Network of Voluntary Associations in Uganda, the Human Rights Network and several others.

8 The Ministries include Education, Agriculture, Animal Husbandry and Fisheries, Trade and Industry, Marketing Cooperatives, and Cooperatives, and Local Government. This is ongoing for the Ministry of Health. MGLSD staff systematically go through the Plans of other Ministries with their key staff, making a gender analysis and thereby producing better Plans. One positive outcome of this process is the current policy of 50 per cent admission of girls to agricultural colleges. In the past, admission was on the basis of merit only, and since there are more qualified boys than girls, most training for agricultural extension workers benefited boys. This policy, it is hoped, will respond more to farmers' needs, the majority of whom are women.

# 11

# The National Commission for Women: the Indian experience

## SHIRIN M. RAI

### Introduction

In this chapter I will examine the brief history of the National Commission for Women in India that was set up in 1990. First, I will provide a background to the political system within which the Commission functions. I will then examine the structure and functions of the Commission itself. I will point to the strengths and weaknesses of the Commission in the context of the politics of the country, as well as the parameters within which it functions. This analysis is based primarily on interviews with Commission members that I undertook in 1994 and 1997. I will conclude by raising some issues for the long-term functioning and efficacy of the Commission.

### The political context

> *Women's issues are the lowest priority for any government.*
> National Commission for Women Chairperson, Dr Mohini Giri
> (*The Economic Times of India*, New Delhi, 12 July 1998).

#### The political system in India

India is a bicameral parliamentary democracy. The lower house is called the Lok Sabha (Peoples' Assembly) and has 545 members. The upper house is called the Rajya Sabha (States' Assembly) with 250 members. Representatives are chosen on the basis of first past the post by single-member constituencies for the lower house and proportional

representation by state assemblies for the upper. In 1991
women formed 5.2 per cent of the membership of the Lok
Sabha and 9.8 per cent of the membership of the Rajya
Sabha (Swarup et al., 1994:362). This was lower than the
preceding Parliament of 1989. Further, 'it can be safely pre-
sumed that membership of women in [political] parties does
not exceed 10 to 12 per cent of their total membership'
(Department of Women and Child Development, 1988:157).

India has had a strong multi-party political system since
its inception in 1947. There was a short period (1975–77)
during the national Emergency declared by Mrs Gandhi
when civil and political rights were suspended. Other than
this, political parties have continued to play an important
role in mobilizing and articulating interests and representing these in the political sphere. While providing political
stability and a degree of accountability through elections,
such strong party systems tend to marginalize issue-based
politics or to expropriate movements that are based on sin-
gular issues. The women's movement in India has had to
confront this issue (Centre for Women's Development Studies (CWDS), 1994, 1995). In particular, women's groups face
this issue because many mass organizations of women are
affiliated to particular political parties, providing them with
assured funding and membership, but also creating political competition and constraints in forming alliances with
other women's organizations.[1]

Another feature of this multi-party system in India is
that while the parties have dominated politics, they have
themselves largely remained organizationally weak and
dependent on local elites (Bjorkman, 1987).[2] The parties
have therefore suffered both in terms of their transparency
in mediating interests within the organizations and in their
capacity to deliver policies as a result of this dependence.
Local elites have had important inputs into policy formula-
tions, and have also been in a position to subvert the
implementation of policies adverse to their interests.
Weak party organizations have also led to the emergence of
dominant party leaders who have been able to impose their
vision of politics on the party. In particular, the Nehru/
Gandhi family was able to provide the leadership of the
Congress Party — the largest national political party —
until the early 1990s. Individual leaders have therefore had

an important role in policy making and in changing established policy. All these factors have played a role in the state addressing women's issues in particular ways.

In the 1990s there was a significant fracturing of the party system.[3] Now there are many political parties based on ascriptive identities. There are others that have primarily a regional political entity. These small political parties have, however, become important players in the national political system because of the erosion of the dominant party system that had provided India with political stability under the Congress Party. Coalition politics is now accepted as the dominant form of politics. Further, the 1990s also saw the political rise of the Bhartiya Janata Party (BJP) within the democratic system. The Party, which has close links with the Rashtriya Swayam Sewak Sangh, a militia-type organization mobilizing through a Hindu fundamentalist discourse, often directed against minority groups such as Muslims and more recently Christians, is now in government as the dominant partner of a coalition. This has implications for the setting up and functioning of organizations such as the National Commission for Women.

In India, the relative stability of the political system has allowed for a significant political space to emerge where women have been able to organize in their various interests. However, the current coalition politics is posing new challenges to women's groups and organizations. So, I would argue, the changing parameters of particular political systems are important to the functioning of public organizations; as are the discourses of legitimacy that the state institutions employ. The first is important to spaces available for the mobilization of women and to the contesting of dominant discourses of gendered power. The second is critical to the nature of negotiations that may or may not accrue between state institutions and women's struggles within a given political context.

## Women's movements

Women have always been active in Indian political life though their visibility and autonomy have varied from one historical phase to another.[4] Women have participated at all levels of public life, from local to national level, and engaged in both non-violent and violent struggles. They have been accepted in public life once they have entered it, both because of the iconography of motherhood — *Bharat Maia* (Mother India) — and because participation in all forms of public life from social service for the disabled or underprivileged, to more conventional political activism, has been described as 'women's role in public life' and somehow in tune with their maternal character. Historically, women have been mobilized in political movements and by political parties in India. While women have provided legitimacy to these movements and organizations, their own gains have been less obvious. The number of women, for example, that have actually been able to participate in public life has been extremely limited. Gender has not been the only variable affecting women's participation in politics; their access to the public sphere has depended on many factors, class, religion and caste being the most important. These categories of difference have, however, not affected their exclusion from public political life. In no social category have women been more able to participate in political life than men.

Women's movements[5] in independent India made significant gains through the 1970s and 1980s. We can chart the growth of women's movements through two periods in Indian politics. The 1970s saw the rise and growth of the civil liberties movement in India in the aftermath of the crisis of the state that led to the imposition of national Emergency in 1975 by Prime Minister Indira Gandhi. The 1980s and 1990s witnessed the mushrooming of women's organizations and movements, as well as the rise of fundamentalism in Indian politics, which have framed the advance of women's causes. The Indian women's movements have pressed for the expanding rights of women as citizens. However, the tension between citizenship as an individual right and the universal appeal of the rights discourse has been carried into the women's movement — women have fought for full citizenship rights but this has made them invisible as women with particular interests, leading to a more ambivalent positioning of women on the political terrain than they had expected (Agnihotri and Mazumdar, 1995:1869). The women's movement has also been able to draw upon the strength of women's movements in other parts of the world, through exchange of ideas, participation in debates and the successful lobbying of international social institutions such as the United Nations (UN). In particular, the activities encouraged by the Women's Conferences sponsored by the UN have helped women's groups successfully to place women's issues on the national political agenda.

## Structures and agents in organizations

As in most countries, political institutions in India have shown a clear male bias in their accessibility and functioning, as well as in the values upon which they rest. The sexual division of labour that exists in society forms the structural basis upon which the exclusion of women is legitimized, or at least accepted. However, the strength of women's movements has elicited responses from state institutions. Most of these responses have been 'adding on' strategies whereby women and women's groups have been added on to existing institutional arrangements.

The demand for greater representation of women in political institutions in India was not taken up in a systematic way until the setting up of the Committee on the Status of Women in India (CSWI), which published its report in 1974. Before this time the focus of the growing women's movement had been on the socio-economic position of women in India, which was regarded as the primary cause of the political marginalization of women. While the women's movement engaged with the project of redefining politics by imbuing it with feminist analysis based on the dictum 'the personal is political', this project focused largely on the improvement of access to participation in this redefined politics (CWDS, 1994:19–25). Most of the groups involved in the women's movement in the 1970s were urban based, and their members were drawn from the educated middle class and from the left of the political spectrum (Kumar, 1989). The women's movement spanned a whole range of issues — civil liberties, consumer action, corruption and workplace rights. The CSWI report, while noting the linkages between the socio-economic marginalization and the political under-representation of women, also suggested that women's representation needed to be increased, especially at the grassroots level through a policy of reservation of seats for women (Government of India, 1974).

The question of political under-representation of women in political institutions did not preoccupy most women's groups during the 1970s and much of the 1980s. The women's movement focused on issues of violence and rape, dowry and sex selection of and the extension of equal opportunities, and their greater inclusion into the economic sphere through the extension of property and inheritance rights for women. In 1988, the National Perspective Plan for Women again focused on political representation of women and suggested that a 30 per cent quota for women be introduced at all levels of elective bodies. Most left-wing women's groups saw this as a strategy of co-option of the gender issue into male-stream politics (CWDS, 1994:21).

However, this view of co-optive politics has been changing. The focus now is on the ways in which institutional politics can be harnessed to expanding possibilities for women (CWDS, 1994). There is a recognition that the 'politics of presence' (Phillips, 1995) matters — that the very presence of women in male-biased institutions disturbs the settled legitimacy of these institutions. There is also the recognition of the difference that individual women committed to changing gender relations can make in the policy-making bodies; that the structural constraints though important are not immutable. Individual agents in organizations may or may not share organizational beliefs; may or may not challenge existing hegemonic practices and ideologies. The question of agency in this context remains more open, and that of structure more contested.

## The National Commission for Women

The momentum of the women's movements and the various Commissions set up to assess the role of women in Indian public life led to the establishment of the National Commission for Women in 1990. The Commission is the result of pressure put upon government by feminist and women's movements for such an organization, which would press for women's interests to be represented in government policy. It is not a ministry of government. It is also not a think-tank in the conventional sense: 'Think-tanks are an organizational expression of the blending of ideas, politics and policy *outside* formal political arenas' (Stone, 1996:2). Yet its members are appointed by the Prime Minister and it was set up to fulfil one of the purposes of think-tanks: to move ideas into politics.

## Setting up the Commission

The setting up of the Commission was a governmental response to the National Perspective Plan for Women. This was done after wide consultation with women's non-governmental organizations (NGOs) and movements, women political representatives, feminist lobbyists and women party members. Most women's groups were in favour of such a Commission, which provided legitimacy for the Commission. There were several reasons for this support. The Indian women's movements had grown considerably in the 1970s and 1980s, bringing a new sense of confidence in making demands upon the political establishment. Second, after twenty years of mobilization, the need for an institutional presence of women in political organizations had become clear; policy formulation and implementation needed to be made gender sensitive. Feminist academics and activists felt able to provide the necessary training on gender issues. The marginalization of women's issues in political parties became a priority. Finally, though the Indian women's groups had largely functioned at the level of social mobilization, there had been a significant group of activists who had argued that an engagement with the state was inevitable in a country such as India where many civil society groups were deeply conservative. Policy change at the top of the political system seemed important to challenge these groups.[6]

At the level of government, support for the move to set up such an organization came from the Prime Minister, Rajiv Gandhi. I have commented above about the importance of individual leaders in addressing women's issues in India. While Mrs Gandhi had felt unable to take up women's issues because she was a woman, Rajiv Gandhi saw himself as a modern, young leader bringing India in line with other countries on this issue (Rai, 1995). Individual leaders can thus become important in the successful start of institutional initiatives.

At the level of political parties, gender issues were also difficult to ignore. This was for two reasons. First, the women's movements had been successful in politicizing gender. Second, as the political parties multiplied, and coalition politics emerged, new constituencies were needed to be mobilized. Women were the obvious targets for political parties. They were numerous and under-represented in the political system. Because of their limited participation in the political processes, most women were not already committed to voting for or supporting a particular party. Speaking for them, then, made political sense in political party terms.

*The structure of the Commission*

The Commission is a statutory body, which was created through parliamentary legislation in January 1992 under the National Commission for Women Act, 1990 (Act No. 20 of 1990 of Government of India) (www.nationalcommissionforwomen.org/about_ncw/about_ncw.html).

The National Commission for Women in India is a cross-party consultative body on women's interests. It includes women from different backgrounds — those who have been active in the women's movements, party women and bureaucrats. It is a permanent Commission with a Chair and a working committee of five members. It has a staff of thirty-six. The Committee is representative of different regions and operates the caste/tribe-based quotas (22.4 per cent) mandatory in government institutions, and therefore it must include at least one member from among persons belonging to the 'Scheduled Castes and Scheduled Tribes respectively'.[7] The Commission has a 'Member-Secretary' nominated by central government who is the administrator of the Commission. The committee has an operational life of three years.[8] The 'parent ministry' of the Commission is the Ministry for Women and Child Development but the Commission liaises closely with other ministries too, depending upon the intervention in policy that it decides to make. The Chair of the committee does not have a Cabinet post, but can be asked by the Cabinet to present the Commission's views on particular issues.

The resources at the disposal of the Commission are meagre. Its starting-up budget was only Rs 1.25 million.[9]

The Commission can bid for individual projects, but it has to compete with other organizations for this. Given its remit as a national advisory organization, this level of resourcing is a significant hindrance to its functioning.

### The Commission's functions

The Commission's mandate is 'to review the Constitutional and legal safeguards for women, recommend remedial legislative measures, facilitate redressal of grievances and advise the Government on all policy matters affecting women' (www.nationalcommissionforwomen.org/about_ncw/about_ncw.html). In the words of its founding Chair, Jayanthi Patnaik, its functions include: 'to review, investigate, examine and recommend'.[10] The Commission investigates matters pertaining to legal safeguards provided for women and recommends amendments; it takes up with the appropriate authorities/ministries cases involving violation of the legal provisions relating to women; and participates in the planning process of socio-economic development of women and evaluates the progress made. The Commission carries out its function at different levels. It sets up committees to investigate particular issues that are urgent or policy related. So, for example, it set up a committee to investigate the rising numbers of female infanticides in the state (province) of Tamil Nadu in 1992. Such a committee would be chaired by the Commission member responsible for the particular area but would be staffed by the local contacts of the Commission. This means that the availability of trained local staff becomes an important issue. This might be affected by the strength of the women's movement in that region and the location of the committee — rural or urban, levels of poverty and education. The poorer the training of the local staff, the more likely it is that either the investigation would be hampered by local patriarchal interests or that there would be 'outsiders' needed to carry out such an investigation, raising its own issues of legitimacy. Commission members were agreed that local mobilization of opinion was the most effective way of furthering the gender agenda, but were also conscious of the lack of infrastructure that the Commission itself could provide.[11]

The Commission presents its findings on particular issues to the appropriate level of government/ministry.

Lobbying individual political leaders for a change in policy is an important part of the Commission's work. Here the question of the accessibility of particular leaders and the commitment of the leader to the agenda of gender equality become important. The lines of communication that the Chair of the Commission is able to establish (or not) with influential political leaders is also important. In this context, the party system becomes relevant. If the Chair is close to the ruling party (the founding Chair was a Congress MP), it is easier for her to establish good working relations with various ministries.

The advisory role of the Commission is strengthened through the mechanism of accountability. Once the Commission recommends changes to existing or new policy, the relevant ministry has to explain to the Commission, to the Cabinet and to Parliament why it has not followed the Commission's recommendations. However, individual ministries do not *have* to consult the Commission; the Commission has to be proactive in monitoring policy making and in identifying areas in which it wants to intercede. This means that, given the poor resourcing of the Commission, its members are unable to cover all the relevant areas that need attention. However, it is possible for the Commission to involve other agencies — women's studies centres, NGOs and grassroots organizations — in its work in order to extend its reach. This is an area that needs greater consideration — how might various civil society groups be brought into the work of the Commission and on what bases? What are the linkages that need to be established and with which organizations? This is not an easy task as it involves negotiating a delicate balance between political activism and a close engagement with the state. I will return to this issue later.

One of the important functions of the Commission is dissemination of information, ideas and good practice. It is involved in publicizing key governmental decisions affecting women, promoting its views about women's status and lobbying media executives regarding the depiction of women in films, telefilms and teleplays. As there is a significant sector of state media in television and radio, the Commission has direct access to it and greater influence in that sector than in the private media sector. It has developed short films on issues of women's social status that the national state television service (Doordarshan) uses as 'fillers'. Again, the Commission is unable to do more than try and 'persuade' the media executive of its cause; it is unable to enforce its preferences through any legislative obligation upon the media.

Another way of both disseminating and examining issues relevant to women in society is organizing and participating in seminars and workshops at different levels. The Commission members do this depending on their area of interests and responsibilities. At these forums the Commission members are able to build networks, and promote an exchange of ideas with different groups and sectors. The Commission has organized successful seminars on diverse issues, such as legal and legislative initiatives, the setting up of micro-enterprises and the mobilization of women, women in the unorganized labour market, women in urban slums and violence against women. Many seminars were organized in 1994 in preparation for the Beijing Fourth World Conference on Women.

At the political level, the Commission can also be involved in new initiatives. One such initiative was taken by the Commission in the run-up to the 1997 elections. The Commission proposed fielding a 'women's candidate' from the prestigious New Delhi constituency. This was to be symbolic of the cross-party support for women's increased representation in the Parliament of the country. As such, political parties were asked not to contest the 'women's candidate' in this constituency. Though most feminist groups and political parties supported this initiative initially (the candidate was selected and her name announced at this stage) this support soon fractured. The Commission was accused of naiveté on the one hand and gimmickry on the other. The 'women's candidate' had to withdraw from the contest.

## Supports and constraints

Given its remit, structure and resourcing, the Commission has had to have strategies of making do, of stretching resources, of making networks, of focusing on particular issues. In this section I will discuss some issues arising in its functioning.

*From the local to the global*

International initiatives such as the UN World Conferences on women provide a great impetus to organizations such as the Commission. The fact that the Indian state is a signatory to the Convention on the Elimination of All Forms of Discrimination against Women meant that participation in the Beijing Conference provided a considerable opportunity to women's groups in general and the Commission in particular to organize for that participation with some financial support from the government. This was a window of opportunity of making use of state resources for furthering their own interests, such as organizing seminars and workshops. In India there was a tremendous activity among the NGO sector in preparation for the Conference, and the draft of the Beijing Declaration and Platform for Action was extensively discussed at different levels of organization and activism. While the Commission was able to bring together many of the academic and governmental actors, the fact that there was an NGO forum at the Beijing Fourth World Conference on Women meant that there was a great deal of discussion and activities that took place at the civil society level, to which the Commission had only limited access.

At the national level, the Commission has had constantly to renegotiate with the government as one coalition after another has come into power. In this context, the stability of government is an issue. The urgency that political parties feel in the task of keeping the coalition together means that issues that are seen as less immediately relevant to that task take a back seat. Further, the discussion on women's social status in India has crystallized into a nationwide debate about the quotas for women in Parliament. In this debate, the Commission has been able to contribute in only a limited way. Various political parties have divergent views on this policy change, and the putting together of coalitions in government has meant that negotiations over the quotas have not gone smoothly.

In terms of the Commission's support at the level of civil society, the picture is also complex. The NGO sector is credited by the Commission members as its strongest ally and support.[12] I have already mentioned that the Commission was set up with the support of a wide cross-section of women's groups and NGOs. These groups provide the Commission with support in different ways — through participation in its programmes, seminars, workshops and investigations; but also through the legitimacy that they provide. The Commission could not have been effective at any level if the civil society groups engaged in feminist activism had not supported its establishment. However, in India's highly politicized context women's groups are engaged in different levels of political activism. Some are closely affiliated to political parties; others are sceptical of governmental funding of women's groups; and still others are suspicious of international funding for some NGOs. So while some NGOs are willing to participate in the Commission's work, others keep away for the fear of conflict of interest with their party or of co-optation into the dominant patriarchal political system.

This multi-layered political situation means that the Commission is caught up in negotiating its position among the many different positions and pressures that it encounters. So, for example, one of the committee members of the first committee left the Commission very soon after joining it because as a member of the Communist Party she felt strongly that the Commission was letting itself be co-opted to serve the Congress government's agendas (Rai, 1997). Over a period of six years of its functioning, women's groups on the left have in large part created a distance from the Commission.[13] It is being cast as an elitist, bureaucratic organization; a pawn in the hands of various governments. This view is supported in part by the system of appointment of the Commission members, which is highly politicized and does not necessarily have regard to the links of the members with women's and feminist groups. The rise of Hindu fundamentalism in the BJP means that the executive of the Commission has been under pressure from the government in terms of changing personnel to suit the current government. The influence of the Commission over the current government led by the BJP is also minimal, even though the BJP is attempting to mobilize women into politics on its own radical-conservative political programme and is supporting the 33 per cent quota for women in legislative bodies.

## Moving forward

The above picture of the Commission tells a complex story of a very young organization. The overall message is that of pessimism — the Commission, which started with a lot of good will, has been unable to sustain that support within the civil society organizations; it has also been marginalized within the party political system. Some of the constraints faced by the Commission have been structural — poor resourcing, for example. Others could be addressed but would require a radical rethinking of the Commission's relationship with the state. In this concluding section I examine the options before the Commission in the light of the consensus that emerged on national machineries at the Beijing Fourth World Conference on Women in 1995.

### National machineries in the Beijing Platform for Action

In its recommendations on national machineries for women, the Beijing Platform for Action suggested the following:
1 Location at the highest possible level in government.
2 Institutional mechanisms or processes that facilitate, as appropriate, decentralized planning, implementation and monitoring with a view to involving NGOs and community organizations from the grassroots upwards.
3 Sufficient resources in terms of budget and professional capacity.
4 Opportunity to influence development of all government policies (PfA, H: paragraph 203).
The Platform for Action further enjoins on national machineries to:
1 facilitate the formulation and implementation of government policies . . . develop appropriate strategies and methodologies, and promote coordination and cooperation within the central government in order to ensure mainstreaming of a gender perspective;
2 promote and establish cooperative relationships with relevant branches of governments . . . and all other actors of civil society;

3 undertake activities focusing on legal reform;
4 promote the increased participation of women as both active agents and beneficiaries of the development process;
5 establish direct links with national, regional and international bodies dealing with the advancement of women;
6 provide training and advisory assistance to government agencies (PfA, H: paragraph 208).

In the following section I examine whether the Commission fulfils these criteria. I then analyse whether these criteria can be met by *any* national machinery for women. I will suggest that we need to rethink what national machineries can achieve realistically and efficiently.

### The Commission through UN criteria

First, the Commission is not located at the highest political level. Its Chair is not a member of government. As the case of the National Service for Women in Chile suggests, membership of Cabinet is not, by itself, a bulwark against marginalization.

Second, the Commission does monitor women's social position in different ways; it does involve NGOs, community organizations, academics and others of its epistemic community in information gathering and dissemination. The issue here is that in a highly party-centred political system such as India's, its choice of partners becomes an issue for its legitimacy. Which NGOs? Which academics? Which leaders of which parties? All these become part of the evaluation of the Commission through deeply tinted party political lenses.

Third, the resourcing of the Commission is poor and, as the examples from different countries show, when national governments need to curtail spending, women's organizations such as the Commission are prime targets for funding cuts (see Goetz and Kwesiga, chapters 3 and 10 of this volume).

Fourth, the opportunity to influence government policy is officially there — that is the Commission's *raison d'être*. However, the Commission has been only partially successful in this for the reasons outlined above.

Fifth, the Commission has tried to review, investigate and examine government policy at different levels — national and provincial. However, it has had limited success in its advocacy function due to the question of political will of governments and leaders, poor resourcing and its weak political position.

Sixth, the Commission has undertaken investigations into legal policy and practice in cooperation with, for example, the National Law School in Bangalore. It has lobbied for some changes in the way the issue of violence against women is dealt with in courts. Its function has, however, mainly been to try and persuade the legal establishment to change. It has had no alternative to this strategy. No major review of the legal procedures has been undertaken as a result of the Commission's advocacy.

Finally, the Commission has established links with regional and international bodies engaged in lobbying for the advancement of women. However, there has been little progress in terms of joint programmes. In the context of the political situation in the sub-continent, in particular the relations between India and Pakistan, regional cooperation is difficult to organize, even though such cooperation would, arguably, be most productive in terms of exchange of ideas and developing new strategies for furthering women's issues.

### Some unresolved issues

Having reflected upon the experience of the National Commission for Women in India, I suggest that the following issues need further thought and research in order to make national machineries for women's equality more effective. First, addressing the issue of legitimacy — the national machinery should be an autonomous body. It could have core funding from the government but should be actively encouraged to look for funding from other sources, such as international social organizations, charitable trusts and even private funding.

Second, defining the remit of the machineries — a focus on mainstreaming gender in public policy would involve considerable lobbying and negotiating skills. To do this effectively, a national machinery could be outreaching to other organizations, networks and lobbying groups rather than getting involved in the process of implementing policies itself (DAW, 1998). It could then be a conduit between civil society organizations and the government.

Third, dealing with political parties — an autonomous identity would allow the Commission greater flexibility in dealing with political parties, as the direct link between the Commission Chair and the ruling political party will be weaker. Also, stronger links with civil society groups would mean that the influence of political parties might be diluted. NGOs and women's groups could be more effectively mobilized to point out the limited nature of cross-party initiatives on women and the common policy bases being camouflaged by party-based rhetoric.

Fourth, there is an obvious case for increasing the funding of such machineries. The focusing of its resources on lobbying the government could also allow for better usage of existing funding, and seeking autonomous funding to enhance it.

Fifth, the issue of location within government — close links with government can be an advantage, but also a serious disadvantage.

Finally, networking — strengthening links with regional and international organizations — can be helpful but would need to be carefully thought through, given the political context in South Asia. Identifying particular networks for particular lobbying initiatives would allow a more focused reach and avoid the charge of 'general foreign junkets' that is laid at the door of many outward-looking semi-official organizations.

*The criteria through the Commission's experience*

In the concluding section, I will reflect upon the criteria set out for national machineries in the Platform for Action and suggest that a second look at these may prompt some thought about the feasibility as well as legitimacy of these machineries. As one reads through the list of functions a national body such as the Commission is supposed to perform according to the Platform for Action, one is struck by how much we expect women to achieve with minimal resources. I wonder if, with the best will in the world, any organization can deliver all that is being asked for in this document. Most governments do not have the best will in the world on the issue of mainstreaming gender. It is an omission to set up expectations without taking on board this central fact. In *A Brief Critique from the All India*

*Democratic Women's Association* of the Platform for Action, it is noted that the draft of section H., dealing with national machineries, does not mention, but should:

> 1) establishment of *autonomous* bodies to monitor Government policies and make recommendations *binding* for the Government which if it does not accept, it will have to submit explanations to elected legislatures; 2) the crucial question of political will; 3) affirmative action to narrow the gender gap in all important spheres. (All India Democratic Women's Association, 1995:12)

Overloading the agenda of national machineries also leads to an enhanced sense of failure of such machineries. No organization, however well resourced, can be asked to carry such a burden of expectation and not be found wanting. The basis of this overloading can be explained in part by what precedes the section on national machineries in the Platform for Action. In the section of 'Women in Power and Decision-Making' it is explicitly stated that: 'Women's equal participation in decision-making is not only a demand for simple justice or democracy but can also be seen as a necessary condition for women's interests to be taken into account' (PfA, G: paragraph 183). There is now a growing body of feminist literature which is problematizing this assumption about a direct co-relation between women's participation in politics and the representation of women's interests (see Coole, 1997; Fraser, 1997; Young, 1997; Hoskyns and Rai, 1998). This issue of representation of interests is a vexed one. Whose interests are being represented by the increased participation of women in political institutions? Who can and will represent these interests? What is the process of interest aggregation? What is gained and what is lost in this process? Can disaggregated interests be represented at all? What are the intersections between various interests and between social variables that affect any aggregation of interests? This is, perhaps, not the place to discuss such issues. However, these questions raise important issues for national machineries such as the National Commission for Women in two ways.

The first is that of legitimacy. If the Commission is to maintain its networks in civil society it needs to demonstrate its autonomy from the dominant political forces.

Without addressing the question of its autonomy through its Constitution, membership, networks and working strategies, charges of elitism and co-optation will be difficult to avoid. The second issue is that of interest aggregation — how does the Commission (or any such national machinery) reach a view on what constitutes a convergence of women's interests which the Commission can then try to mainstream? The different interests of class and, in the current political situation in India, of caste and religion, make for different interests of women such that the assumptions of women's interests become highly problematic. Also, the different social profiles of women mean that the urgency given to policy formulation in one area might not meet the needs of another group of women. Policy implementation makes these issues of difference even more prominent. Reviewing policy then becomes a highly politically sensitive task.

In conclusion, however, I would suggest that the work of the Commission provides a useful focal point not only to address specific policy issues but also to allow us to raise the broader issues of differences among women. It is through the democratization of discussion, agenda setting, monitoring and reviewing of its programme that the Commission can build a legitimate profile for itself and, its work, as well as acting as a forum for discussion of wider social issues affecting gender relations in India.

## Notes

1 For example, the All India Women's Conference is affiliated to the Congress Party, the All India Women's Federation to the Communist Party of India, and the All India Democratic Women's Association to the Communist Party of India (Marxist).

2 The exceptions are the two Communist Parties, which are highly structured and disciplined and cadre based.

3 The first challenge to the Congress Party's domination of Indian politics came in the wake of the Emergency, when Mrs Gandhi lost the elections to a coalition of Opposition parties brought together under the umbrella of the Janata Party. The Communist Party of India (Marxist) and the BJP supported this coalition.

4 Women were active in the nationalist movement in both the Congress-led non-violent struggle and also in the militant armed struggles.

5 I use the term 'women's movements' here as a shorthand for all the various groups of women and feminists that are engaged in political and social life and have as their central concerns justice and equality for women. I do not include in this group any right-wing women's groups whose concerns are with cultural authenticity.

6 Interview with Dr Vina Mazumdar, CWDS, January 1998.

7 The Indian Constitution provides for population-based quotas for the lowest castes and tribes under its 9th Schedule — hence the 'Scheduled Castes and Tribes' category. This quota is operative at every level of educational and professional organizations run by any governmental agency. In 1993, a quota of 33 per cent was instituted for women in the village and township level government under the 73rd Amendment to the Constitution. Currently, a Bill extending this quota to women in the provincial assemblies and the national Parliament is being discussed.

8 The First Commission was constituted on 31 January 1992 with Mrs Jayanti Patnaik as the Chairperson. The Second Commission was constituted in July 1995 with Dr (Mrs) Mohini Giri as the Chairperson. The Third Commission has been constituted and the government has nominated Mrs Vibha Parthasarathy as the Chairperson (www.nationalcommissionforwomen.org/about_ncw/about_ncw.html).

9 The current exchange rate between the British Pound and Indian Rupee is 1:70.

10 Interview with Jayanthi Patnaik, Chair of the Commission, January 1994. Constitutionally it is mandated to: 'a. investigate and examine all matters relating to the safeguards provided for women under the Constitution and other laws; b. present to the Central Government, annually and at such other times as the Commission may deem fit, reports upon the working of those safeguard; c. make in such reports recommendations for the effective implementation of those safeguards for the improving the conditions of women by the Union or any state; d. review, from time to time, the existing provisions of the Constitution and other laws affecting women and recommend amendments thereto so as to suggest remedial legislative measures to meet any lacunae, inadequacies or shortcomings in such legislation; e. take up cases of violation of the provisions of the Constitution and of other laws relating to women with the appropriate authorities; f. look into complaints and take *suo moto* notice of matters relating to: — i. deprivation of women's rights; ii. non-implementation of laws enacted to provide protection to women and also to achieve the objective of equality and development; iii. non-compliance of policy decisions, guidelines or instructions . . . ; g. call for special studies or investigations into specific problems or situations . . . ; h. undertake promotional and educational research . . . i. participate and advise on the planning process . . . j. evaluate the progress of the development of women under the Union and any State; l. fund litigation involving issues affecting a large body of women; m. make periodical reports to the Government; n. any other matter which may be referred to it by Central Government' (www.nationalcommissionforwomen.org/about_ncw/about_ncw.html).

11 Interviews at the Commission offices in New Delhi, January 1994.

12 Interview with Padma Seth, committee member, January 1994.

13 Interviews at CWDS, New Delhi, January 1998.

# 12

# The life and times of women's policy machinery in Australia[1]

MARIAN SAWER

Historically in Australia women have been policy shapers as well as policy takers and have called on the state to promote social reform and equal opportunity. This was the path that led to the appearance of 'femocrats' in government in the 1970s and 1980s, with a mandate to achieve more gender equality policy outcomes. Australia became well known for its femocrats, a term that Australia gave the world, and for their innovations in governance. However, at the same time another group was increasing its policy influence — the economic rationalists, who believed that intervention in the market to promote equity or other social goals was counter-productive.

This resurgence of market liberalism preceded, but was reinforced by, the election of conservative governments in the 1990s. To varying degrees these governments had engaged in their election campaigns in populist discourse concerning the excessive power of special interest groups over government and the need to end regimes of 'political correctness'. In practice this often meant views that 'feminism had gone too far' in its policy influence and that the pendulum needed to be readjusted in favour of men. Not surprisingly, such views were unfavourable to the kind of close analysis of the gender effects of policy for which Australia had been noted.

In this chapter, I survey the impact of these discursive shifts on women's policy machinery, primarily at the federal level but with some broader comments relating to subnational levels of government (states and territories). The sources for this chapter include a survey of federal women's policy units conducted in May–June 1998 and outcomes of a workshop involving state and territory women's advisers in February 1998.

### The Australian model of women's policy machinery

It should be noted that Australia has a Westminster system of responsible government, deriving from the United Kingdom but complicated by federalism and strong upper houses. There are six states and two territories, in addition to the federal level of government (known as the Commonwealth government, not to be confused with the British Commonwealth). A historic two-party system, made up of the Australian Labor Party on the one hand and a conservative coalition of various political parties on the other, has been diluted by the appearance of minor parties and Independents holding the balance of power, both at Commonwealth and at state and territory levels of government. This development has been facilitated by the use of proportional representation in six of Australia's houses of parliament, but has not been restricted to chambers elected in this way.

The first Australian Women's Adviser was appointed by Labor Prime Minister Gough Whitlam in 1973. At her first press conference she articulated what was to be the central focus of the Australian model — the need to audit all Cabinet submissions for their impact on women. The functional priority given to gender audit of all policy meant in turn a related structural focus on locating women's policy machinery within the central policy coordinating agency of government. In Australia, this is the Prime Minister's, Premier's or Chief Minister's Department, depending on the level of government.

One important aspect of the Australian model of women's policy machinery was that it was originally developed by the women's movement rather than invented by government. Members of the Women's Electoral Lobby (WEL) inside and outside government worked on a model for women's machinery, which they presented to the Royal Commission on Australian Government Administration set up by the Labor government in 1974. The model consisted of a women's coordination unit within the central policy coordinating agency of government linked to a network of departmental women's units responsible for monitoring policy at the point of initiation. This kind of women's movement debate over the most effective form of government machinery was absent at the time in comparable countries such as Canada (Arscott, Rankin and Vickers, 1997).

Australian feminists decided against a self-standing bureau or ministry on the grounds that it might simply become a 'waste-paper basket for women's problems' and an alibi for gender-blind policy in the rest of government. It was also perceived that a self-standing ministry would lack policy clout and have difficulty in accessing crucial Cabinet submissions and Cabinet processes. Location within the Prime Minister's portfolio made access to Cabinet and coordinating work across government much easier. In order to strengthen gender advocacy within Cabinet itself, a minister assisting the Prime Minister for the status of women was subsequently appointed, briefed by the women's unit within the Prime Minister's department. After some misadventures, including exile in a low-ranking portfolio, the Office of the Status of Women (OSW) returned to the Prime Minister's Department in 1983.

While women's coordination units such as OSW focused on across-the-board gender analysis of policy rather than programme delivery, they were also responsible for co-ordinating cross-portfolio initiatives and for the development of new policy to the point where it could be handed over to another agency for implementation. Examples of the latter at the federal level were the development of federal sex discrimination and affirmative action legislation. Femocrats inside and outside OSW also influenced policy over a range of sectors at this time — such as the quintupling of the national child-care programme; the development of the home and community care programme; increased funding of women's services; improved access of women, including married women and sole parents, to labour market assistance; shifting of family support to primary carers; and national programmes on violence against women and women's health. Where government could not be swayed from policy directions disadvantaging women, such as the reintroduction of fees for tertiary education or the introduction of enterprise bargaining instead of centralized wage fixing, there were policy 'saves' to try to minimize their impact.

The Australian model of women's policy machinery was not only developed by feminists, it was even justified in terms of the compatibility of the matrix structure with the women's movement's philosophy. Undoubtedly, however, the location of the central unit within the central policy arena made the modelling of the feminist process more difficult, if not impossible. Hence the paradox that it was 'sisters in suits' who acted as the internal advocates for the funding of the quite unconventional models of service delivery developed by the women's movement (Eisenstein, 1995).

Mediation by femocrats both in coordinating and line departments contributed to the ability of women's services to resist pressure to become conventional service deliverers and to persist in modelling feminist organizational forms. Most women's services, such as refuges, domestic violence referral services, women's health centres, rape crisis centres, women's legal centres and working women's centres, were government funded but largely run on semi-collectivist lines by community-based groups. Representatives of such services were brought into policy advisory bodies and played an important role in policy development and law reform. Governments themselves took on the responsibility of providing women's information services from the 1970s, but these were shaped by the organizational philosophy of the community-based women's services.

Another Australian innovation was the women's budget process. This was a major coordinating exercise, pioneered at the federal level in 1984, whereby all departments and agencies were required to account for the impact of their activities on women in a budget document. The Women's Budget Program was a world first in terms of educating bureaucrats to disaggregate the impact of their 'mainstream' programmes rather than simply highlighting programmes for women. Many departments had not previously collected data relating to their programmes on a gender basis. The idea of insisting on gender disaggregation of budgetary outlays was an inspired one. In one state it was found that specifically targeted allocations to women and girls in the community made up only 0.75 per cent of global budgets (Sharp and Broomhill, 1990:3). This meant that it was the disaggregation of general outlays that was crucial to see who benefited from government activity.

Departments were not allowed to escape with unsubstantiated claims that because their policies were directed towards some public benefit such as the health of the economy that they would therefore have the same impact on men and women. They were required to maintain sex-disaggregated statistics relevant to policy and programmes. The need to examine the different location of men and women in the labour market in order to assess the impact of industry restructuring, for example, was a useful lesson for bureaucrats in how rare it is for public policy to be gender neutral in its effects.

The idea of the women's budget programme was to be an attractive one for feminists in other countries trying to mainstream gender accountability and the (British) Commonwealth Secretariat is now assisting countries interested in developing pilot women's budget programmes (Budlender and Sharp, 1998).

In taking up this Australian model, other countries have improved upon it, for example by the incorporation of parliamentary oversight (a parliamentary committee with some expert technical support) to ensure it remains a meaningful accountability exercise. In Australia, the federal prototype became 'captured by the bureaucracy' and became more a public relations exercise concerned with specific initiatives for women than the intended longitudinal analysis of progress in improving gender equality within mainstream programmes. By 1998, the women's budget had been abolished at the federal level and in most jurisdictions. It was not replaced, as recommended in 1993, by the inclusion of gender-reporting requirements within the format used for budget reporting to Parliament.

WEL lobbied for the original model of women's policy machinery to be adopted by state and territory governments and it was eventually replicated in all jurisdictions, including the women's budget process. The quarterly meetings of federal, state and territory women's advisers inaugurated in 1978 helped to ensure that best practice from whichever government was picked up and reproduced. These meetings were originally off-the-record exchanges of strategic information by feminists and were unlike other intergovernmental meetings. This changed with the establishment of the Ministerial Conference on the Status of Women in 1991, after which the officials' meetings took on more familiar traits of political competitiveness. Today the intergovernmental arrangements for women's policy are far from satisfactory.

As already noted, location in a central policy area was a drawback in terms of feminist process; the confidentiality of policy advice at Cabinet level caused tensions with non-governmental organizations (NGOs) expecting more sisterly sharing of information. Nonetheless, policy success was most likely when there was joint work from inside and outside government, as with the eventual ratification of the International Labour Organization Convention 156 on Equal Opportunities for Workers with Family Responsibilities in 1990.

Under the federal Labor governments of the 1980s and 1990s, bureaucratic monitoring of policy was reinforced at the political level by the Parliamentary Labor Party (Caucus) Status of Women Committee, meeting weekly. There was no multi-party parliamentary committee with oversight of bureaucratic forms of gender accountability (e.g. requirements relating to annual reports, preparation of estimates or budget documents).

To summarize, the characteristics of the Australian model at its best were as follows:

- location of the central unit in the chief policy coordination agency;
- Prime Minister taking portfolio responsibility, assisted by a woman Cabinet minister;
- focal points in other government agencies;
- emphasis on gender audit through analysis of Cabinet submissions and budget outlays;
- reinforcement of bureaucratic monitoring by a parliamentary party committee;
- funding of women's advocacy groups as well as women's services;
- community representation on policy advisory bodies;
- use of intergovernmental bodies to share best practice.

## Diversification and/or disappearance

In this context of unfavourable ideological and political shifts, it is perhaps not surprising that the original Australian model of women's policy machinery, with its strengths and weaknesses, no longer exists. Instead, there has been diversification of structures, ranging from almost complete disappearance in the Australian Capital Territory to the creation of a self-standing Department for Women in New South Wales.[2] In this section, I draw on structural issues nominated by members of the Standing Committee of Commonwealth/State Women's Advisers during a workshop in February 1998.[3] The section is biased towards subnational issues.

A major issue for women's advisers is that of location — in all states the variously named women's policy coordination units have been moved out of the central location they originally enjoyed. In addition to the loss of central location and the authority of the Premier, there have been the mobility costs of following ministers to different portfolios. Movement out of Premier's Departments also raises the issue of Cabinet seniority of the minister or, in the worst case, location of that minister outside Cabinet.

Another major issue in the context of a federal system, and one related to the location issue, is the accessibility and accountability of intergovernmental bodies responsible for financial arrangements and programme coordination. The lack of effective gender input into intergovernmental agreements has become increasingly evident, with Premier's and Treasury Departments playing the predominant role. The Ministerial Conference on the Status of Women has very limited influence on other ministerial councils, in particular on the Council of Australian Governments or its predecessor, the Special Premiers' Conferences. This is a matter of considerable concern when decision making is moving out of the public domain into these 'closed door' intergovernmental bodies. In 1991 the Ministerial Conference did attempt to query the gender impact of 'new federalism' proposals that would have untied Commonwealth grants in areas such as community services, health and housing. By the mid 1990s, however, major new intergovernmental agreements, such as those underpinning competition policy, received little contestation from this quarter. A paper on the gender implications of competition policy did not go to the Ministerial Conference until two years after the competition policy agreements had been signed.

The women's sub-committees that advised ministerial councils in areas such as health, housing, education, employment and training have also been allowed to wither on the vine. The new push to devolve Commonwealth responsibilities in areas such as health and to untie funding for specific programmes such as the National Women's Health Program and the Alternative Birthing Services Program has been accompanied by the decision to abolish the Women's Health Sub-Committee of the Health Ministers' Advisory Council (from October 1998). While the focus on gender audit of policy and programme delivery had been seen as a strength of the Australian model, it has not extended to the increasingly important intergovernmental arena.

Another problem for women's policy structures is a more general issue arising from the nature of the new public sector management — the increased volatility of bureaucratic structures and the environment of continuous change. Within this environment it is difficult to sustain the structures needed for long-term projects such as improving the status of women and there is a continuing loss of corporate memory. Moreover, within the commercial product format and outcomes focus associated with the new public sector management there is a devaluing of process, including the information sharing that has been central to feminist work.

Also related to the new public sector management is the devaluing of policy expertise of all kinds, including the expertise in gender analysis necessary if policy is to be adequately evaluated at source for gender impact. Such expertise is also needed for the purpose of accountability. Without adequate means of external accountability, including requirements for disaggregated statistical data, gender 'mainstreaming' will not take place. Accountability through performance agreements between chief executive officers and ministers, without an external element, is unlikely to result in such expert scrutiny. Too often 'mainstreaming' becomes a code word for killing off gender audit.

Another topical issue is the need for more effective use of information technology to improve the interface between women's policy structures across and between governments and between women's policy structures and women in the community. At the time of the February 1998 workshop, many women's policy units lacked web links to women's policy areas in other portfolios or levels of government or to women's policy units in the Asia-Pacific region. There have been some improvements since the workshop — for example, the federal rural women's website installed excellent links to other federal and state women's units as well as NGO sites. There is also now some participation by feminist bureaucrats in Ausfem-Polnet, the main electronic feminist policy discussion list in Australia.

A longstanding issue in women's affairs has been the lack of a consistent approach to creating a 'national voice for women' in public policy debate to ensure that gender perspectives are always heard on policy issues of the day. Alternatives that have been pursued in a half-hearted manner are: strengthening the forum which links women's advisory councils from the different jurisdictions and supporting greater coordination among women's NGOs through funding networking or peak bodies as in other sectors.

International work on state feminism (e.g. Stetson and Mazur, 1995) suggests that one of the most important functions of women's policy machinery is making resources available to community organizations, including funding, information and access to the policy process. Today, governments often express doubt that community organizations are really representative of women and prefer to engage in market research to test women's attitudes to government policies. This is far from the citizenship empowerment or capacity-building model of the past and seeks to bypass the mediated expression of women's views.

A different issue is the need to clarify the relationship between advisory and policy structures. Incoming governments sometimes place more trust in 'their' women, who they can place directly on advisory bodies. Partisan bias in appointments to advisory bodies contributes to failure to develop bipartisan support for women's policy structures, quite apart from the issue of appropriate functional roles. By contrast, where there is broad political representation on advisory bodies, this can act as a parachute for internal women's policy structures during a change of government.

State women's advisers have also raised the importance of 'international learning' — of borrowing approaches to gender mainstreaming that have been successful elsewhere. Such international borrowing or 'model mongering' can give a strategic advantage to those otherwise low in power resources (Braithwaite, 1994). If it can be argued that something has worked in the European Union or Canada, this can provide significant leverage in Australia. As discussed further below, international instruments and associated reporting requirements are another important resource.

## Changes at the federal level between 1996 and 1998

Some of the broader changes occurring in women's affairs have been sketched above. This section deals with more specific changes that have occurred at the federal level since the election of the conservative coalition government in March 1996. This government was elected with promises to end the reign of 'political correctness' and to 'govern for the mainstream'. In line with the general delegitimizing of equity agendas, OSW suffered a budget cut of 40 per cent in 1996, quite disproportionate to the rest of the Prime Minister's portfolio. The cut in staff numbers and the departure of all but eleven of the former staff during the accompanying demoralization affected all aspects of the Office's work. A new Head was appointed to the Office with no background in the women's movement or policy experience. A radio journalist, she was co-author of a very flattering biography of the Prime Minister.

As a result of the 1996 budget cut, OSW was no longer able to provide its share of funding for the Women's Statistics Unit in the Australian Bureau of Statistics, which consequently closed in June 1997. The Unit had produced Women's Year Books since 1994, replacing the gender equality indicators used previously to measure outcomes of government activity to advance the status of women. Both forms of statistical monitoring had received favourable international attention. At the same time another form of gender audit, the federal women's budget process, was finally abolished completely. As noted above, it was not replaced by the requirement for gender accountability in estimates reporting, as originally intended.

Abolition of the women's budget process was accompanied by a more general withdrawal by OSW from a role in coordinating or supporting women's policy work across government. Its new self-description in the Commonwealth Government Directory referred only to its role in providing strategic advice on specific areas of policy, not to any role in mainstreaming gender perspectives. By default, coordination initiatives tended to come from elsewhere.

The minister assisting the Prime Minister for the status of women was one of the most conservative members of the government, Senator Jocelyn Newman, known for the confrontational style she adopted towards NGOs. After a brief period during which a junior minister was Minister for the Status of Women, Newman resumed portfolio responsibility in 1998. The following year she allocated $100,000 (over two years) in operational funding to a men's rights group, Lone Fathers' Association Australia.

Newman announced the funding of Lone Fathers at their national conference, saying it was 'to redress the gender imbalance in policy development'. In this, she echoed men's rights discourse, which positions men as victims of all-powerful bureaucratic feminism. A couple of weeks later, Newman announced the defunding of the National Council of Single Mothers and Their Children. These moves were particularly controversial as they mirrored the government's amendments to the Child Support Scheme, which reduced transfers to custodial parents and increased control of non-custodial parents over the remaining transfers. Newman was subsequently forced by public furore to refund single mothers.

In the meantime, the funding for women's NGOs was reduced by half (to $500,000 per annum) and by 1999 operational funding was provided only to more conservative and less policy active NGOs. Under the new regime, the ministerial round tables (meetings between national women's NGOs and government ministers) were reduced in frequency from twice to once a year, and agendas were much more closely controlled by government. The information-sharing network set up by national women's organizations to coordinate advocacy work (and input into round tables) was defunded and replaced, after a tendering process, by a commercially provided and inferior website.

Round tables are a common form of consultation in Australia, with NGO representatives being paid to come to

Canberra to attend. This enables face-to-face meetings between NGO representatives before the meetings with government, something much prized in a country where distances make such face-to-face meetings difficult. In 1999 the majority of national women's NGOs (some forty out of sixty) received letters 'disinviting' them from the round table, being informed that selected 'prominent individual women' would be invited in their place.

Meanwhile, the fate of women's policy structures across federal portfolios varied markedly. The Department of Education, Training and Youth Affairs provided the worst-case scenario, with the loss of all its women's policy structures, including its Women's Bureau dating from 1963. The Women's Bureau had already been fatally weakened by a 'mainstreaming' exercise under the previous government and it was finally abolished in 1997. Its research funding programme, the Women's Research and Employment Initiatives Program, dating from 1984, was also abolished.

As can be seen from Figures 3(a) and 3(b), another loss was the Office of Indigenous Women in the Aboriginal and Torres Strait Islander Commission (ATSIC) — responsibility for women was to be 'mainstreamed' to programme managers and to the one remaining officer with responsibility for the Indigenous Women's Issues Program. Meanwhile, the Work and Family Unit and the Equal Pay and Workplace Relations Section in the Department for Workplace Relations and Small Business survived and even grew during the period, thanks to particularly dedicated and skilful bureaucrats. Policy monitoring in these areas was of major importance because of the effects of 'workplace reforms' (shifts to decentralized wage bargaining) on family-friendly hours and pay relativities.

The Work and Family Unit oversees the Working Women's Centres set up to provide assistance to women workers under the more decentralized wage-bargaining system. The Centres were also intended to be an important source of policy input, but under the coalition government they no longer receive operational funding and so are too busy chasing government contracts.

The Equal Pay Section acquired extra temporary staff because of its responsibility for servicing an independent review of the Affirmative Action Act, one of a series of

**Figure 3(a)** Federal women's policy machinery, February 1996

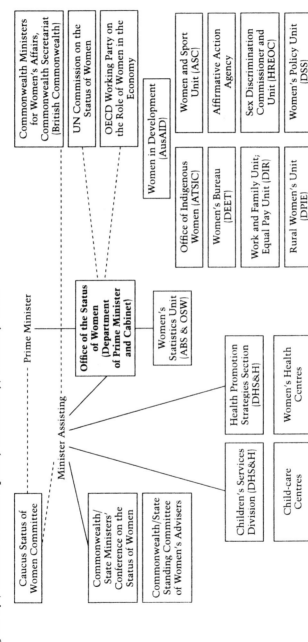

Key: ABS — Australian Bureau of Statistics; ASC — Australian Sports Commission; ATSIC — Aboriginal and Torres Strait Islander Commission; AusAID — Australian Agency for International Development; DEET — Department of Employment, Education and Training; DHS&H — Department of Human Services and Health; DIR — Department of Industrial Relations; DPIE — Department of Primary Industries and Energy; DSS — Department of Social Security; HREOC — Human Rights and Equal Opportunity Commission; OECD — Organization for Economic Cooperation and Development.

**Figure 3(b)** Federal women's policy machinery, September 1999

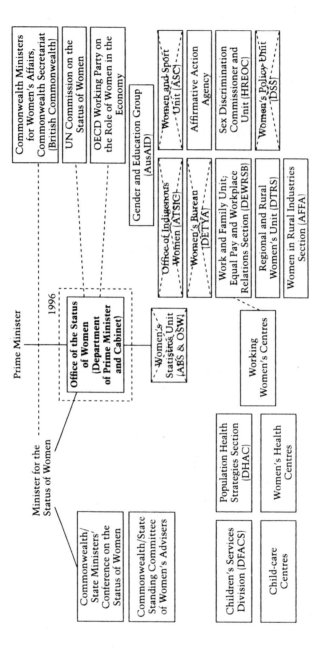

*Key*: ABS — Australian Bureau of Statistics; AFFA — Agriculture, Fisheries and Forestry–Australia; ASC — Australian Sports Commission; ATSIC — Aboriginal and Torres Strait Islander Commission; AusAID — Australian Agency for International Development; DETYA — Department of Education, Training and Youth Affairs; DFACS — Department of Family and Community Services; DHAC — Department of Health and Aged Care; DEWRSB — Department of Employment, Workplace Relations and Small Business; DTRS — Department of Transport and Regional Services; HREOC — Human Rights and Equal Opportunity Commission; OECD — Organization for Economic Cooperation and Development.

regulatory reviews required by the 1995 intergovernmental Competition Policy Agreement. Unexpectedly, the review was very positive and recommended strengthening the powers of the Affirmative Action Agency. The response of the federal government was, however, lukewarm. Many believed the view of the government had been signalled by a letter sent to ministers on 30 April 1997 telling them that departments should not deter the private sector by drawing attention to the need for government contractors to be in compliance with the Affirmative Action Act.

In the Australian Sports Commission, the Women's Sports Unit was gradually whittled away under the new government, finally disappearing completely in 1999. In the same year, the main NGO in the area, Womensport Australia, was also defunded.

While much of the impact of the federal coalition government on women's policy machinery was negative, an exception was the rural affairs area, where policy advisory and consultative arrangements were expanded. The coalition government included the rural-based National Party, under threat from the rise of rural-based populism and anxious to shore up its constituency. During 1996–98 the Rural Women's Unit in the Department of Primary Industries and Energy increased in size and initiated new consultative arrangements bringing together senior policy makers and rural women's NGOs.

After the 1998 federal election, portfolio restructuring resulted in the renamed Regional and Rural Women's Unit migrating with its National Party minister (now Party Leader) to the Department of Transport and Regional Services. A round table with NGO women in mid 1999 was notable for the fact that, unlike the recent round tables serviced by the Office of the Status of Women, the minister actually listened to NGO women. Shortly afterwards a Regional Women's Advisory Council was established, headed by the energetic President of Australian Women in Agriculture (a leading NGO).

A new women's unit called the Women in Rural Industries Section was also established in the Ministry of Agriculture, Fisheries and Forestry — Australia. This unit inherited the Women in Rural Industries NGO grants programme established in 1998, which provided operational funding to two NGOs in 1999 and seed funding for another.

An isolated example of a new intergovernmental structure being created during this period is the Australasian Women in Policing Advisory Committee, which has a mandate to advise Police Commissioners on gender issues.

Meanwhile, the Human Rights and Equal Opportunity Commission had been less fortunate — between 1997 and 1999 its budget was reduced from $19.3 million to $12.3 million — a decrease of 36 per cent over the two years and quite disproportionate in relation to the rest of the Attorney-General's portfolio. The cuts meant the halving of the staff in the Sex Discrimination Unit — although, in fact, turnover was almost complete as a result of demoralization. Moreover, the statutory position of Sex Discrimination Commissioner was left vacant for a year while the government considered abolishing it along with the other specialist Commissioners. This meant not only a policy hiatus in 1997–98, but also a loss of visibility. Other matters of concern included future accessibility of remedies under a new and expensive federal court regime and large cuts to legal aid. Symptomatically the Human Rights branch of the Attorney-General's Department also lost the bulk of its staff at this time.

Under the new federal government, there was a loss of political as well as bureaucratic accountability, with no backbench committee on the status of women. This was explained in terms of the very divergent views among coalition women MPs, from feminists to outspoken anti-feminists as well as individualist philosophies, limiting the possibilities of collective work. The lack of collective strength was very evident as government cuts left children's services in crisis.

### The international dimension

Historically, Australian feminists have put considerable effort into international work. The development of international instruments and platforms has provided an important form of domestic leverage, both through international standard setting and related reporting processes (see Sawer, 1998). Usually there has been close cooperation between NGOs and femocrats over international status-of-women issues. The Australian women's movement has rarely been involved in the kind of politics of embarrassment or international shaming that has been part of the repertoire of other social movements.

More recently, the women's movement has felt pushed into an oppositional stance at the international level, most notable on the occasion of Australia's presentation of its periodic report to the Committee on the Elimination of Discrimination Against Women (CEDAW) in July 1997. A joint NGO report was prepared and seventeen organizations were signatories to it.[4] A representative travelled to New York and briefed CEDAW members over lunch the day before Australia's report was presented.

NGOs had not been consulted, as in the past, over Australia's official report, which was not, in fact, a proper periodic report at all. It was the resubmission of supplementary material provided at the time that Australia's Second Report was considered in 1994. The information had been rendered very out-of-date by the change of federal government.

The NGO report detailed, as the official report did not, the policy impact of the new federal government in areas of special concern to women. This was also covered in a report prepared for CEDAW by the Federal Labor Party Status of Women Committee entitled 'Back to the 1960s? Progress Report on the Australian Government's CEDAW Obligations and Beijing Platform for Action' (Coalition of Australian Participating Organizations of Women, 1997).

The subsequent comments by CEDAW on the Australian official report were a far cry from those when Australia had presented its first report. In 1988, the Australian report was described as exemplary in terms of both the substance of machinery and programmes it described and its self-critical nature. In 1997, Australia was criticized by CEDAW for its retreat from international leadership on gender equality issues and for the erosion of women's policy structures at home (CEDAW, 1997).

In expressing concern over the government's apparent shift in attention away from gender equality and the weakened role of national machinery, CEDAW specifically noted the abandonment of initiatives such as the women's budget statement and the Register of Women, which had served as models for other governments. It also expressed concern over the consequences for women of policy changes affecting child care, housing and labour market assistance. The Committee recommended that the government carefully monitor the impact of recent policy changes for the purpose of its next periodic report, including an evaluation of the impact of the new decentralized wage-fixing system on different groups of women and the impact of the shift in responsibility for health care from the federal to the state level. As we have seen, the mechanisms for performing such a role have been eroded at the intergovernmental level as well as within Australian governments.

CEDAW's criticisms of the Australian government's retreat on gender equality received wide media coverage and in turn provoked a furious reaction from the government. The Minister Assisting the Prime Minister on the Status of Women slammed NGOs for 'bagging their country from overseas'. The government's operational funding for the NGO network, the Coalition of Australian Participating Organizations of Women, which had helped to initiate the NGO shadow report, expired on 30 June 1997 and was not renewed.[5]

Unfortunately, the coalition government appeared less interested than its predecessors in its international reputation in Human Rights areas, as exemplified by the cavalier attitude adopted towards findings by the Human Rights Committee that it was in breach of the International Covenant on Civil and Political Rights (Evatt, 1988). So just when the women's movement has been mobilized to use the shaming tactic, it has become less effective. Nonetheless, there were some effects, including a backdown over the position of Sex Discrimination Commissioner.

## Conclusion

The structures for gender accountability within government, which Australia helped to pioneer, have been threatened by discursive shifts within the government. Women have been discursively repositioned as a 'special interest group' rather than as a majority of citizens with legitimate claims on government. Processes for promoting gender equality in policy design and service delivery have been recast as a form of rent seeking as well as an obstacle to international competitiveness.

At a broader level, ruling concepts now include those of 'competition' (reducing the role of the public sector) and 'micro-economic reform' (reducing the role of unions and centralized wage fixing). In the face of these fundamental shifts away from Australia's historical traditions, feminists have been successful only in establishing some monitoring and mitigating regimes. And at the intergovernmental level, which has become increasingly important in terms of frame-work agreements, feminists have had even less success.

Nonetheless, women's policy machinery still exists in most Australian jurisdictions and, where it has been abolished, the government is often very coy about the fact (e.g. suggesting that women's policy functions are still being carried, even if there are no longer dedicated positions for this purpose). A number of governments have recently changed and national NGOs have been considering what machinery improvements they would like to see under a new federal government. Discussion of such issues is very important in creating a sense of ownership and a political base for them in the women's movement. Suggestions include the greater use of the Australian National Audit Office in auditing the mainstreaming of gender account-ability in government and a return to some form of gen-der accountability in budgetary reporting to Parliament. Another issue is how to increase gender accountability in the intergovernmental arena, where important framework decisions such as competition policy are now being made.

One machinery possibility is a (multi-party) parliament-ary standing committee on the status of women. Such a committee would oversee requirements for gender account-ability in, for example, annual reporting to Parliament and in budgetary reporting, and would require a secretariat with technical expertise in gender analysis. The main problem with such a proposal in the Australian context is the very adversarial nature of the party system and the fact that it is the Labor Party that has been more identified with supporting gender accountability than the coalition parties. It could be argued that such a multi-party body would help to educate all participants in the unintended gender effects of policy making; if so, it would be a triumph over current ideological positions.

In terms of NGO input into policy making, one important decision is whether to support the existence of women's advisory bodies, serviced by government, or whether money is better spent supporting community-based peak organizations independent of government. Women's advisory bodies, serviced by women's policy units, have played an important role as a public voice for issues on which femocrats cannot speak out. When carefully constituted they have also helped to broaden awareness and political support for women's policy machinery (the parachute function). On the other hand, advisory bodies are inevitably constrained by government agendas and are frequently frustrated in their attempts to establish greater independence.

The lessons from the Australian experience are not wholly negative. Despite the unfavourable discursive shifts, there is still institutionalized acknowledgement that all government policy needs to be analysed for gender effects and that no policy can be assumed to be gender neutral. This has now been in place for twenty-five years. And, as in the past, Australian women will look to multilateral forums to help provide the impetus for further progress. The relationship between domestic and international work on the status of women in Australia has been a close one. Both the League of Nations and the United Nations have played an invaluable role in standard setting for us, a process in which we have participated as both agents and beneficiaries.

## Notes

1 With thanks to Lani Russell for the 1998 survey of federal women's policy units and to Sarah Miskin for editing.

2 In the Australian Capital Territory, policy units were 'mainstreamed' in the mid 1990s, leaving only the Women's Information and Referral Service and a Women's Consultative Council. As of June 1998, New South Wales had the best staffing for its women's policy machinery of

any jurisdiction — for example, fifty-two staff in the Department for Women and ten in the Women's Equity Bureau (Department of Industrial Relations).

3 The workshop, entitled 'The Future of Women's Policy Structures in Australia', was held on 12 February at the Research School of Social Sciences, Australian National University, and was attended by Women's Advisers from all jurisdictions including New Zealand but excluding the Commonwealth.

4 The signatories to the NGO report were as follows: Association of Non-English Speaking Background Women of Australia; Australian Feminist Law Foundation; Australian National Committee on Refugee Women; Australian Reproductive Health Association; Australian Women Lawyers' Association; Bahai Office for the Advancement of Women; Coalition of Activist Lesbians; Coalition of Women's Right to Choose; International Women's Development Agency; National Pay Equity Coalition; National Women's Media Centre; School of Women Artists; United Nations Association of Australia Status of Women Committee, SA; Women's Economic Think Tank; Women's Electoral Lobby Australia; Women's International League for Peace and Freedom; Young Women's Christian Association of Australia.

5 Other 'peak' bodies defunded following criticism of coalition government policies included the Australian Pensioners' and Superannuants' Federation, National Shelter, and the Australian Youth Policy and Action Coalition.

# Conclusions: looking forward

SHIRIN M. RAI

The chapters in this volume have provided a comparative and critical assessment of national machineries in different countries and geographical regions. This brief concluding chapter will provide an overview of the main issues raised by the contributors. These include both the success stories of, and the challenges faced by, national machineries for women.

As national machineries are at the cusp of an expanded role, there is a need to review current practices, lessons learnt and organizational effectiveness, and to strategize for the new challenges. The first section examines the issue of accountability of national machineries themselves as a means of strengthening machinery–civil society relations which in turn may strengthen the position of the machinery within the state structure. The second section briefly summarizes the lessons learnt from the various case studies in this volume and determines what may be an enabling environment for national machineries.

## Accountability and legitimacy of national machineries

It can be argued that the legitimacy of national machineries is an important political capital. This capital is needed to invest in efficient, pragmatic and normative work of the machineries. Further, it must be recognized that this capital is not static but rather that it can expand, as well as decrease. To increase this capital, national machineries need to build strong relationships with civil society organizations on the one hand, and demonstrate effectiveness in influencing policy *outcomes* on the other (see Staudt, chapter 2 of this volume). In order to do so, national machineries need to be aware of issues of accountability to their constituencies in their multiplicity — women's movements and groups, academics, policy makers and activists. As the various chapters in the book reveal, women's groups have only recently begun to shed their entrenched scepticism of 'working with the state'; therefore, one way of ensuring that activists do not 'give up trying to be "partners" and stick to the role of "adversaries" ' is for national machineries seriously to take into consideration the accountability issue (Balasubrahmanyan, 1993:31–5).

The legitimacy of national machineries is also bound up with how far they are able to, and are seen to, represent the interests of the majority of women. This issue becomes important with the increased pressures of globalization on national and local economies. It is also important in multi-ethnic and -cultural societies and in political contexts where established democracies are not yet operating. In all these contexts the interests of some groups are more readily visible than those of others. If organizations such as national machineries represent these changing interests, and indeed participate in articulating and sometimes aggregating these, then the *processes* by which this happens need to be taken seriously. It is in this context of representing interests and influencing outcomes (policies) that we need to examine the question of accountability of national machineries.

Accountability can be defined as the 'requirement for representatives [and representative organizations] to answer [for] the disposal of their powers and duties, act upon criticisms or requirements made of them, and accept (some) responsibility for failure, incompetence, or deceit' (McLean, 1996, p. 1). Accountability can be discussed in *normative* terms — that women bring a different style of politics to the public sphere. For this an open, dialogical and listening style of functioning and being is essential. In this context, the accountability of national machineries would be discussed in terms of openness to different standpoints and to varied strategic and practical interests. Thus accountability, with its focus on responsibility, allows us to discuss a new form of politics. A *pragmatic* reason for taking accountability seriously is that without engaging in a dialogue with varied interest groups, without creating a trust between non-governmental organizations (NGOs) and women's groups on the one hand, and national machinery on the other, the *raison d'être* collapses. If national machineries are unable to generate a dialogue with civil society because they are perceived as unaccountable, arrogant and removed from concerns of women's groups organizing in the field, the purpose for which national machineries have been created would not be achieved. Finally, there is a strong *efficiency* argument attached to accountability. As pointed out in chapter 1, national machineries function at different levels of governance — national/local, regional and international. In articulating 'women's interests', national machineries become representatives of 'women's movements', and civil society groups to governments, regional and international bodies. The support of these various groups increases the legitimacy of national machineries; the scepticism and opposition of these groups to the national machineries' style of functioning, agendas and programmes, would erode their legitimacy. National machineries are stronger in their position *vis-à-vis* governance circuits if they have strong legitimacy signals from their constituencies (see United Nations, 1998:12–14). This is particularly important as they hold their mandate of representing women's interests in tension with the need to function effectively and democratically by engaging in negotiation, bargaining and strategizing which might result in positive outcomes for women.

In support of increasing autonomy for national machineries, it could be argued that a mainstreaming of gender agendas requires negotiating across ministries, sectors of government bureaucracy and with civil society organizations. Such negotiations can be effective only when the leadership of the machineries is 'freed from stricter forms of political accountability if they are to be freed to engage in discussion' (Phillips, 1991:156). The argument for deliberative democratic practice presupposes a level of autonomy for representatives of interests which allows them to shift their positions if persuaded by the arguments had in a deliberative space. Without such autonomy representatives have no role to play other than as 'carriers'. Without autonomy there is no flexibility and therefore practical politics becomes impossible, leading to an impasse and breakdown of communication.

Here a focus on the leadership of national machineries, and the question of politics in general, becomes important. Committed, intelligent and resourceful individuals make a

**Table 5** Enabling national machineries

| Areas of work of the state | Areas of work of civil society associations | Issues for national machinery |
|---|---|---|
| • Supportive legislation<br>• Clear mandate<br>• Well-defined space within the state, preferably at the top of the state hierarchy<br>• Increasing levels of women's participation in political institutions through quota or other appropriate policies<br>• Administrative infrastructure<br>• Access to the highest policy-making bodies<br>• Access to information needed to monitor state bodies<br>• Transparency of bureaucratic/state procedures in gender mainstreaming | • Lobby the government to establish a national machinery for women in order to mainstream gender equality issues in policy at all levels<br>• Monitor the government's work on gender mainstreaming from the outside<br>• Enable national machineries to articulate a gender equality agenda which is widely acceptable<br>• Monitor the work of national machineries<br>• Insist upon transparency in the work of the machinery<br>• Develop innovative links with the national machinery | • Be clear about the mandate<br>  • What is the constitutional provision and status of the machinery?<br>  • What is the core area of work for the machinery?<br>• Clarify the channels of communication within government<br>• Insist upon access to relevant information in order to audit governmental policy making and implementation, especially for gender audit of the budget<br>• Make the case of taking both processes and outcomes of gender mainstreaming seriously |

- Adequate number of trained personnel
- Staff demographics within the state to be more gender equal
- Resources
- Political support for the agenda for mainstreaming gender
- Political support for the national machinery and its work
- Supporting autonomy of the machinery within the state structure
- Economic provision at an appropriate level
- Technology to enable 'outreach' work of the machineries at national and international levels through the internet
- Support of innovative linkages between the machineries and civil society organizations
- Skills and training resources for personnel of the machineries on an ongoing basis

- Establish regular communication channels
- Share information and experience with the machinery to increase the knowledge and skills base of the machinery

- Establish and maintain links with civil society organizations on a non-partisan basis
- Be transparent about intra-organizational procedures
- Use the internet to consult widely and feed back on the work of the machinery
- Learn from other machineries by participating in regional and international conferences and exchanges

difference to organizations. Leaderships have to choose, at times, between different types of political capital — governmental or non-governmental. As Kardam and Acuner argue, 'Leadership is a matter of entrepreneurship; it involves the combination of imagination in inventing institutional options and skill in brokering the interests of numerous actors to line up support for such options ... within [the structural] constraints' (p. 112 of this volume). These choices can be more or less urgent and difficult depending upon the nature of government itself. The wider issue of democratic governance is relevant here (see Fox and Brown, 1998:15–17; Staudt, chapter 2 of this volume).

Picking a path through these different choices cannot be easy, requiring strong leadership on the one hand, and strong allies on the other. While it is not necessary that these choices are as stark as delineated here, they alert us to the need for distinguishing between processes and outcomes where the work of national machineries is concerned. The question of autonomy goes hand in hand with the question of accountability. It is the balance between accountability and autonomy that needs to be got right for national machineries to be effective. National machineries thus need to be advocates as well as deliberators and critics, otherwise co-optation becomes a real danger. 'Reasonableness' in government — linked to autonomy for shifting positions — can undermine the oppositional/challenge politics that might be required to shift the status quo. The examples of the various national machineries in this book suggest that some machineries are better able to face challenges than others. In most part it is the context in which they operate that is crucial to their success, as it is to the weakness of others. So what makes for an enabling environment for women's national machineries?

## An enabling environment for the national machineries

The chapters in this volume have identified several elements of an enabling environment for the national machineries for women. Broadly, these include the role of the state, civil society organizations and the work of the national machineries themselves (see table 5).

An enabling environment, however, is also a contextualized environment. As we have seen in the various chapters of this book, the embeddedness of national machineries cannot be disregarded. The *politics* of national machineries thus becomes important. The political system within which the machineries are situated, whether or not they are autonomous from the state and political parties, whether there is a strong civil society, whether there are civil associations supportive of the broad agendas of the machineries and whether there is adequate resourcing of the machineries are all factors that impact on the functioning of these bodies. The international community becomes an important source of strength in some political contexts, but poses difficult issues of independence of machineries in others, especially where nationalist rhetoric is available to, and deployed by, the major political players. The economic strength of the state is also important to the strength of the machinery — under-resourcing and vulnerability due to restructuring of state bodies often depend on the state of a particular economy. Finally, the ways in which gender mainstreaming is understood and accepted as a frame of reference within particular political contexts are also critical. As Goetz points out, gender mainstreaming as 'de-institutionalizing male preference' faces enormous obstacles, especially as 'No government or bureaucracy feels it has anything to fear from women' (1995:211–12). However, the possibility of national machineries working effectively becomes higher where women's movements have been able to produce a long-term discursive shift in the way gender mainstreaming is discussed. The Nordic example, however imperfect, does suggest this.

## Conclusions

This book reflects both the longer-term strategic and shorter-term practical needs of national machinery functioning. While these analyses are made in the context of the national/local space, the arguments presented here are also valid for assessing the work of national machineries at the regional and international levels. Different contexts bring different

strains and tensions on the one hand, and also varied possibilities of alliances and negotiations. These need to be
mapped and used by national machineries.

*Challenges for the future*

In conclusion, the most pressing issue for national
machineries is how to create an enabling environment.
Capacity building of these machineries in times of economic and political restructuring of the state is difficult,
but imperative (see Goetz and Kwesiga, chapters 3 and 10
of this volume). Second, there needs to be acknowledgement of the political process that is crucial to gender
mainstreaming. Here it is important to consider the point
made by Goetz in chapter 3: 'The "lack of political will"
explanation for failure in promoting women's rights and
interests is too vague to be of much use; it does not direct
attention to the real problems of generating political support for socially unpopular policies' (p. 70). However, it is
also important to note that 'political will', defined to
include the leadership of political parties, civil bureaucracies
and state bodies, can be an accountability measure available to the national machineries for assessing progress on
the achievement of the gender mainstreaming agenda. Here,
leaderships of national machineries, their links with NGOs
and civil society organizations and networks at local/global
levels, and their visibility at the global level are important
factors.

Third, the nature of national machineries is important
— decentralized organizational structures, even within a
context of strong central state control, are important to
link in with civil society organizations at the grassroots, as
well as to lobby and monitor the functioning of state-level
bodies at local levels which are so critical for implementation of national policy. As Silvia Vega Ugalde argues in
this volume, 'Experience demonstrates that there is greater
mobilization, greater public visibility, greater impact on
public opinion, a greater degree of participation by women
when such an initiative arises from below, from civil society [rather than from the state]' (p. 129).

Fourth, democratization of state institutions, and of politics more generally, is crucial. The demographic map of state
institutions needs to be changed to reflect gender equality.

The work of national machineries within the state can result in an 'expanded sisterhood with women in government staking out their claims as much for themselves as for the whole bureaucracy, networking among each other and with women in the GO–NGO community for mutual growth and . . . a common agenda' (Honculada and Ofreneo, p. 142 of this volume; see also Stokes, chapter 9 of this volume). The nature of political systems is critical to capacity building of national machineries, as it is to the developing of networks as well as innovative institutionalization of gender equality agendas through the work of national machineries. As Jezerska argues in chapter 8 of this volume, 'International, intergovernmental and regional institutions should be encouraged to provide financial and technical assistance in support of institutional mechanisms and the development and implementation of tools for gender equality' (p. 183; see also Åseskog, chapter 7 of this volume).

Fifth, democratization in this context also means crucially a democratic and accountable functioning of national machineries themselves, as without such accountability the legitimacy of the machineries themselves can be brought into question. As Sawer argues in chapter 12 of this volume, 'Accountability through performance agreements between chief executive officers and ministers, without an external element is unlikely to result in . . . expert scrutiny' (p. 250). One way that this could be strengthened is to have stronger consultative mechanisms, not only with the participating governments such as questionnaires for states, but also with civil society organizations (www.un.org/womenwatch/daw/followup/question.htm). Sixth, democratization needs to be embedded in the framework of mainstreaming itself if mainstreaming is not to become a 'code word for killing off gender audit' (Sawer, p. 250). As Staudt argues in chapter 2 of this volume, 'Good governance is about many things, ranging from opening democratic spaces to performing governance tasks well, justly and equitably' (p. 61). The Economic Commission for Latin America and the Caribbean also suggests that 'the subject of the [democratic] agenda is central to all debates about the State, not just because democratic governance depends on the ability to define the social, political and economic aspects of the public agenda . . . , but because this very definition is a necessary precondition for social cohesion' (1998:21), as well as for gender equality. Finally, more comparative research needs to be done to establish a more sophisticated analysis of best practice and common pitfalls. To quote the Secretary-General of the UN: 'Despite the international presence of national machineries, little research has been done to assess their increasingly important role on the international and regional level' (p. 3).

It is by negotiating these different agendas that national machineries become important instruments of gender mainstreaming and supports for women's empowerment.

# Bibliography

Acker, J., 1990, 'Hierarchies, Jobs, Bodies: A Theory of Gendered Organisation', *Gender and Society*, Vol. 2, No. 4.

Acuner, Selma, 1999, *Gender Equality and the Process of Institutionalization* (in Turkish), doctoral dissertation, Ankara University.

Aduki Pty Ltd, 1995, *Poverty in Vietnam: A Report for SIDA*, Canberra.

African Agenda, 1998, 'National Machinery for Women . . . Can the State Deliver?', No. 1, pp. 13–27.

African Centre for Women, 1995, *Guidelines for the Implementation of the African Platform for Action: African Common Position for the Advancement of Women*, June, Addis Ababa: ECA.

African Development Bank, 1993, *Governance and Development in Africa: Issues, and the Role of the African Development Bank and other Multilateral Institutions*, Abidjan.

Agarwal, Bina (ed.), 1988, *Structures of Patriarchy: State, Community and Household in Modernising Patriarchy*, Delhi: Kali for Women.

Agnihotri, Indu and Veena Mazumdar, 1995, 'Changing Terms of Political Discourse: Women's Movement in India, 1970s–1990s', *Economic and Political Weekly*, Vol. 30, No. 29, July.

Ahmed, Rehnuma, 1985, 'Women's Movement in Bangladesh and the Left's Understanding of the Woman Question', *The Journal of Social Studies*, Vol. 30, October.

Akerkar, Supriya, 1995, 'Theory and Practice of the Women's Movement in India: A Discourse Analysis', *Economic and Political Weekly*, Vol. 30, No. 27, April.

Alam, Bilquis Ara, 1987, 'Women in Local Government: Profiles of Six Chairmen [sic.] of Union Parishads', *The Journal of Local Government*, Vol. 16, No. 1.

Ali, Shaheen Sardar, 2002, 'Women's Rights, CEDAW, and International Human Rights Debates: Toward Empowerment?', in Jane Parpart, Shirin M. Rai and Kathleen Staudt (eds), *Rethinking Empowerment, Gender and Development in a Global/Local World*, London: Routledge.

All India Democratic Women's Association, 1995, *The UN 'Platform for Action' Draft (May '95): A Brief Critique from the All India Democratic Women's Association*, New Delhi: AIDWA.

Allen, J., 1990, 'Does Feminism Need a Theory of the State?', in S. Watson (ed.), *Playing the State*, London: Verso.

Alvarez, Sonia, 1990, *Engendering Democracy in Brazil*, Princeton: Princeton University Press.

Anderson, Mary, 1993, *Focusing on Women: UNIFEM's Experience in Mainstreaming*, New York: UNIFEM.

Anthias, F. and N. Yuval-Davis, 1990, *Woman–Nation–State*, London: Routledge.

Arscott, Jane, Pauline Rankin and Jill Vickers, 1997, 'Canadian Experiments with State Feminism: Status-of-Women-Machinery in a Federal State', unpublished ms.

Åstrom, Gertrud, 1994, 'Into the Main Building', *Shared Power/Responsibility* (a magazine on the Government Bill on policy for equality between women and men). Ministry of Health and Social Affairs, Sweden.

Baden, Sally and Anne Marie Goetz, 1997, 'Who Needs [Sex] When You Can Have [Gender]? Conflicting Discourses on Gender at Beijing', in Kathleen Staudt (ed.), *Women, International Development and Politics: The Bureaucratic Mire*, Philadelphia: Temple University Press, second edition.

Baden, Sally, Cathy Green, Anne Marie Goetz and Meghna Guhathakurta, 1994, *Background Report on Gender Issues in Bangladesh*, IDS Bridge Report, IDS: Brighton.

Balasubrahmanyan, Vimal, 1993, 'Uneasy Partners: Activists and the State', *Mainstream*, 11 September.

Bangladesh Bureau of Statistics, 1986, *Statistical Yearbook of Bangladesh*, Dhaka.

Bangladesh Bureau of Statistics, 1992, *Statistical Pocketbook of Bangladesh*, Dhaka.

Bangura, Yusuf, 1996, *The Concept of Policy Dialogue and Gendered Development: Understanding its Institutional and Ideological Constraints*, Geneva: UNRISD.

Bangura, Yusuf, 1997, *Policy Dialogue and Gendered Development: Institutional and Ideological Constraints*, Geneva: UNRISD Discussion Paper 87.

Barkallil, Nadira, 1994, 'Technical Cooperation and Women's Lives: Integrating Gender into Development Policy: Morocco', UNRISD mimeo, Geneva: UNRISD.

Begum, Najmir Nur, 1987, *Pay or Purdah: Women and Income Earning in Rural Bangladesh*, Dhaka: Winrock and BARD.

Belic, M., 1999, Interview, (November) B.a. .B.e. . (Grupa za ženska ljudska prava).

Bennis, A., 1994, '*Elements de Strategie Pour La Promotion de la Femme Rurale*', Draft Statement, Ministry of Agriculture.

Bjorkman, James W., 1987, 'India: Party, Personality and Dynasty', in Alan Ware (ed.), *Political Parties*, Oxford: Blackwell.

Blackden, C. Mark and Elizabeth Morris-Hughes, 1993, *Paradigm Postponed: Gender and Economic Adjustment in Sub-Saharan Africa*, Technical Note No. 13, Human Resources and Poverty Division, Technical Department, Africa Region, Washington DC: World Bank.

Bouchier, David, 1993, *The Feminist Challenge*, London: Macmillan.

Boyd, Rosalind, 1989, 'Empowerment of Women in Uganda: Real or Symbolic?', *Review of African Political Economy*, No. 45/46.

Braithwaite, John, 1994, 'A Sociology of Modelling and the Politics of Empowerment', *British Journal of Sociology*, Vol. 45, No. 3.

Budlender, Debbie and Rhonda Sharp, 1998, *How To Do a Gender-Sensitive Budget Analysis: Contemporary Research and Practice*, London: Commonwealth Secretariat.

Buvinic, Mayra, 1983, *Women and Poverty in the Third World*, Baltimore: Johns Hopkins University Press.

Byrne, B. and J. Koch Laier with S. Baden and R. Marcus, 1998, 'National Machineries for Women in Development', *BRIDGE Report* No. 36, Institute of Development Studies, Sussex.

Cabinet Office (UK), 1998, *Report on the Review of the Women's National Commission*.

Campbell, Beatrix, 1984, 'Town Hall Feminism', *New Socialist*, November.

CEDAW, 1997, Report of the Committee on the Elimination of Discrimination against Women, sixteenth and seventeenth sessions, doc. A/52/38, Rev.1, third periodic report of Australia, paras 365–408.

Centre for Women's Development Studies, 1994, *Confronting Myriad Oppressions: The Western Regional Experience*, New Delhi.

Centre for Women's Development Studies, 1995, *Towards Beijing: A Perspective from the Indian Women's Movement*, New Delhi.

Charlton, Sue Ellen, Jana Everett and Kathleen Staudt (eds), 1989, *Women, The State, and Development*, New York: State University of New York Press.

Chhachhi, Amrita, 1989, 'The State, Religious Fundamentalism, and Women', *Economic and Political Weekly*, Vol. 24, March.

Chowdhury, Najma, 1985, 'Women in Politics in Bangladesh', in Ahmed et al. (eds), *The Situation of Women in Bangladesh*, Dhaka: Ministry of Social Welfare and Women's Affairs.

Chuchryk, Patricia M., 1989, 'Feminist Anti-authoritarian Politics: The Role of Women's Organisations in the Chilean Transition from Dictatorship to Democracy', in J. Jaquette (ed.), *The Women's Movement in Latin America*, London: Unwin Hyman.

Coalition of Australian Participating Organizations of Women (COMP.), 1997, *Australian NGO Report to CEDAW*, Canberra: Women's Electoral Lobby.

Cockburn, Cynthia, 1991, *In The Way of Women: Mwn'a Resistance to Sex Equality in Organisations*, London: Macmillan.

Cockburn, Cynthia, 1996, 'Strategies for Gender Democracy: Strengthening the Representation of Trade Union Women in the European Social Dialogue', *The European Journal of Women's Studies*, Vol. 3.

Comerzan, A. (State Chancellor, Director of Social Issues, Chief of Social Protector Sector) and V. Bodrug-Lungu, Director of Gender Centre, State University of Moldova, 1999, interviews (December).

Committee on the Status of Women, 1975, *Towards Equality*, Government of India, Ministry of Social Welfare.

Commonwealth Secretariat, Gender and Youth Affairs Division, 1998, *Gender Management System*, Proceedings of the Pan Commonwealth Workshop on Gender Management Systems, Malta, 27–30 April.

Connell, R. W., 1990, 'The State, Gender and Sexual Politics', *Theory and Society*, Vol. 19.

Constantin, A. M., 1999, Ministry of Labour and Social Protection of Romania, interview (December).

Coole, Diana, 1997, 'Is Class a Difference that Makes a Difference?', *Radical Philosophy*, No. 77, May–June.

Coote, Anna and Bea Campbell, 1987, *Sweet Freedom*, Oxford: Blackwell.

Coote, Anna and Polly Patullo, 1990, *Power and Prejudice: Women and Politics*, London: Weidenfeld and Nicholson.

Council of Europe, 1994, *National Machinery to Promote Equality between Women and Men in Central and Eastern European Countries*, Proceedings from seminar, Ljubljana.

Council of Europe, 1997, *4th European Ministerial Conference on Equality between Women and Men, Democracy and Equality between Women and Men: Declaration and Resolutions*.

Dahlerup, Drude, 1988, 'From a Small to a Large Minority: Women in Scandinavian Politics', *Scandinavian Political Studies*, Vol. 11, No. 4.

David, Karina Constantino, 1990, 'The Philippine Development Plan for Women: Conception, Birth and Infancy', paper written for the Asia-Pacific Development Centre, Kuala Lumpur, Malaysia.

Davin, Delia, 1992, 'Population Policy and Reform in the Soviet Union, Eastern Europe and China, in Shirin M. Rai, Hilary Pilkington and Annie Phizacklea (eds), *Women in the Face of Change: Eastern Europe, the Soviet Union and China*, London: Routledge.

Del Leon, Corazon Alma, 1998, 'Women's Workplace Issues: Contingent Employment in the Public Sector', Manila.

Deles, Teresita Quintos, 1987, 'Talk Given at the Symposium on "The 1987 Constitution and Women"', Manila.

Deles, Teresita Quintos and Eleanor Dionisio, 1990, 'Field Assessment of UNIFEM's Assistance to the National Commission on the Role of Filipino Women', paper written for the United Nations Fund for Women (UNIFEM).

Department for Promotion of Gender Equality, Ministry of Labour and Social Policy, 1999, *Background Paper to the Conference CEE Workshop in Preparation for Beijing +5 Conference*, Macedonia, December.

Department of Women and Child Development 1988, *National Perspective Plan for Women 1988–2000*, Delhi: Government of India.

Dietz, Mary, 1992, 'Context is All: Feminism and Theories of Citizenship', *Daedalus* Vol. 116, No. 4; also in Chantal Mouffe (ed.), *Dimensions of Radical Democracy*, London: Verso.

Dominelli, L. and A. G. Jonasdottir, 1988, 'Feminist Political Action in Iceland: Some Reflections on the Experience of Kwenna Frambothid', *Feminist Review*, Vol. 48, No. 1.

Economist Development Unit, 1993, *Indochina: Vietnam, Laos, Cambodia*, London.

Einhorn, Barbara, 2000, 'Gender and Citizenship in the Context of Democratisation and Economic Reform in East Central Europe', in Shirin M. Rai (ed.), *International Perspectives on Gender and Democratisation*.

Eisenstein, Hester, 1990, 'Femocrats, Official Feminism and the Uses of Power', in S. Watson (ed.), *Playing the State*, London: Verso.

Eisenstein, Hester, 1995, *Inside Agitators: Australian Femocrats and the State*, Philadelphia: Temple University Press.

Eisenstein, Zillah R., 1978, *Capitalist Patriarchy and the Case for Socialist Feminism*, New York and London: Monthly Review Press.

Elson, Diane, 1996a, 'Gender-Neutral, Gender-Blind, or Gender-Sensitive Budgets?: Changing the Conceptual Framework to Include Women's Empowerment and the Economy of Care', Paper presented to the Commonwealth Ministers Responsible for Women's Affairs, Fifth Meeting, Port of Spain, Trinidad, 25–28 November.

Elson, Diane, 1996b, 'Integrating Gender Issues into National Budgetary Policies and Procedures within the Context of Economic Reform: Some Policy Options', Paper presented to the Commonwealth Ministers Responsible for Women's Affairs, Fifth Meeting, Port of Spain, Trinidad, 25–28 November.

Evans, A., 1993, ' "Contracted out" — Some Reflections on Gender, Power, and Agrarian Institutions', *IDS Bulletin — The Political Analysis of Markets*, Vol. 24, No. 3.

Evatt, Elizabeth, 1998, 'Meeting Universal Human Rights Standards: The Australian Experience', Senate Occasional Lecture, Parliament House, Canberra, 22 May.

Faundez, Julio (ed.), 1994, *Good Government and Law*, Basingstoke: Macmillan.

Fine, Robert and Shirin M. Rai, 1997, *Civil Society, Democratic Perspectives*, London: Frank Cass.

Fox, Jonathan A. and L. David Brown, 1998, *The Struggle for Accountability*, Cambridge, Mass.: The MIT Press.

Franzway, Suzanne, Diane Court and R. W. Connell, 1989, *Staking a Claim: Feminism, Bureaucracy, and the State*, Cambridge: Polity Press.

Fraser, Nancy, 1989, *Unruly Practices: Power, Discourse, and Gender in Contemporary Social Theory*, Cambridge: Polity Press.

Fraser, Nancy, 1997, 'From Redistribution to Recognition? Dilemmas of Justice in a Poststructuralist Age', *New Left Review*, No. 212, July–August.

Gallagher, Anne, 1997, 'Ending the Marginalization: Strategies for Incorporating Women into the United Nations Human Rights System', *Human Rights Quarterly*, Vol. 19.

Gladwin, M., 1993, *We are Counting on Equality: Monitoring Equal Opportunities at Work in Relation to Sex, Race, Disability, Sexuality, HIV/AIDS and Age*, London.

Goetz, Anne Marie, 1994, 'From Feminist Knowledge to Data for Development: The Bureaucratic Management of Information on Women and Development', *IDS Bulletin: Knowledge is Power? The Use and Abuse of Information in Development*, Vol. 25, No. 2.

Goetz, Anne Marie, 1995, 'The Politics of Integrating Gender to State Development Processes. Constraints in Bangladesh, Chile, Jamaica, Mali Morocco and Uganda', UNRISD Occasional Paper No. 2, Geneva.

Goetz, Anne Marie, 1997, *Getting Institutions Right for Women in Development*, London and New York: Zed Books.

Gondwana Foundation, 1998, *Slovak Women on the Move: Strategies to Improve the Women's Status and Enhance their Contribution to the Development of the Slovak Republic*, Gondwana: Bratislava.

Goss, Sue, 1988, *Local Labour and Local Government*, Edinburgh: Edinburgh University Press.

Government of Bangladesh, Ministry of Planning, *Five-Year Plans from 1973 to 1990*, Dhaka.

Government of Bangladesh, Planning Commission, 1989, *Memorandum for the Bangladesh Aid Group 1989–90*, Dhaka.

Government of India, 1974, *Towards Equality: Report of the Committee on the Status of Women in India*, New Delhi.

Government of Jamaica, Bureau of Women's Affairs, n.d.(a), *Gender Monitoring Checklist*, Kingston.

Government of Jamaica, Bureau of Women's Affairs, n.d.(b), *Project Profile Format and Preparation Procedures for Project Profiles*, Kingston.

Government of Jamaica, Bureau of Women's Affairs, 1987, *National Policy Statement on Women*, Kingston.

Government of Jamaica, Bureau of Women's Affairs, 1990, *Summary of the Five Year Plan on Women*, Kingston.

Government of Morocco, Ministry of Employment and Social Affairs, 1989, *Strategie Nationale de Promotion de la Femme Marocaine a l'Horizon 2000*, Marrakesh.

Government of Morocco, Ministry of Employment and Social Affairs, 1993, *Strategie de Developpement Social Pour la Decennie 90*, Ministere du Plan, Rabat, June, Marrakesh.

Gyford, John, 1985, *The Politics of Local Socialism*, London: Allen and Unwin.

Hale, M. and M. K. Kelly (eds), 1989, *Gender, Bureaucracy, and Democracy: Careers and Equal Opportunity in the Public Sector*, New York: Greenwood Press.

Hamid, S., 1989, *Women's Non-Market Work and GDP Accounting*, Dhaka: Bangladesh Institute of Development Studies Research Monograph, Dhaka.

Heilbroner, Robert, 1989, 'Reflections: The Triumph of Capitalism', *The New Yorker*, 23 June.

Heilbroner, Robert, 1989, 'Reflections: The Triumph of Capitalism', *The New Yorker*, 23 January.

Hirschman, David, 1991, 'Women and Political Participation in Africa: Broadening the Scope of Research', *World Development*, Vol. 19, No. 12.

Honculada, Jurgette and Rosalinda Pineda Ofreneo, 1998, *Transforming the Mainstream: Building a Gender-Responsive Bureaucracy in the Philippines*, UNIFEM.

Hoskyns, Catherine and Shirin M. Rai, 1998, 'Gender, Class and Representation: India and the European Union', *European Journal of Women's Studies*, Vol. 5, nos 3–4.

Humphries, J. and J. Rubery (eds), 1995, *The Economics of Equal Opportunities*, Manchester: Equal Opportunities Commission.

Hurt, Karen and Debbie Budlender, 1998, *Money Matters: Women and the Government Budget*, Cape Town: Institute for Democracy in South Africa.

Illo, Jeanne Frances I. et al., 1996, *Gender Analysis of Selected Philippine Concerns Under APEC*, seven Policy Research Papers commissioned by the National Commission on the Role of Filipino Women, for the Senior Women Leaders Network Manila Conference on 'Trade Liberalization and Investment and Economic and Technical Cooperation for Sustained Growth and Equitable Development — The Gender Dimension', 2–4 October.

Indsheva, R., Interview (November 1999), Karat Coalition.

Islam, Mohsena, 1994, 'Technical Cooperation and Women's Lives: Integrating Gender into Development Policy: Bangladesh', UNRISD mimeo, Geneva.

Jahan, Rounaq, 1982, 'Purdah and Participation: Women in the Politics of Bangladesh', in Hannah Papnek and Gail Minault (eds), *Separate Worlds: Studies of Purdah in South Asia*, Mussoori: South Asian Books.

Jahan, Rounaq, 1995, *The Elusive Agenda: Mainstreaming Women in Development*, London: Zed Books.

Jaquette, J. and S. Wolchick (eds), 1998a, *Women and Democracy: Latin America and Central and Eastern Europe*, Baltimore: The Johns Hopkins University Press.

Jaquette, J. and S. Wolchick, 1998b, 'Women and Democratization in Latin America and Central and Eastern Europe, A Comparative Introduction', in *Women and Democracy: Latin America and Central and Eastern Europe*, Baltimore.

Jaquette, Jane, 1994, 'Women's Movements and the Challenge of Democratic Politics in Latin America', *Social Politics*, Vol. 1, No. 3, Autumn.

Jayawardena, K., 1989, *Women and Nationalism in the Third World*, London: Zed Books.

Jonasdottir, Anna G., 1988, 'On the Concept of Interest, Women's Interests, and the Limitations of Interest Theory', in Anna G. Jonasdottir and Kathleen B. Jones (eds), *The Political Interests of Gender: Developing Theory and Research with a Feminist Perspective*, London, Sage.

Kabeer, Naila, 1989, 'The Quest for National Identity: Women, Islam and the State in Bangladesh', *IDS Discussion Paper* No. 268, Sussex.

Kabeer, Naila, 1991, 'Gender Dimensions of Rural Poverty: Analysis from Bangladesh', *Journal of Peasant Studies*, Vol. 18, No. 2, January.

Kabeer, Naila, 1994, *Reversed Realities: Gender Hierarchies in Development Thought*, London: Verso.

Kandiyoti, Deniz, 1988, 'Women and Rural Development Policies: The Changing Agenda', *IDS Discussion Paper* No. 244, Sussex.

Karam, Azza, 1998, *Women in Parliament: Beyond Numbers*, Stockholm: International Institute for Democracy and Electoral Assistance.

Karat Coalition, 1999, *Regional Report on Institutional Mechanisms for the Advancement of Women in the Countries of Central and Eastern Europe*, Warsaw.

Karat Coalition and UNIFEM, (1999), conference 'Women and Peacebuilding in Balkan', Budapest, November.

Kardam, Nüket, 1990, 'The Adaptability of International Development Agencies,' in Kathleen Staudt (ed.), *Women, International Development and Politics: The Bureaucratic Mire*, Philadelphia: Temple University Press.

Kardam, Nüket, 1991, *Bringing Women In: Women's Issues in International Development Programs*, Boulder: Lynne Rienner.

Kardam, Nüket, 1994, 'The State, Gender Policy and Social Change: An Analysis from Turkey', in Gay Young (ed.), *Color, Class and Country: Experiences of Gender*, London: Zed Books.

Kardam, Nüket, 1997, 'Changing Institutions in Women's Interests', *Development and Gender in Brief*, May.

Kardam, Nüket and Yakin Erturk, 1999, 'Towards Expanded Accountability? Women's Organizations and the State in Turkey', *International Journal of Organization Theory and Behavior*, Vol. 2, Nos 1&2.

Krasniqi, A. (public relations specialist), 1999, Albania, interview (December 1999).

Kumar, Radha, 1989, 'Contemporary Indian Feminism', *Feminist Review*, No. 3, Autumn.

Kwesiga, J. C., 1994, 'Technical Co-operation and Women's Lives: Integrating Gender into Development Policy', Uganda Case Study Report, prepared for UNRISD, Geneva, March.

Kwesiga, J. C., 1995, 'The Women's Movement in Uganda: An Analysis of Present and Future Prospects', *Uganda Journal*, Vol. 42, December.

Kwesiga, J. C., 1996, 'Institutional Framework for the Advancement of Women in Uganda', Paper presented at the Post Beijing Debriefing Seminar for District Women and Youth Leaders in Uganda, Uganda Management Institute, Kampala, 26 March, organized by the British Council and Ministry of Gender and Community Development.

Kymlicka, Will (ed.), 1995, *The Rights of Minority Cultures*, Oxford: Oxford University Press.

Landell-Mills, Pierre, 1992, 'Governance, Civil Society, and Empowerment', The Journal of Modern African Studies, Vol. 30, No. 4.

Lasswell, Harold, 1979, 'Politics: Who Gets What, When, How', in *The Political Writings of Harold D. Lasswell*, Glencoe, Ill.: Greenwood Press.

Lehman, David A., 1994, 'Women and Protestantism in Brazil', paper presented at the Social Sciences Congress, July, Lisbon.

Lewis, Barbara, 1990, 'Farming Women, Public Policy, and the Women's Ministry: A Case Study from the Cameroons', in Kathleen Staudt (ed.), *Women, International Development and Politics: The Bureaucratic Mire*, Philadelphia: Temple University Press.

Loach, Loretta, 1985, 'The Pains of Women in Labour', *Spare Rib*, No. 59, October.

Lohmann, K. (Regional Co-ordinator) Karat Coalition, Poland, 2000, interview, January.

Lokar, S., CEE Network for Gender Issues and Gender Task Force, Interview, January 2000.

London–Edinburgh Weekend-Return Group, 1979, *In and Against the State*, London: Pluto Press.

Lovenduski, Joni and Vicky Randall, 1993, *Contemporary Feminist Politics*, Oxford: Oxford University Press.

Lovenduski, Joni and Pippa Norris (eds), 1993, *Gender and Party Politics*, London: Sage.

MacKinnon, Catharine, 1987, *Feminism Unmodified: Discourses on Life and Law*, Cambridge, Mass.: Harvard University Press.

MacKinnon, Catharine, 1989, *Towards a Feminist Theory of the State*, Cambridge, Mass.: Harvard University Press.

Mariott, Christine, 1994, 'Technical Cooperation and Women's Lives: Integrating Gender Into Development Policy: The Jamaican Report', UNRISD mimeo.

McBride Stetson, Dorothy and Amy G. Mazur, 1995, *Comparative State Feminism*, London: Sage.

McLean, Iain, 1996, *Oxford Concise Dictionary of Politics*, Oxford: Oxford University Press.

Mehdid, Malika, 1996, 'En-gendering the Nation-State: Women, Patriarchy and Politics in Algeria', in Shirin M. Rai and Geraldine Lievesley (eds), *Women and the State: International Perspectives*, London: Taylor and Francis.

Miller, Carol and Shahara Razavi (eds), 1998, *Missionaries and Mandarins: Feminist Engagement with Development Institutions*, London: IT Publishers.

Ministry of Gender and Community Development, 1995, *County Report in Preparation for the Fourth World Conference on Women*, Kampala, Uganda.

Ministry of Gender and Community Development, 1997, *The National Gender Policy*, Directorate of Gender, Kampala, Uganda.

Ministry of Gender and Community Development and Statistics Department, Ministry of Planning and Economic Development, 1998, *Women and Men in Uganda: Facts and Figures 1998*, Kampala, Uganda.

Ministry of Labour and Social Policy, Bulgaria, 1999, 'Background paper' to the conference 'CEE Workshop in Preparation for Beijing +5 Conference'.

Moghadam, Valentine, 1994, 'Market Reforms and Women Workers in Vietnam', WIDER *Working Paper* No. 116, United Nations University, Helsinki.

Mohanty, Chandra T., Ann Russo and Lourdes Torres, 1991, *Third World Women and the Politics of Feminism*, Bloomington: Indiana University Press.

Molyneux, Maxine, 1985, 'Mobilisation Without Emancipation? Women's Interests, the State, and Revolution in Nicaragua', *Feminist Studies*, Vol. 11, No. 2.

Molyneux, Maxine, 1994, 'Women's Rights and the International Context: Some Reflections on the Post-Communist States', *Millennium*, Vol. 23, No. 2.

Molyneux, Maxine, 1998, 'Analysing Women's Movements', *Development and Change*, Vol. 29.

Monsod, Toby C., n.d., *Budgeting for GAD: A Review and Refocusing*, Manila: NCRFW.

Moser, Caroline O. N., 1993, *Gender Planning and Development: Theory, Practice and Training*, London: Routledge.

Moser, Caroline, 1996, *Confronting Crisis: A Comparative Study of Household Responses to Poverty and Vulnerability in Four Poor Urban Communities*, Washington, DC Environmentally Sustainable Development Studies and Monographs Series No. 8.

Mouffe, Chantal, 1988, 'Towards a New Concept of Democracy', in C. Nelson and L. Grosberg (eds), *Marxism and the Interpretation of Culture*, Basingstoke: Macmillan.

Mouffe, Chantal (ed.), 1992, *Dimensions of Radical Democracy*, London: Verso.

National Association of Women's Organizations in Uganda (NAWOU), 1997a, *A Directory of Women's Organisations Affiliated to NAWOU*, Kampala.

National Association of Women's Organisations in Uganda (NAWOU), 1997b, *Women Community Based Organisations (CBO)*, Kampala.

National Commission on the Role of Filipino Women, n.d.(a), 'Annotated List of Gender and Development Reference Materials, Tools and Manuals', Manila.

National Commission on the Role of Filipino Women, n.d.(b): 'The Final Report of the 1997 NCRFW Organizational Development Project', Manila.

National Commission on the Role of Filipino Women, n.d.(c): *GAD Budget Q & A*, Manila.

National Commission on the Role of Filipino Women, *Development of a Gender-Responsive Statistical System* (Module D), Manila.

National Commission on the Role of Filipino Women, *Gender Training and Advocacy*, (Module E), Manila.

National Commission on the Role of Filipino Women, *Gender-Responsive Planning and Budgeting*, Manila.

National Commission on the Role of Filipino Women, *The National Commission on the Role of Filipino Women: Historical Background (The Philippine Development Plan for Women in Focus)*, Manila.

National Commission on the Role of Filipino Women, 1980, *Women in the Philippines: A Country Report*, published for the 'World Conference of the UN Decade for Women', Copenhagen 14–20 July.

National Commission on the Role of Filipino Women, 1985, *The Women's Decade in the Philippines — Analysis of Significant Changes in Women's Roles and Status*, Manila.

National Commission on the Role of Filipino Women, 1989a, *Philippine Development Plan for Women*, Manila.

National Commission on the Role of Filipino Women, 1989b, *Philippine Development Report on Women*, Manila.

National Commission on the Role of Filipino Women, 1989c, *NEWS-WINGS, An Annual Newsletter of Women in Government Service*, Manila.

National Commission on the Role of Filipino Women, *Mid-Term Report 1992–95*, Manila.

National Commission on the Role of Filipino Women, *Term Report 1986–92*, Manila.

National Commission on the Role of Filipino Women, 1992a, *NEWS-WINGS, An Annual Newsletter of Women in Government Service*, Manila.

National Commission on the Role of Filipino Women, 1992b, *Focal Point NEWS*, July–September, Vol. 1, No. 3; October–December, Vol. 1, No. 4, Manila.

National Commission on the Role of Filipino Women, *From the Margins to the Mainstream — Six Years of Advancing Gender and Development in Government* (NCRFW Term Report, 1992–98), Manila.

National Commission on the Role of Filipino Women and National Economic Development Authority Region 10, 1993a, *Guidelines for Integrating Gender Concerns in the Development Processes*, Manila.

National Commission on the Role of Filipino Women and National Economic Development Authority, 1993b, *Guidelines for Developing and Implementing Gender-Responsive Principles and Practices*, Manila.

National Commission on the Role of Filipino Women, 1994a, *NEWS-WINGS, An Annual Newsletter of Women in Government Service*, Manila.

National Commission on the Role of Filipino Women, 1994b, *Focal Point NEWS*, July–September, Vol. 3, No. 3; Vol. 3, No. 4, Manila.

National Commission on the Role of Filipino Women, 1995a, *Philippine Plan for Gender-Responsive Development 1995-2025*, Manila.

National Commission on the Role of Filipino Women, 1995b, *GST Trainers' Pool Get-Together — Reflections on Our Gender Sensitizing Practice.* 24–28, April White Rock Resort Hotel, Subic, Zambales, Manila.

National Commission on the Role of Filipino Women, *The Women's Budget Philippines 1995–96*, Manila.

National Commission on the Role of Filipino Women, 1996, GAD Mainstreaming Evaluation Report, Manila.

National Commission on the Role of Filipino Women, 1997, *Highlights of the 1997 GAD Budget Reports*, Manila.

National Commission on the Role of Filipino Women in cooperation with the Deutsche Gesellschaft fuer Technische Zusammenarbeit (GTZ), Canadian International Development Agency (CIDA), National Economic Development Authority (NEDA-Regional Offices I, VII and X) and Department of Agriculture, 1997, *Gender Mainstreaming: A Handbook for Local Development Workers*, Manila.

National Commission on the Role of Filipino Women, 1998a, *FactSheet* No. 4 on Women and Public Life, Manila.

National Commission on the Role of Filipino Women, 1998b, *Gender Focus*, semestral publication of the National Commission on the Role of Filipino Women, January–June, Vol. 1, No. 1, Manila.

National Economic Development Authority Region I, n.d.(d) 'Briefing Set on the Gender and Development Focal Point' from Reference Project Report, Part II.

Nelson, Barbara J. and Najma Chowdhury (eds), 1994, *Women and Politics Worldwide*, London: Yale University Press.

Nelson, C. and L. Grosberg (eds), 1988, *Marxism and the Interpretation of Culture*, Basingstoke: Macmillan.

NGO Coordinating Committee for Beijing +5, 2000, *Pakistan NGO Review, Beijing +5, Gender Equality, Development and Peace for the 21st Century*, February; http://www.un.org.pk/NGOReport.htm.

Nordic Council of Ministers, 1994, *Women and Men in the Nordic Countries. Facts on Equal Opportunities Yesterday, Today and Tomorrow*, Copenhagen: Nordic Council of Ministers.

North, Douglass, 1990, *Institutions, Institutional Change and Economic Performance: Political Economy of Institutions and Decisions*, Cambridge: Cambridge University Press.

Nyberg, Anita, 1997, *Women, Men and Incomes. Gender Equality and Economic Independence*. (A report to the committee set up by the Swedish government on the distribution of economic power and economic resources between women and men, Stockholm).

OECD, 1992, *Third Monitoring Report on the Implementation of the DAC Revised Guiding Principles on Women in Development*, Paris: OECD.

Olin, Ulla, 1988, *Needs Assessment of Women in Development in Vietnam*, unpublished report for UNIFEM.

Oxhorn, Philip, 1994, 'Where Did All the Protesters Go? Popular Mobilisation and the Transition to Democracy in Chile', *Latin American Perspectives*, Vol. 21, No. 3.

Papnek, Hannah and Gail Minault (eds), *Separate Worlds: Studies of Purdah in South Asia*, Mussoori: South Asia Books.

Parpart, Jane, Shirin M. Rai and Kathleen Staudt (eds), 2002, *Rethinking Empowerment, Gender and Development in a Global/Local World*, London: Routledge.

Pateman, Carole, 1985, *The Sexual Contract*, Cambridge: Polity.

Perrigo, Sarah, 1986, 'Socialist Feminism and the Labour Party', *Feminist Review*, No. 23, Summer.

Phillips, Anne, 1991, *Engendering Democracy*, Cambridge: Polity.

Phillips, Anne, 1995, *The Politics of Presence*, Oxford: Oxford University Press.

Pintat, Christine, 'Democracy through Partnership: The Experience of the Inter-Parliamentary Union', in Azza Karam (ed.), *Women in Parliament: Beyond Numbers*, Stockholm: International Institute for Democracy and Electoral Assistance.

Pollack, Molly, 1994a, 'Technical Cooperation and Women's Lives: Integrating Gender into Development Policy: Chile, Civil Servants, Report', UNRISD mimeo.

Pollack, Molly, 1994b, 'Technical Cooperation and Women's Lives: Integrating Gender into Development Policy: Chile — NGOs', UNRISD mimeo.

Pringle, Rosemary and Sophie Watson, 1992, 'Women's Interests and the Post-Structuralist State', in Michele Barrett and Anne Phillips (eds), *Destabilising Theory: Contemporary Feminist Debates*, Cambridge: Polity Press.

Rai, Shirin M., 1995, 'Women and Public Power: Women in the Indian Parliament', *IDS Bulletin* , Vol. 26, No. 3, July.

Rai, Shirin M., 1996, 'Women, Representation and Good Government: Perspectives on India and Chile', in Julio Faundez (ed.), *Good Government and Law*, Basingstoke: Macmillan.

Rai, Shirin M., 1997, 'Gender and Representation: Women MPs in the Indian Parliament 1991–96', in Anne Marie Goetz (ed.), *Getting Institutions Right for Women in Development*, London: Zed Books.

Rai, Shirin M. (ed.), 2000, *International Perspectives on Gender and Democratisation*, Basingstoke: Macmillan.

Rai, Shirin M. and Geraldin Lievesley (eds), 1996, *Women and the State: International Perspectives*, London: Taylor and Francis.

Rao, Aruna, Rieky Stuart and David Kelleher, 1991, *Gender Training and Development Planning: Learning from Experience*, Bergen and New York: Chr. Michelsen Institute and Population Council.

Rathgeber, Eva, 1990, 'WID, WAD, GAD: Trends in Research and Practice', *Journal of Developing Areas*, Vol. 24.

Razavi, Shahra and Carol Miller, 1995a, 'Gender Mainstreaming: A Study of Efforts by the UNDP, the World Bank, and the ILO to Institutionalise Gender Issues', UNRISD Occasional Paper No. 4.

Razavi, Shahra and Carol Miller, 1995b, *From WID to GAD: Conceptual Shifts in the Women and Development Discourse*, Geneva: UNRISD, OP #1.

Republic of Uganda, 1995, *Constitution of the Republic of Uganda 1995*, Kampali.

Rivington, Diana, 1997, *Workshop on Gender Mainstreaming*, Geneva, 15–17 September.

Robezniece, G., Ministry of Welfare, Latvia, 1999, Interview (December).

Roelofs, Sarah, 1989, 'In and Against the State', *Spare Rib*, March.

Rogers, Lenore and Jeanne Illo, 1995, *Final Report of an Evaluation of the National Commission on the Role of Filipino Women (NCRFW) Institutional Strengthening Project 23*, March, Manila.

Rowbotham, Sheila, 1990, *The Past is Before Us*, Harmondsworth: Penguin.

Safilios-Rothschild, C. and S. Mahmud, 1989, *Women's Roles in Agriculture: Present Trends and Potential for Growth*, Dhaka: UNDP/UNIFEM.

Salman, Tom, 1994, 'The Diffident Movement: Generation and Gender in the Vicissitudes of the Chilean Shantytown Organisations, 1973–1990', *Latin American Perspectives*, Vol. 21, No. 3.

Sawer, M., 1995, 'Femocrats and Ecocrats: Women's Policy Machinery in Austria, Canada, and New Zealand', UNRISD Occasional Paper No. 6.

Sawer, Marian, 1996, *Femocrats and Ecorats: Women's Policy Machinery in Australia, Canada and New Zealand*, Geneva: UNRISD, March, Op # 6.

Sawer, Marian, 1998, 'Femocrats and Ecorats: Women's Policy Machinery in Australia, Canada and New Zealand', in Carol Miller and Shahra Razavi (eds), *Missionaries and Mandarins: Feminist Engagement with Development Institutions*, London: IT Publications.

Schalkwyk, Johanna and Beth Woroniuk, 1997, 'Source Book: Prepared in Conjunction with the Draft Principles for Development Cooperation on Equality Between Women and Men', Prepared for the Expert Group on Women in Development OECD–DAC, March, Paris: OECD.

Sen, Amartya, 1990, 'Gender and Cooperative Conflicts', in Irene Tinker (ed.), *Persistent Inequalities*, New York: Oxford University Press.

Sen, Gita and Caren Grown, 1987, *Development, Crises, and Alternative Visions: Third World Women's Perspectives*, New York: Monthly Review Press.

Sharp, Rhonda and Roy Broomhill, 1990, 'Women and Government Budgets', *Australian Journal of Social Issues*, Vol. 25, No. 1.

Siemienska, R., 1998, 'Consequences of Economic and Political Changes for Women in Poland', in Jane Jaquette and S. Wolchick, *Women and Democracy: Latin America and Central and Eastern Europe*, Baltimore.

Simerska, L. (Karat Coalition) and Novakova, J. (Division for Equality for Men and Women, Ministry of Labour and Social Affairs, Czech Republic), Interviews, (December 1999).

Sorensen, Georg (ed.), *Democracy and Democratization: Processes and Prospects in a Changing World*, Boulder: Westview.

South Africa Report of the Gender Study Visit to Uganda and Australia, 27 November 1995 to 6 January 1996.

Staudt, Kathleen, 1985, *Women, Foreign Assistance, and Advocacy Administration*, New York: Praeger.

Staudt, Kathleen (ed.), 1990, *Women, International Development and Politics: The Bureaucratic Mire*, Philadelphia: Temple University Press.

Staudt, Kathleen (ed.), 1997, *Women, International Development and Politics: The Bureaucratic Mire*, Philadelphia: Temple University Press, second edition.

Staudt, Kathleen, 1998, *Policy, Politics and Gender: Women Gaining Ground*, West Hartford, CT: Kumarian Press.

Stetson, Dorothy M. and Amy Mazur (eds.), 1995, *Comparative State Feminism*, Newbury Park, CA: Sage.

Stokes, Wendy, 1998, 'Feminist Democracy: The Case for Women's Committees', *Contemporary Politics*, Vol. 4, No. 1.

Stone, Deborah, 1997, *Policy Paradox: The Art of Political Decision Making*, New York: W. W. Norton.

Stone, Diane, 1996, *Capturing the Imagination: Think Tanks and the Policy Process*, London: Frank Cass.

Stund, K., 1984, 'Public Women — Private Policies and Development: A Review Essay' *Women's Politics*, Vol. 4, No. 1.

Subido, Tarrosa, 1989, *The Feminist Movement in the Philippines 1905–1985*, Manila: National Federation of Women's Clubs of the Philippines.

Swarup, Hem Lata, Niroj Sinha, Chitra Ghosh and Pam Rajput, 1994, 'Women's Political Engagement in India', in Barbara Nelson and Nupur Chowdhury (eds), *Women and Politics Worldwide*, London: Yale University Press.

Tadjbakhsh, Sh. 2000, 'National Machinery for Gender Equality and the Advancement of Women in Transition Countries', prepared for ECE Regional Preparatory meeting , Geneva, January.

Tetreault, Mary Ann, 1991, 'Women and Revolution in Vietnam', *Working Paper* No. 223, Michigan State University, Michigan.

Tinker, Irene (ed.), 1990, *Persistent Inequalities*, New York: Oxford University Press.

Tomlinson, Marlene H., 1992, 'Jamaica: Context Report, WID Evaluation Study', Canadian Cooperation office, Kingston, Jamaica, mimeo.

Torres, Amaryllis T. and del Rosario, Rosario S., 1994, *Gender and Development — Making the Bureaucracy Gender-Responsive*, United Nations Fund for Women, Manila.

Trakymiene, R. (State Counsellor, Prime Minister Office) and Peciurienie J. (Women's Issuse Information Centre, Lithuania) interviews (December 1999).

Tran, Thi, Van Ahn (in collaboration with Nguyen Nhat Tuyen), 1994, 'The Vietnam Case Study for UNRISD', mimeo, Geneva: UNRISD.

Tsikata, Dzodzi, 1999, 'Location is not Everything', *African Agenda*, No. 1.

Uganda Media Women's Association, 1998, *The Other Voice*.

United Nations, 1994, *Technical Assistance and Women: Mainstreaming Towards Institutional Accountability*, Report of the Secretary-General to the Commission on the Status of Women Doc E/CN.6/1995/6.

United Nations, 1996, *The Beijing Declaration and the Platform for Action*. Fourth World Conference on Women, Beijing, China 14–15 September, 1995. Department of Public Information, UN, New York.

United Nations, 1999a, *Atlas of Women in Politics: 2000*, Map No. 4136 (The World Today), December, New York.

United Nations, 1999b, *Thematic Issues Before the Commission on the Status of Women*, Report of the Secretary-General (E/CN.6/1999/4), New York.

UN/DAW, 1998a, *Report of the Expert Group Meeting on 'National Machineries for Gender Equality'*, organized by the United Nations Division for the Advancement of Women and the Economic Commission for Latin America and the Caribbean, Santiago, Chile, 31 August–4 September (EGM/NM/1998/Rep. 1), New York: UN.

UN/DAW, 1998b, 'Recommendations to the Expert Group Meeting on National Machineries for Gender Equality by NGO Committee on the Status of Women Task Force on Institutional Mechanisms for the Advancement of Women' (EGM/NM/1998/OP.1), August.

UN/DAW, 1998c, 'National Machineries for Gender Equality — A Global Perspective' Background paper prepared by DAW for the Expert Group Meeting (EGM/NM/1998/BP.1), August.

UNDP, 1990, *Human Development Report 1990*, New York: Oxford University Press.

UNDP, 1991, *Situation Analysis of the Status of Children and Women in Jamaica*, Kingston: Planning Institute of Jamaica.

UNDP, 1993, 'Fifth Country Programme for Jamaica, 1993–96' mimeo, Kingston.

UNDP, 1994, *Human Development Report 1994*, New York: Oxford University Press.

UNDP, 1995, *Human Development Report 1995*, Oxford: Oxford University Press.

UNDP and DAW, 1996, *Sub-Regional Conference of Senior Governmental Experts on the Implementation of the PFA Adopted by the 1995 Fourth World Conference on Women in Beijing, in Central and Eastern Europe*, Regional Bureau for Europe and CIS; Bucharest, Romania, United Nations, September.

United Nations Economic Commission for Africa (ECA) and Organization of African Unity (OAU), 1994, *African Platform for Action: African*

*Common Position for the Advancement of Women Adopted at the Fifth African Regional Conference on Women*, Dakar, Senegal 12–23 November.

United Nations Economic Commission for Europe, 1999a, *Developing Tools for Enforcing and Monitoring Policies of Equality*, Draft conclusions on the theme of Institutional Mechanisms for the Advancement of Women; revision proposed by UNIFEM Workshops on CEE and CIS Preparations for Beijing +5; Budapest, Almaty, United Nations.

United Nations Economic Commission for Europe, 1999b, *Draft Conclusions on the theme of Institutional Mechanisms for the Advancement of Women*; revision proposed by UNIFEM Workshops on CEE and CIS Preparations for Beijing +5; Budapest, Almaty, United Nations, December.

United Nations Economic Commission for Latin America and the Caribbean, 1998, *The Institutionality of Gender Equity in the State: A Diagnosis for Latin America and the Caribbean*, United Nations, August.

UN/ECOSOC, 1994, *Regional Platform for Action — Women in a Changing World — Call for Action from an ECE Perspective*, United Nations October, Vienna.

UNIFEM, 1999, *Sub-Regional Workshop in Preparation for the Beijing +5 Review for the CEE countries*, December, Budapest.

UNIFEM, 1999, *Sub-Regional Workshop in Preparation for the Beijing +5 Review for the CIS countries*, December, Almaty.

United Nations International Research and Training Institute for the Advancement of Women (INSTRAW), 1999, *Engendering the Political Agenda: A South African Case Study*, Gender Research Project, University of the Witwatersrand, South Africa, July.

United Nations International Research and Training Institute for the Advancement of Women (INSTRAW), 2000, *Engendering the Political Agenda: The Role of the State, Women's Organizations and the International Community*, Santo Domingo, Dominican Republic: INSTRAW.

USAID, 1991, 'Gender and Adjustment', mimeo, prepared for the Office of Women in development, USAID, by the Mayatech Corporation.

Veitch, Janet, 1999, *Institutional Mechanisms for Women within the UK Government*, London: WNC.

Watson, S. (ed.), 1990, *Playing the State*, London: Verso.

Waylen, Georgina, 1992, 'Rethinking Women's Political Participation and Protest: Chile 1970–1990', *Political Studies*, Vol. 15, No. 2.

Waylen, Georgina, 1994, 'Women and Democratisation: Conceptualising Gender Relations in Transition Politics', *World Politics*, Vol. 46, April.

Waylen, Georgina, 1996, 'Women's Movements, the State and Democratization in Chile: The Establishment of SERNAM', in Anne Marie Goetz (ed.), *Getting Institutions Right for Women in Development*, London and New York: Zed Books.

Weber, Max, 1972, *Politics as a Vocation*, Philadelphia: Fortress Press.

White, Christine Pelzer, 1982, 'Socialist Transformation of Agriculture and Gender Relations: The Vietnamese Case', *IDS Bulletin*, Vol. 13, No. 4.

Women's National Commission, Cabinet Office (UK), 2000, *WNC News*, Issue 16, February.

WNC, 1999, *Women 2000: Report from the Women's National Commission on the Implementation of the Beijing Platform for Action in the UK*, London, December.

World Bank, 1989a, *Bangladesh: Public Expenditure Review — Public Resource Management During the Forth Five-Year Plan, FY1991–95*, Washington DC.

World Bank, 1989b, *Bangladesh Strategy Paper on Women in Development: Towards a Better Understanding of Women's Roles in the Development Process*, Population and Human Resources Division, Country Department 1, Asia Region, Washington DC.

World Bank, 1989c, www.uneca.org/eca_resources/cdroms/status-of-african_women/pages/publions2a.htm#4

World Bank, 1990, *Vietnam: Stabilisation and Structural Reforms*, Washington DC.

World Bank, 1992, *Governance and Development*, Washington DC.

World Bank, 1993a, *Poverty Reduction Handbook*, Washington DC.

World Bank, 1993b, *Governance: The World Bank Experience*, Operations Policy Department, Washington DC.

World Bank, 1993c, *Trends in Developing Economies*, Washington DC: Johns Hopkins Press.

World Bank, 1994a, *World Development Report*, Washington DC.

World Bank, 1994b, *Social Indicators of Development*, Washington DC: Johns Hopkins Press.

Young, Gay (ed.), 1994, *Color, Class and Country: Experiences of Gender*, London: Zed Press.

Young, Iris Marion, 1995, 'Together in Difference: Transforming the Logic of Group Political Conflict', in Will Kymlicka (ed.), *The Rights of Minority Cultures*, Oxford: Oxford University Press.

Young, Iris Marion, 1997, 'Unruly Categories: A Critique of Nancy Fraser's Dual Systems Theory', *New Left Review*, 222, March–April.

Zalewski, Marysia and Jane Parpart, 1998, *The 'Man' Question in International Relations*, Boulder, CO: Westview Press.

Zoldyne, E. S., Ministry of Family and Social Affairs, Hungary, interview (December 1999).

Zulu, Lindiwe, 2000, 'Institutionalising Changes: South African Women's Participation in the Transition to Democracy' in Shirin M. Rai (ed.), *International Perspectives on Gender and Democratisation*, Basingstoke: Macmillan.

# Index